Word 2002
Level 1

ESSENTIALS

Word 2002
Level 1

KEITH MULBERY
UTAH VALLEY STATE COLLEGE

E
S
S
E
N
T
I
A
L
S

Prentice
Hall

Upper Saddle River, New Jersey

Publisher and Vice President: Natalie E. Anderson
Executive Editor: Jodi McPherson
Managing Editor: Monica Stipanov
Assistant Editor: Jennifer Cappello
Editorial Assistant: Mary Ann Broadnax
Developmental Editors: Joyce J. Nielsen and Jan Snyder
Media Project Manager: Cathleen Profitko
Executive Marketing Manager: Emily Knight
Manager, Production: Gail Steier de Acevedo
Project Managers: Tim Tate and April Montana
Associate Director, Manufacturing: Vincent Scelta
Manufacturing Buyer: Natacha St. Hill Moore
Design Manager: Pat Smythe
Interior Design: Kim Buckley
Cover Design: Pisaza Design Studio, Ltd.
Manager, Print Production: Christy Mahon
Full-Service Composition: Impressions Book and Journal Services, Inc.
Printer/Binder: Courier Companies, Inc. Kendallville

Credits and acknowledgments borrowed from other sources and reproduced, with permission, in this textbook appear on the appropriate page within the text.

10 9 8 7 6 5 4 3 2 1
ISBN 0-13-092795-3

What Does This Logo Mean?

It means this courseware has been approved by the Microsoft® Office User Specialist Program to be among the finest available for learning **Microsoft Word 2002.** It also means that upon completion of this courseware, you may be prepared to become a Microsoft Office User Specialist.

What Is a Microsoft Office User Specialist?

A Microsoft Office User Specialist is an individual who has certified his or her skills in one or more of the Microsoft Office desktop applications of Microsoft Word, Microsoft Excel, Microsoft PowerPoint, Microsoft Outlook, or Microsoft Access, or in Microsoft Project. The Microsoft Office User Specialist Program typically offers certification exams at the "Core" and "Expert" skill levels.* The Microsoft Office User Specialist Program is the only Microsoft-approved program in the world for certifying proficiency in Microsoft Office desktop applications and Microsoft Project. This certification can be a valuable asset in any job search or career advancement.

More Information:

To learn more about becoming a Microsoft Office User Specialist, visit www.mous.net

To purchase a Microsoft Office User Specialist certification exam, visit www.DesktopIQ.com

To learn about other Microsoft Office User Specialist approved courseware from Prentice Hall, visit www.prenhall.com/phit/mous_frame.html

---

* The availability of Microsoft Office User Specialist certification exams varies by application, application version, and language. Visit www.mous.net for exam availability.

Microsoft, the Microsoft Office User Specialist Logo, PowerPoint, and Outlook are either registered trademarks or trademarks of Microsoft Corporation in the United States and/or other countries.

Dedication

I would like to dedicate this book to my parents—Kenneth and Mary Lu—and grandparents—Herman, Billie, and Orpha—for their support and encouragement. I further dedicate this book to the memory of Grandpa (Raymond) Mulbery. Through them, I learned the value of hard work, a passion for my work, and the importance of education.

Acknowledgments

This book is a result of collaborative effort from the essentials team. First, I'd like to express sincere appreciation to **Monica Stipanov** and **Tim Tate** at Prentice Hall for their professionalism and dedication to the essentials series. They have been a reliable force throughout the years for ensuring continuity, accuracy, and pedagogical strength throughout the series. The team at Impressions converted the manuscript and individual screen shots into actual pages. The essentials series would not be the popular series it is today without the Prentice Hall marketing team: **Kris King, Sharon Turkovich,** and **Jason Smith.**

A special thanks to **Larry Metzelaar** and **Marianne Fox** for providing a positive direction as series editors. I appreciate the valuable advice provided by Developmental Editor **Jan Snyder.** Her suggestions definitely strengthened the content of this book. In addition, Copy Editor **Nancy Sixsmith** ensured the grammatical accuracy of the manuscript—thanks for catching those sneaky little typos that almost slipped by!

Some final acknowledgments: **Nancy Bartlett,** Director of Human Resources at Utah Valley State College, gave me permission to use AAEO documentation as data files; **Rick Bradshaw** took me to Cold Stone Creamery for ice cream to relieve stress; my colleagues at Utah Valley State College gave me their support and ideas; and my students provided valuable feedback while working through previous editions of this book.

About the Series Editors

Marianne Fox—Series editor and coauthor of *essentials Excel 2002 Level 1, Level 2,* **and** *Level 3.* Marianne Fox is an Indiana CPA with B.S. and M.B.A. degrees in Accounting from Indiana University. For more than 20 years, she has enjoyed teaching full-time—initially in Indiana University's School of Business; since 1988 in the College of Business Administration at Butler University. As the co-owner of an Indiana-based consulting firm, Marianne has extensive experience consulting and training in the corporate and continuing education environments. Since 1984, she has co-authored more than 35 computer-related books; and has given presentations on accounting, computer applications, and instructional development topics at a variety of seminars and conferences.

Lawrence C. Metzelaar—Series editor and coauthor of *essentials Excel 2002 Level 1, Level 2,* **and** *Level 3.* Lawrence C. Metzelaar earned a B.S. in Business Administration and Computer Science from the University of Maryland, and an Ed.M. and C.A.G.S. in Human Problem Solving from Boston University. Lawrence has more than 30 years of experience with military and corporate mainframe and microcomputer systems. He has taught computer science and Management Information Systems (MIS) courses at the University of Hawaii, Control Data Institute, Indiana University, and Purdue University; currently, he is a full-time faculty member in the College of Business Administration at Butler University. As the co-owner of an Indiana-based consulting firm, he has extensive experience consulting and training in the corporate and continuing education environments. Since 1984, he has co-authored more than 35 computer-related books; and has given presentations on computer applications and instructional development topics at a variety of seminars and conferences.

About the Series Authors

Linda Bird—Author of *essentials PowerPoint® 2002 Level 1* **and** *Level 2.* Linda Bird specializes in corporate training and support through her company, Software Solutions. She has successfully trained users representing more than 75 businesses, including several Fortune 500 companies. She custom designs many of her training materials. Her clients include Appalachian Electric Power Co., Goodyear, Pillsbury, Rockwell, and Shell Chemical. Her background also includes teaching at Averett College and overseeing computer training for a business training organization.

Using her training experience as a springboard, Linda has written numerous books on Power-Point, Word, Excel, Access, and Windows. Additionally, she has written more than 20 instructor's manuals and contributed to books on a variety of desktop application programs. She has also penned more than 150 magazine articles, as well as monthly how-to columns on Power-Point and Excel for *Smart Computing* magazine.

Linda, a graduate of the University of Wisconsin, lives near the Great Smoky Mountains in Tennessee with her husband, Lonnie, and daughters, Rebecca and Sarah. Besides authoring books, Linda home-educates her daughters. If she's not writing, you can probably find her trekking around the mountains (or horseback riding) with her family.

Keith Mulbery—Author of *essentials Word 2002 Level 1, Level 2,* **and** *Level 3.* Keith Mulbery is an associate professor in the Information Systems Department at Utah Valley State College, where he teaches computer applications courses and assists with curriculum development. Keith received his B.S. and M.Ed. (majoring in Business Education) from Southwestern Oklahoma State University. Keith has written several Word and WordPerfect textbooks. His previous book, *MOUS essentials Word 2000*, received the Utah Valley State College Board of Trustees Award of Excellence in January 2001. In addition, he was the developmental editor of *essentials Word 2000 intermediate* and *essentials Word 2000 advanced*. Keith also conducts hands-on computer application workshops at the local, state, and national levels, including at the National Business Education Association convention.

Dawn Parrish Wood—Author of *essentials Access 2002 Level 1*, *Level 2*, and *Level 3*. Dawn Parrish Wood is an independent contractor, and provides software training through her own business, Software Support. She teaches customized courses to local businesses and individuals in order to upgrade employee skills and knowledge of computers. Dawn has written materials for these specialized courses for her own use. She also provides software consultation to local businesses. Previously, she was the computer coordinator/lead instructor for the Business & Industry Services division at Valdosta Technical Institute in Valdosta, Georgia. The majority of the coursework she taught was in continuing education. Prior to teaching, she worked as a technical support representative and technical writer for a software firm. She lives in Valdosta, Georgia, with her husband, Kenneth, and their two daughters, Micaela (4 1/2 years) and Kendra (2 1/2 years). Both girls have been her superlative students, learning more on the computer every day.

Contents at a Glance

Table of Contents

Introduction

Essentials courseware from Prentice Hall Information Technology is anchored in the practical and professional needs of all types of students.

The *essentials* series has been conceived around a "learning-by-doing" approach that encourages you to grasp application-related concepts as you expand your skills through hands-on tutorials. As such, it consists of modular lessons that are built around a series of numbered, step-by-step procedures that are clear, concise, and easy to review. The end-of-chapter exercises have likewise been carefully constructed from the routine Checking Concepts and Terms to tasks in the Discovery Zone that gently prod you into extending what you've learned into areas beyond the explicit scope of the lessons proper. Following, you'll find out more about the rationale behind each book element and how to use each to your maximum benefit.

Key Features

❏ **Step-by-Step Tutorials.** Each lesson in a project includes numbered, bold step-by-step instructions that show you how to perform the procedures in a clear, concise, and direct manner. These hands-on tutorials let you "learn by doing." A short paragraph may appear after a step to clarify the results of that step. To review the lesson, you can easily scan the bold numbered steps. Accompanying data files eliminate unnecessary typing.

❏ **End-of-Project Exercises.** Check out the extensive end-of-project exercises (generally 20 percent of the pages in each project) that emphasize hands-on skill development. You'll find three levels of reinforcement: Skill Drill, Challenge, and Discovery Zone. Generally, each exercise is independent of other exercises, so you can complete your choices in any order. Accompanying data files eliminate unnecessary typing.

> **Skill Drill** Skill Drill exercises reinforce project skills. Each skill reinforced is the same, or nearly the same, as a skill presented in the project. Each exercise includes a brief narrative introduction, followed by detailed instructions in a step-by-step format.
>
> **Challenge** Challenge exercises expand on or are somewhat related to skills presented in the lessons. Each exercise provides a brief narrative introduction, followed by instructions in a numbered-step format that are not as detailed as those in the Skill Drill section.
>
> **Discovery Zone** Discovery Zone exercises require advanced knowledge of topics presented in lessons, application of skills from multiple lessons, or self-directed learning of new skills. Each exercise provides a brief narrative introduction. Numbered steps are not provided.

Two other sections precede the end-of-project exercises: **Summary** and **Checking Concepts and Terms**. The Summary provides a brief recap of tasks learned in the project, and guides you to topics or places where you can expand your knowledge. The Checking Concepts and Terms section includes Multiple Choice and Discussion questions that are designed to check your comprehension and assess retention. Projects that introduce a new work area include a Screen ID question.

❏ **Notes.** Projects include two types of notes: "If you have problems..." and "To extend your knowledge..." The first type displays between hands-on steps. These short troubleshooting notes help you anticipate or solve common problems quickly and effectively. Many lessons in the projects end with "To extend your knowledge..." notes that provide extra tips, shortcuts, and alternative ways to complete a process, as well as special hints. You may safely ignore these for the moment to focus on the main task at hand, or you may pause to learn and appreciate the additional information.

❐ **Task Guide.** The Task Guide, which follows the Overview of Windows, lists common procedures and shortcuts. It can be used in two complementary ways to enhance your learning experience. You can refer to it while progressing through projects to refresh your memory on procedures learned. Or, you can keep it as a handy real-world reference while using the application for your daily work.

❐ **Illustrations.** Multiple illustrations add visual appeal and reinforce learning in each project. An opening section titled "Visual Summary" graphically illustrates the concepts and features included in the project and/or the output you will produce. Each time a new button is introduced, its icon displays in the margin. Screen shots display after key steps for you to check against the results on your monitor. These figures, with ample callouts, make it easy to check your progress.

❐ **Learn-How-to-Learn Focus.** Software has become so rich in features that cater to so many diverse needs that it is no longer possible to anticipate and include everything that you might need to know. Therefore, a learn-how-to-learn component is provided as an "essential" element in the series. Selected lessons and end-of-project exercises include accessing onscreen Help for guidance. References to onscreen Help are also included in selected project summaries and "To extend your knowledge..." notes.

How to Use This Book

Typically, each *essentials* book is divided into seven to eight projects. A project covers one area (or a few closely related areas) of application functionality. Each project consists of six to eight lessons that are related to that topic. Each lesson presents a specific task or closely related set of tasks in a manageable chunk that is easy to assimilate and retain.

Each element in the *essentials* book is designed to maximize your learning experience. Following is a list of the *essentials* project elements and a description of how each element can help you:

❐ **Project Objectives.** Starting with an objective gives you short-term, attainable goals. Using project objectives that closely match the titles of the step-by-step tutorials breaks down the possibly overwhelming prospect of learning several new features of an Office XP application into small, attainable, bite-sized tasks. Look over the objectives on the opening page of the project before you begin, and review them after completing the project to identify the main goals for each project.

❐ **Key Terms.** Key terms introduced in each project are listed, in alphabetical order, immediately after the objectives on the opening page of the project. Each key term is defined during its first use within the text, and is shown in bold italic within that explanation. Definitions of key terms are also included in the Glossary.

❐ **Why Would I Do This?** You are studying Office XP applications so you can accomplish useful tasks. This brief section provides an overview of why these tasks and procedures are important.

❐ **Visual Summary.** This opening section graphically illustrates the concepts and features that you will learn in the project. One or more figures, with ample callouts, show the final result of completing the project.

 ❐ **If You Have Problems...** These short troubleshooting notes help you anticipate or solve common problems quickly and effectively. Even if you do not encounter the problem at this time, make a mental note of it so that you know where to look when you (or others) have difficulty.

 ❐ **To Extend Your Knowledge...** Many lessons end with "To extend your knowledge..." comments. These notes provide extra tips, shortcuts, alternative ways to complete a process, and special hints about using the software.

Typeface Conventions Used in This Book

Essentials 2002 uses the following conventions to make it easier for you to understand the material.

❐ Key terms appear in ***italic and bold*** the first time they are defined in a project.

❐ Monospace type appears frequently and looks `like this`. It is used to indicate text that you are instructed to key in.

❐ *Italic text* indicates text that appears onscreen as (1) warnings, confirmations, or general information; (2) the name of a file to be used in a lesson or exercise; and (3) text from a dialog box that is referenced within a sentence, when that sentence might appear awkward if the dialog box text were not set off.

❐ Hotkeys are indicated by underline. Hotkeys are the underlined letters in menus, toolbars, and dialog boxes that activate commands and options, and are a quick way to choose frequently used commands and options. Hotkeys look like this: File, Save.

Accessing Student Data Files

The data files that students need to work through the projects can be downloaded from the Custom PHIT Web site (www.prenhall.com/customphit). Data files are provided for each project. The filenames correspond to the filenames called for in this book. The files are named in the following manner: The first character indicates the book series (e=essentials); the second character denotes the application (w=Word, e=Excel, and so forth); and the third character indicates the level (1=Level 1, 2=Level 2, and 3=Level 3). The last four digits indicate the project number and the file number within the project. For example, the first file used in Project 3 would be 0301. Therefore, the complete name for the first file in Project 3 in the *Word Level 1* book is ew1-0301. The complete name for the third file in Project 7 in the *Excel Level 2* book is ee2-0703.

Instructor's Resources

❐ **Customize Your Book (www.prenhall.com/customphit).** The Prentice Hall Information Technology Custom PHIT Program gives professors the power to control and customize their books to their course needs. The best part is that it is done completely online using a simple interface.

Professors choose exactly what projects they need in the *essentials* Office XP series, and in what order they appear. The program also allows professors to add their own material anywhere in the text's presentation, and the final product will arrive at each professor's bookstore as a professionally formatted text.

To learn more about this new system for creating the perfect textbook, go to www.prenhall.com/customphit, where you can go through the online walkthrough of how to create a book.

❐ **Instructor's Resource CD-ROM.** This CD-ROM includes the entire *Instructor's Manual* for each application in Microsoft Word format. A computerized testbank is included to create tests, maintain student records, and provide online practice testing. Student data files and completed solutions files are also on this CD-ROM. The *Instructor's Manual* will contain a reference guide of these files for the instructor's convenience. PowerPoint slides, which give more information about each project, are also available for classroom use.

❐ **Test Manager.** Prentice Hall Test Manager is an integrated, PC-compatible test-generation and classroom-management software package. The package permits instructors to design and create tests, maintain student records, and provide online practice testing for students.

Prèntice Hall has also formed close alliances with each of the leading online platform providers: WebCT, Blackboard, and our own Pearson CourseCompass.

❐ **WebCT and Blackboard.** This custom-built distance-learning course features exercises, sample quizzes, and tests in a course-management system that provides class administration tools as well as the ability to customize this material at the instructor's discretion.

❐ **CourseCompass.** CourseCompass is a dynamic, interactive online course-management tool powered by Blackboard. It lets professors create their own courses in 15 minutes or less with preloaded quality content that can include quizzes, tests, lecture materials, and interactive exercises.

Training and Assessment (www.prenhall.com/phit)

Prentice Hall's Train Generation IT is a computer-based training software a student can use to preview, learn, and review Microsoft® Office application skills. Delivered via intranet, network, CD-ROM, or the Web, Train IT offers interactive, multimedia, computer-based training to augment classroom learning. Built-in prescriptive testing suggests a study path based on not only student test results, but also the specific textbook chosen for the course.

Prentice Hall
ASSESS Generation it

Prentice Hall's Assess Generation IT is separate computer-based testing software used to evaluate a student's knowledge about specific topics on Word, Excel, Access, and PowerPoint®. More extensive than the testing in Train IT, Assess IT offers more features for the instructor and many more questions for the student.

Getting Started with Word

Objectives

In this project, you learn how to

- ✔ Explore the Word Screen
- ✔ Use Menus and Toolbars
- ✔ Enter Text in a Document
- ✔ Save a Document
- ✔ Correct Spelling and Grammatical Errors
- ✔ Print a Document
- ✔ Get Help
- ✔ Close a Document and Exit Word

Key terms in this project include

- ❏ Click and Type feature
- ❏ close
- ❏ defaults
- ❏ document window
- ❏ end-of-document marker
- ❏ exit
- ❏ Formatting toolbar
- ❏ full menu
- ❏ grayed-out
- ❏ Help
- ❏ horizontal scrollbar
- ❏ hypertext links
- ❏ icons
- ❏ insertion point
- ❏ menu
- ❏ menu bar
- ❏ Office Assistant
- ❏ ruler
- ❏ saving
- ❏ ScreenTip
- ❏ short menu
- ❏ shortcuts
- ❏ Standard toolbar
- ❏ status bar
- ❏ submenu
- ❏ task pane
- ❏ title bar
- ❏ vertical scrollbar
- ❏ view buttons
- ❏ word-wrap feature

Why Would I Do This?

Word-processing software is possibly the most commonly used type of software. People around the world—students, office assistants, managers, and business professionals—use word-processing programs such as Microsoft Word for a variety of tasks. You can create letters, research papers, newsletters, brochures, and other documents with Word. You can even create and send e-mail and produce Web pages with Word.

After creating your documents, you need to edit and format them. These tasks are a snap with Word. But first, you need to learn your way around the Word window and understand how to create, save, and print your documents. In this project, you learn all of that, plus how to use the built-in Help feature. Let's get started!

Visual Summary

In this project, you learn about the Word interface—the screen and common tools—and how to create a short document, as shown in Figure 1.1.

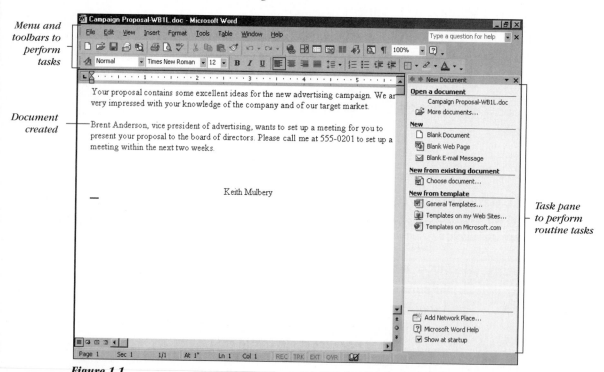

Menu and toolbars to perform tasks

Document created

Task pane to perform routine tasks

Figure 1.1

Lesson 1: Exploring the Word Screen

Starting Word is the first step to learning and using the software. Your exciting experience with Word all begins with the Start button on the taskbar. After you start Word, you learn your way around the Word screen.

To Start Word and Explore the Word Screen

1 **Click the Start button on the left side of the Windows taskbar.**

The Start menu appears. Use this menu to start programs, get help, choose computer settings, and shut down your computer.

2 **Move the mouse pointer to the Programs menu item.**

The <u>P</u>rograms menu appears on the right of the Start menu, as shown in Figure 1.2.

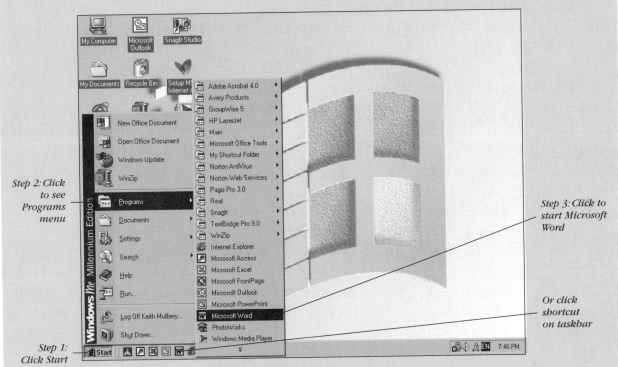

Step 2: Click to see Programs menu

Step 3: Click to start Microsoft Word

Or click shortcut on taskbar

Step 1: Click Start

Figure 1.2

3 **Move the mouse pointer to Microsoft Word on the Programs menu, and click it once.**

? If you have problems...

If you don't see Microsoft Word on the <u>P</u>rograms menu, ask your instructor for further assistance.

Word is loaded into the computer, and a blank document appears (see Figure 1.3). The Word window consists of a large area on which you place your text, graphics; and many different buttons, icons, and menus. They are all designed to help you create the perfect document for any occasion.

(Continues)

To Start Word and Explore the Word Screen (Continued)

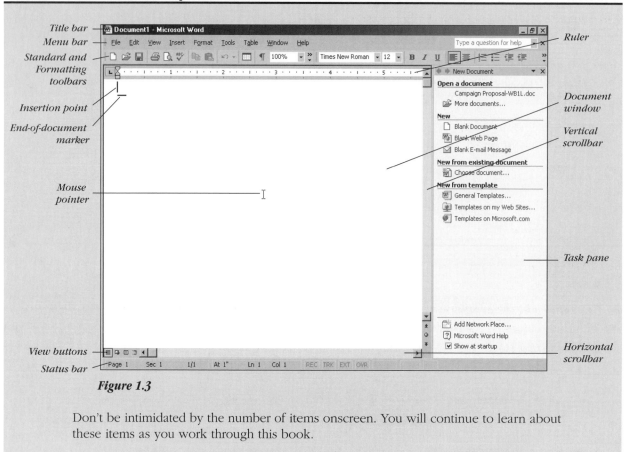

Figure 1.3

Don't be intimidated by the number of items onscreen. You will continue to learn about these items as you work through this book.

Table 1.1 lists the default screen elements and gives a brief description of each element.

Table 1.1 Elements of the Microsoft Word Screen

Element	Description
Insertion point	Shows your location in the document.
End-of-document marker	Indicates the end of the document. Appears only in Normal view.
Title bar	Shows the name of the file you are currently working on. If you haven't saved the document, Word displays a document number, such as Document2. Word also shows the name of the program, such as Microsoft Word.
Menu bar	Lists the categories of menus that contain options from which to choose.
Standard toolbar	Contains a row of buttons that perform routine tasks such as opening, saving, and printing a file. Other toolbars are available for specific types of tasks.
Formatting toolbar	Contains a row of buttons that perform functions to enhance the appearance of your documents.

Table 1.1 Elements of the Microsoft Word Screen	
Element	**Description**
Ruler	Shows the location of tabs, indents, and left and right margins.
Document window	Displays text and formats for documents you create.
Vertical scrollbar	Moves up and down in a document.
View buttons	Switch between different view modes. These options are also available on the View pull-down menu.
Horizontal scrollbar	Adjusts horizontal view (left to right).
Status bar	Displays the current page number and location of the insertion point. Also displays active modes, such as Overtype.
Task pane	A window pane that displays frequently used features. It displays different tasks, based on what you are doing—such as options for creating a new document, document recovery, and styles and formatting.

To extend your knowledge...

Using the Word Shortcut Icon

If you see the Word icon on the Windows taskbar, you can click it to immediately start Word, instead of using the Start menu.

Lesson 2: Using Menus and Toolbars

Word's commands are organized in menus. The menu bar lists nine command categories, such as File. When you click a menu category name, you see a ***menu***—a list of commands that relate to the category. Word's menus appear as short or full menus. The ***short menus*** display a list of commonly used commands (see Figure 1.4).

Click down-pointing arrows to see full menu

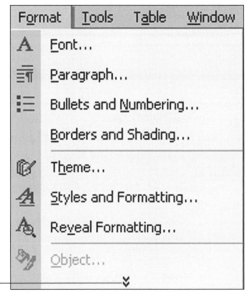

Figure 1.4

After a few seconds, or when you click the down-pointing arrows, you see the ***full menu***, which includes all commands in that menu category (see Figure 1.5). When you select a command from the full menu, Word adapts the short menu by including that command the next time you display the menu.

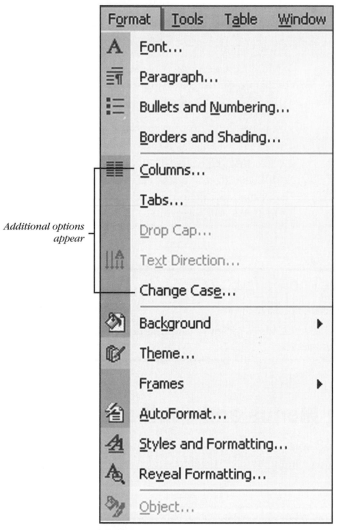

Additional options appear

Figure 1.5

To Use the Menu Bar

❶ Click File on the menu bar.
The File menu displays, listing the last four to nine documents used on your computer (see Figure 1.6). Your list will show different document names.

To Use the Menu Bar

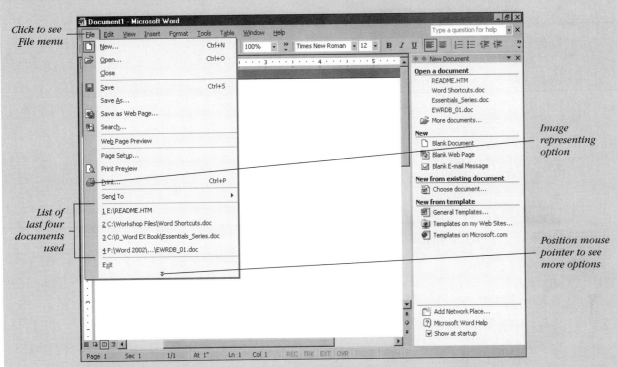

Figure 1.6

You see images on the left side of some menu options. These images, called *icons*, represent various tasks. For example, the Print icon looks like a printer. Notice that some of the icons in the menu also appear on the toolbar.

❷ Move the mouse pointer to the bottom of the File menu, where you see the arrows.

You now see the full menu, which contains additional options, such as Send To and Properties. The following table describes the different types of menu options that you encounter as you study the other menus.

Characteristic	Description	Example
… (ellipsis)	Displays a dialog box with specific task-related options.	Print…
▶ (triangle)	Displays a *submenu*, a menu of more specific options, to the side of the current menu.	Send To ▶
No symbol	Performs the task immediately without providing additional options.	Exit
✔ (check mark)	Indicates that an option is turned on or active.	✔ Standard
Gray option name	Indicates that the option is currently unavailable (*grayed-out*).	Cut

(Continues)

To Use the Menu Bar (Continued)

3 **Click** <u>F</u>**ile again on the menu bar to close the menu.**
If you decide not to select a menu bar option, close the menu by clicking the menu name.

You can close the task pane if it's visible onscreen. If the task pane does not appear on the right side of your screen, as shown in Figure 1.3, skip the next two steps of this exercise.

4 **Choose** <u>V</u>**iew.**
You see a check mark to the left of Tas<u>k</u> Pane, indicating that it is visible.

5 **Choose Tas**<u>k</u> **Pane to deselect it.**
The task pane is no longer visible.

To extend your knowledge...

Closing Menus

You can also close a menu by pressing Esc twice; by pressing Alt once; or by clicking outside of the menu, such as in the document window.

Selecting Menus from the Keyboard

You can use the keyboard to select from the menu bar. Notice that one letter (often the first) of each menu bar option is underlined. For example, <u>F</u> is underlined in <u>F</u>ile. To choose a particular menu, press Alt and the underlined letter. For example, pressing Alt+F displays the <u>F</u>ile menu.

When the menu displays, press ↓ or ↑ to highlight an option; then press ↵Enter to select that option. You can also press the underlined letter to immediately select the option of your choice. For example, press C for <u>C</u>lose on the <u>F</u>ile menu.

The menus also display keyboard ***shortcuts***, such as Ctrl+S for <u>S</u>ave (refer to Figure 1.6). By using keyboard shortcuts, you can keep your hands on the keyboard and maybe save a little time.

The Standard and Formatting toolbars are rows containing icons or buttons to perform various tasks. For example, click the Save button to save a file. Clicking the Save button is often faster than opening the <u>F</u>ile menu and choosing the <u>S</u>ave command.

Currently, the Standard and Formatting toolbars share one row. In the next exercise, you learn how to separate them to see all icons on both toolbars at the same time. Plus, you learn about ScreenTips.

To Use Toolbars

1 **Move the mouse pointer to the New Blank Document button on the Standard toolbar.**
When you position the mouse pointer on an icon, Word displays the icon's name in a little box, called a ***ScreenTip***. You should see the ScreenTip *New Blank Document (Ctrl+N)* now.

If you have problems...

If the menus and ScreenTips do not show the shortcut keys, choose <u>T</u>ools, <u>C</u>ustomize; click the <u>O</u>ptions tab; and click the *Show ScreenTips on toolbars* check box. Make sure that the *Show s<u>h</u>ortcut keys in ScreenTips* check box is selected, and click Close.

To Use Toolbars

2 **Click View on the menu bar to see the View menu.**

3 **Choose Toolbars.**

You see a list of different toolbars, plus the Customize option (see Figure 1.7). The check marks indicate the active toolbars.

Active toolbars indicated by check marks

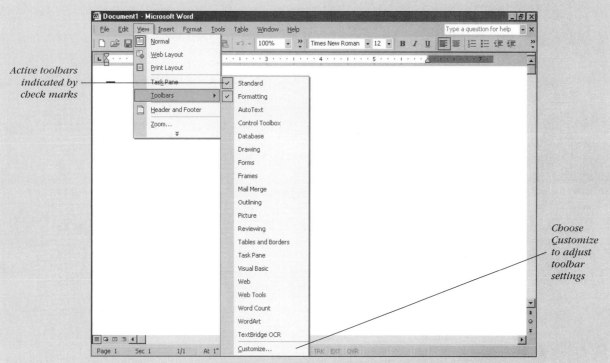

Choose Customize to adjust toolbar settings

Figure 1.7

4 **Click Customize at the bottom of the menu.**

The Customize dialog box appears, in which you can adjust the way the toolbars appear on your screen (see Figure 1.8).

(Continues)

To Use Toolbars (Continued)

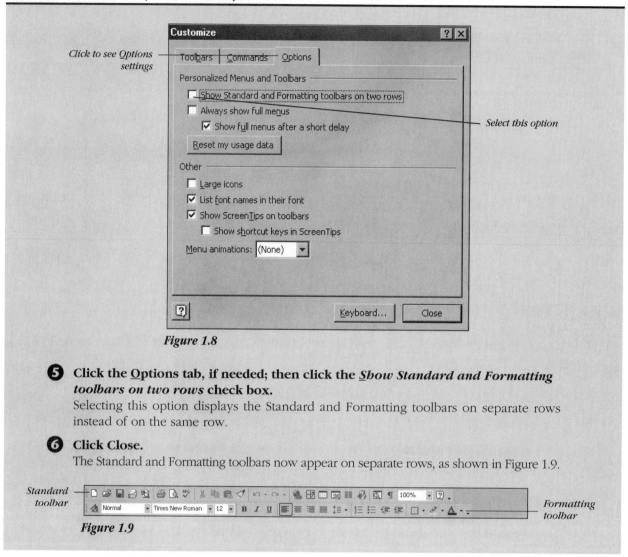

Figure 1.8

5 **Click the Options tab, if needed; then click the *Show Standard and Formatting toolbars on two rows* check box.**
Selecting this option displays the Standard and Formatting toolbars on separate rows instead of on the same row.

6 **Click Close.**
The Standard and Formatting toolbars now appear on separate rows, as shown in Figure 1.9.

Figure 1.9

 ## To extend your knowledge...

Customizing the Toolbar

Instead of choosing View, Toolbars, Customize, you can right-click anywhere on the toolbar and choose Customize.

Lesson 3: Entering Text in a Document

You can begin entering text for your document as soon as you start Word. When you begin a new document, Word's *defaults*, predefined settings such as margins and font size, control the original format of the document. The document window is where you type and format your documents, and the *insertion point* should appear below the ruler. The insertion point, sometimes called a *cursor*, is the thin vertical blinking line that indicates where you are about to insert text.

In this lesson, you enter text using the default settings.

To Enter Text in a Document

1 **Type the following text, including the misspelled words and grammatical error, in the document window:**

Your proposal contain some excelant ideas for the new advertising campagn. We are very impressed with your knowledge of the company and of our target market.

Don't press 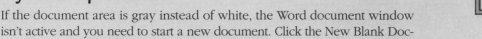(←Enter) when you reach the end of a line. When you enter more text than can fit on the current line, the ***word-wrap feature*** continues text to the next line when it runs out of room on the current line.

If you have problems...

If the document area is gray instead of white, the Word document window isn't active and you need to start a new document. Click the New Blank Document button on the left side of the Standard toolbar.

2 **Press** (←Enter) **twice when you reach the end of a single-spaced paragraph.**
Pressing (←Enter) tells Word to go to the next line. Pressing (←Enter) a second time leaves one blank line between paragraphs.

3 **Continue by typing the following paragraph:**

Brent Anderson, vice president of advertising, wants to set up a meeting for you to present your proposal to the board of directors. Please call me at 555-0201 to set up a meeting within the next two weeks.

Figure 1.10 shows what your document should look like.

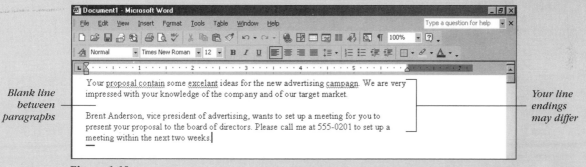

Blank line between paragraphs

Your line endings may differ

Figure 1.10

4 **Leave the text you typed onscreen to continue with the next exercise.**

To extend your knowledge...

Correcting Mistakes

If you make a mistake as you type, press (←Backspace) to delete text to the *left* of the insertion point, or press (Del) to delete text to the *right* of the insertion point. After deleting incorrect letters, type the correct letters.

Seeing Dots and Symbols

You might see dots between words and a paragraph (¶) symbol at the end of the paragraphs. You learn about these marks in Project 3, "Formatting Text." For now, click the Show/Hide ¶ button on the Standard toolbar to hide the symbols.

The **Click and Type feature** lets you double-click in any area of the document, and type new text in Print Layout View. Depending on where you double-click, you can type text at the left margin, tabbed in from the left margin, centered between the margins, or flush with the right margin.

To Use Click and Type

1 **Choose <u>V</u>iew and then choose <u>P</u>rint Layout from the <u>V</u>iew menu.**
The end-of-document marker disappears in Print Layout view. However, you can use the Click and Type feature.

2 **Position the mouse pointer about one-half inch below your last paragraph and centered between the left and right edges of the screen.**
Figure 1.11 shows the mouse pointer. The horizontal lines below the mouse pointer indicate that text will be centered when you double-click.

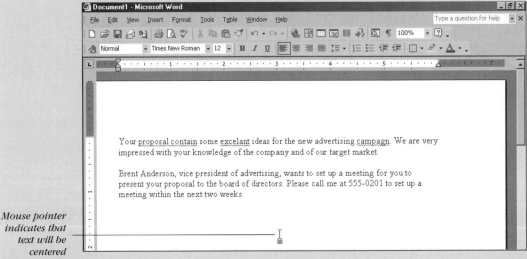

Mouse pointer indicates that text will be centered

Figure 1.11

 If you have problems...
If you don't see the horizontal lines by the mouse pointer, you might be in Normal view instead of Print Layout view. Click the Print Layout View button above the left side of the status bar.

If Click and Type is still not working, you need to activate it. To do this, choose <u>T</u>ools and choose <u>O</u>ptions from the <u>T</u>ools menu. Click the Edit tab, click the *Enable <u>c</u>lick and type* check box, and click OK.

3 **Double-click in the center point, and type your name.**
Your name is centered between the left and right margins.

4 **Leave the document onscreen to continue with the next lesson.**

Lesson 4: Saving a Document

After creating part of a document, you should save it. **Saving** is the process of storing a document with a unique filename in a particular location, such as a data disk or hard drive. Currently, the document you created exists only in the computer's random access (RAM) memory. RAM is temporary; it is cleared when you shut off your system, or if the system crashes or locks up on you. Therefore, you should save your documents to use them in the future.

In this lesson, you save the two-paragraph document with the name *Campaign Proposal-WB1L*. When saving lesson files in this book, you assign realistic filenames, such as *Campaign Proposal*, followed by a code. *WB* stands for the Word Basic (Level I) book, *1* represents the project number, and *L* represents a file you save within a lesson.

To Save a Document

① **Insert a new formatted disk into the appropriate disk drive if you plan to save to a floppy disk or Zip disk.**

② **With your new Word document open, choose File, Save As.**
The Save As dialog box appears (see Figure 1.12). The first step in saving your document is to choose a location where you want to keep it.

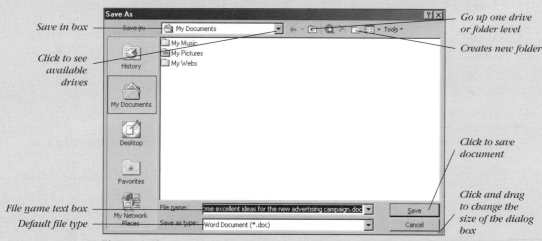

Save in box
Click to see available drives
File name text box
Default file type

Go up one drive or folder level
Creates new folder
Click to save document
Click and drag to change the size of the dialog box

Figure 1.12

By default, Word saves documents in the My Documents folder on the hard drive.

③ **Click the drop-down arrow on the right side of the *Save in* text box.**
You see a list of available storage devices on your computer system (see Figure 1.13). You may choose to save to a floppy disk, a hard drive, a Zip disk, or a network drive. If you want to save the file in a different folder, select the folder from the *Save in* list, or click the Create New Folder button to create and name a new folder. Ask your instructor if you are not sure about the location for saving the files you create.

(Continues)

To Save a Document (Continued)

Saves to floppy disk

Saves to Zip disk

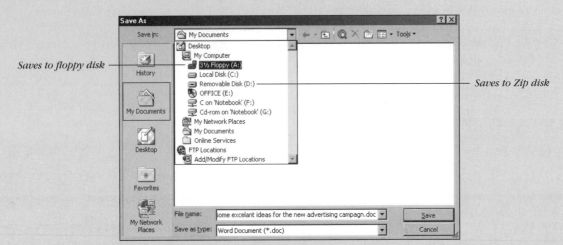

Figure 1.13

4 Select the drive and folder in which you want to save the current document.

If you have problems...

If the *Save in* option displays Desktop and you don't see a list of drives, ask your instructor how to proceed.

5 Press Alt+N to make the *File name* text box active.
Now, you can type over the suggested filename.

6 Type `Campaign Proposal-WB1L` in the *File name* text box.
When you type a filename, it replaces the default name suggested by Word. You can assign long filenames based on Windows limitations, including upper- and lowercase letters, numbers, some symbols, and spaces.

7 Click Save in the bottom-right corner of the dialog box.

8 Leave your document onscreen to continue with the next lesson.

If you have problems...

If you try to save to a floppy disk and get an error message, make sure that you have correctly inserted a disk in the disk drive, and make sure that you have selected the correct drive. Some network drives may prohibit users from storing files in these locations.

To extend your knowledge...

Using Save versus Save As

The first time you save a document, you can use either Save or Save As. Either way, you see the Save As dialog box. After you save a document, however, Save and Save As have two different effects.

If you modify a document and use Save, Word saves the changes under the same filename without displaying the Save As dialog box. Use Save to save a document under the same filename and then continue entering text and formatting it.

At other times, you might want to assign a different name to a modified document, so you have the original document as well as the modified document. Use Save As to save the document with a different filename or to a different location. For example, you might want to save a document in two different locations: on a Zip disk and your hard drive. To do this, click the *Save in* drop-down arrow, and choose the drive and folder in which to save the modified document. Furthermore, you might want to save a document in a non-Word format. To do this, click the *Save as type* drop-down arrow, and choose the file type, such as *Plain Text (*.txt)*.

Saving Methods

You can also press Ctrl+S, or click the Save button on the Standard toolbar to save a document. Note that the toolbar does *not* contain a button for Save As, although the Save button displays the Save As dialog box if you have *not* saved the document yet.

Lesson 5: Correcting Spelling and Grammatical Errors

A wavy red underline below a word indicates that the word is not in Microsoft's main dictionary. You see these wavy red lines below misspelled words and proper nouns. For example, you see a wavy red underline below *excelant*.

A wavy green underline below a word or phrase indicates a potential grammatical error. For example, you see a wavy green underline below *proposal contain*.

You can correct spelling and grammatical errors by right-clicking the text above the wavy underline and choosing the correct spelling or grammar from the menu that appears.

To Correct Spelling and Grammatical Errors

❶ **Right-click *proposal contain* in the first paragraph in the *Campaign Proposal-WB1L* document.**
You see a shortcut menu that displays possible corrections, as shown in Figure 1.14.

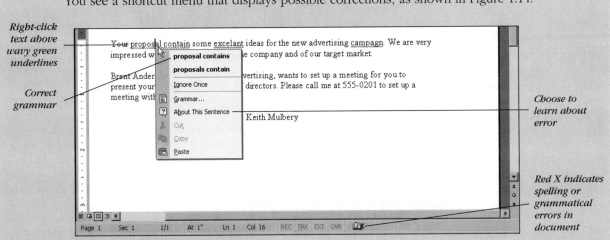

Right-click text above wavy green underlines

Correct grammar

Choose to learn about error

Red X indicates spelling or grammatical errors in document

Figure 1.14

❷ **Select *proposal contains* from the menu.**
Word replaces the grammatical error with the correct grammar you select from the menu.

(Continues)

To Correct Spelling and Grammatical Errors (Continued)

③ Right-click *excelant*.
Word displays a list of suggested spellings (see Figure 1.15).

Misspelled word

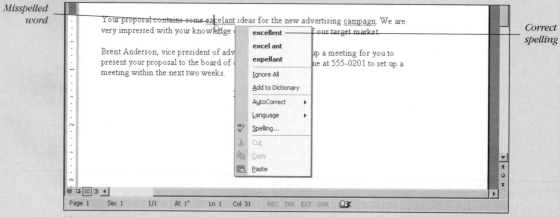

Correct spelling

Figure 1.15

④ Choose *excellent* from the menu that appears.
Word replaces *excelant* with *excellent*.

⑤ Right-click *campagn* and choose *campaign* from the menu.
Word replaces *campagn* with *campaign*. Notice that the red X changes to a red check mark on the status bar, indicating that the document does not contain any spelling or major grammatical errors.

⑥ Click the Save icon on the Standard toolbar.

To extend your knowledge...

Spelling and Grammar Dialog Box

Instead of looking through your document to find text with wavy red or green underlines, you can use the Spelling and Grammar dialog box to find and correct these types of errors.

Click the Spelling and Grammar button on the Standard toolbar. Figure 1.16 shows a sample error in the dialog box.

Click appropriate suggestion

Display additional options

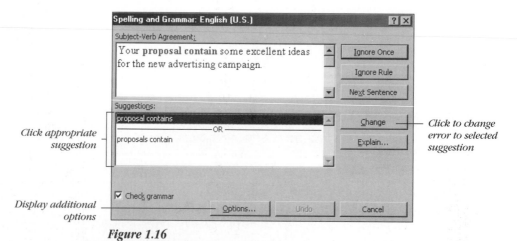

Click to change error to selected suggestion

Figure 1.16

The top of the Spelling and Grammar dialog box tells you the type of error, such as Subject-Verb Agreement. You see the error in a different color and suggestions to choose from. You can ignore the detected word or phrase if it is really correct.

Lesson 6: Printing a Document

Before printing a document, you should preview it to make sure it looks the way you want it to look. If the document is formatted correctly, you can then print it. If not, you can correctly format the document before printing it.

To Use Print Preview

1 Click the Print Preview button on the Standard toolbar.
You see a preview of what the printed document will look like (see Figure 1.17).

Click to print

View percentage

Close Print Preview window

Figure 1.17

If your document is formatted correctly, you can print from within the Print Preview window by clicking the Print button on the Print Preview toolbar.

2 Click Close on the Print Preview toolbar to close the Print Preview window.

To extend your knowledge...

Print Preview Options

You can press ↵Enter to move text down or display the Ruler to change margins to balance text on a page if needed. The Print Preview toolbar contains buttons for magnifying the page onscreen, displaying one page, displaying multiple pages, or shrinking the document to fit.

After previewing a document and adjusting the format, if needed, you are ready to print it. You can quickly print the entire document by clicking the Print button on the Standard toolbar. If you need to specify print settings, such as the number of copies to print, you need to display the Print dialog box.

To Print a Document

1 **Make sure the printer is turned on, has paper, and is online.**
Ask your instructor if you need further assistance in using the printer.

2 **Click File and then choose Print from the menu.**
The Print dialog box appears (see Figure 1.18).

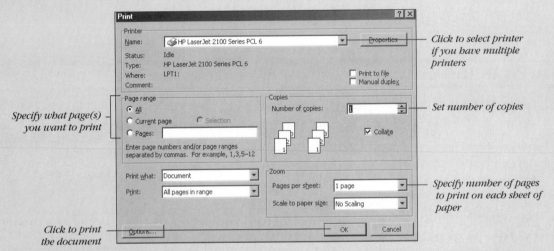

Click to select printer if you have multiple printers

Specify what page(s) you want to print

Set number of copies

Specify number of pages to print on each sheet of paper

Click to print the document

Figure 1.18

3 **Ask your instructor which printer name is correct for the system you're using. If needed, click the down arrow to the right of the *Name* text box and choose the correct printer name from the list.**

4 **Click OK to print your document.**
Word sends a copy of the document to the printer. After you print a document, make sure the text looks good on paper. Check the format. You might need to adjust the formatting and print the document again.

5 **Leave your Word document onscreen to continue with the next lesson.**

To extend your knowledge...

Print Keyboard Shortcut

You can press Ctrl+P to display the Print dialog box.

Clicking the Print Button

Clicking the Print button on the Standard toolbar sends the entire document to the printer without displaying the Print dialog box. Although this is a fast way to print a document, it doesn't give you the opportunity to select print options.

Print Options

The Print dialog box contains many useful options. For example, you can print only the page that contains the insertion point (Current page) or a range of pages, such as pages 3–10 (Pages). Furthermore, you can print several copies of the document (Number of copies), print miniature copies of pages on a single sheet of paper (Pages per sheet), or adjust the document text size to fit on a particular type of paper (Scale to paper size).

Lesson 7: Getting Help

When you work with Word, you might need to know about a specific feature or how to perform a certain task. Although you are learning a lot about Word by completing this book, you might run across a situation in which you need assistance. Word contains an onscreen assistance feature called Help. **Help** provides information about Word features and step-by-step instructions for performing tasks.

You can get quick assistance by using Word Version 2002's Ask a Question text box, which is located to the right of the menu bar. Figure 1.19 shows the Ask a Question box to the right of the menu bar.

Figure 1.19

In this lesson, you want to find out how to recover a document when Word locks up and you haven't saved it recently.

To Get Help from the Ask a Question Box

❶ Type How do I recover a document? **in the Ask a Question text box, and then press** ⏎Enter**.**
Figure 1.20 shows the options that appear for the topic you entered in the Ask a Question text box.

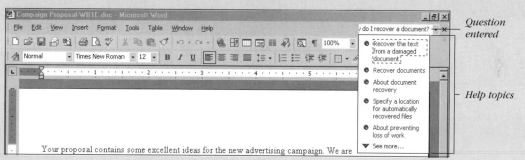

Figure 1.20

❷ Choose *Recover documents*.
The Microsoft Word Help window appears (see Figure 1.21).

(Continues)

To Get Help from the Ask a Question Box (Continued)

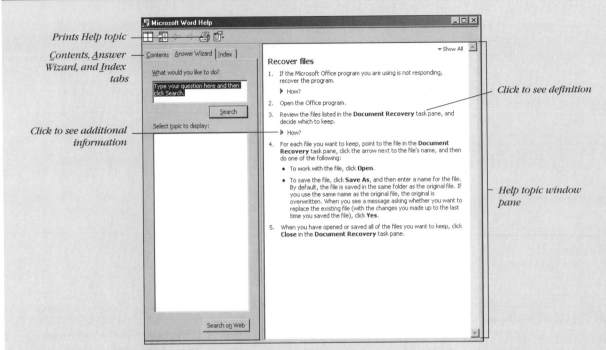

Figure 1.21

The left side contains tabs for different ways of accessing Help: Contents, Answer Wizard, and Index. The right side contains information about the topic you selected. The Help window covers part or all of the document. Don't worry about this; the document window enlarges when you close the Help feature. Keywords and phrases appearing in a different color—usually blue—are called *hypertext links*. When you click a hypertext link, you see additional information.

 If you have problems...

If you don't see the Navigation pane, click the Show button on the Help toolbar.

❸ Click the blue words *task pane* on the right side of the window.
A definition appears in green letters.

❹ Click *How?* below step 1 in the Help window.
When you click a hyperlink preceded by a triangle, Word displays additional information, such as specific steps or explanations. If you click the hyperlink again, the additional information is hidden again.

❺ Click the Print button on the Microsoft Word Help toolbar to display the Print dialog box.

❻ Click OK to print the Help topic.
Word sends the Help topic to the printer so that you'll have a hard copy of the information as you perform the step-by-step instructions, if needed.

❼ Click the Close button—the X in the top right corner of the Help window—to close the Microsoft Word Help window.

❽ Keep the document onscreen to continue to the next lesson.

To extend your knowledge...

Help Index

The Index feature lets you type a topic and search through the alphabetical index of topics. The first step is to enter keywords (particular words that might be found in the Help topics) and then click the Search button. Alternatively, you can scroll through the list of keywords in the index to find what you're looking for.

You see a list of topics in the *Choose a topic* list box. Double-click the topic listed in the *Or choose keywords* list box.

What's This? Feature

The What's This? Feature displays a ScreenTip about a screen item. To use this feature, choose Help, What's This, or press ⬆Shift+F1. When the pointer resembles a question mark with an arrow, click the mouse pointer on the screen item that you don't understand. Word then provides a ScreenTip that describes that feature. Press ⬆Shift+F1 to turn off the What's This? feature. If you click within text with the What's This? mouse pointer, the task pane appears with information describing the formats of the text you click in.

Office Assistant

You might see the **Office Assistant**, which is an animated image, onscreen. The Office Assistant offers suggestions and lets you click it and type in questions or topics like you do in the Ask a Question text box. You can display or hide the Office Assistant by choosing the option you want from the Help menu.

Help on the Web

If you can't find the information you need within Word, you can access resources available on the World Wide Web. Assuming you have Internet access, you can choose Help, Office on the Web to view information on Microsoft's Web site for Word.

Lesson 8: Closing a Document and Exiting Word

When you finish working on your documents, you should properly **close** the files (that is, remove them from the screen). When you finish using Word, you should **exit** (close down) the Word software. If you simply turn off the computer, you might lose valuable work and create problems within the computer itself. Because you saved the document in Lesson 4 and have not made any changes to it, you can close the document without having to save again.

To Close a File and Exit Word

① **Choose File, Close from the menu.**
The file closes immediately. If you haven't saved the document after modifying it, Word displays a dialog box that asks if you want to save the changes. Click Yes to save the file before closing it, or click No to close the document without saving the changes.

② **Choose File, Exit from the menu to close Word.**
If other Word files are open, they close immediately if you saved them. If other files have been modified since you last saved them, Word prompts you to save them before the program closes. After Word closes, you see the Windows Desktop if no other programs are running.

This concludes Project 1. You can reinforce and expand your knowledge and skills by completing the end-of-project activities that follow the summary.

Summary

You are now familiar with some of the Word screen components. You can also use the menu bar and toolbars to access commands easily. You can enter text, check the spelling and grammar, and save and print the document.

You can extend your learning by studying the menu bar and toolbars to see how commands are organized. Use the Office Assistant and the Help feature to learn more about the exciting things you can do with Word. Remember to use the index at the back of this book; it's an excellent way to find the *exact* pages that discuss particular topics. These sources provide a vast array of information to help you become comfortable with and proficient at using Word.

Checking Concepts and Terms

Multiple Choice

Circle the letter of the correct answer for each of the following.

1. How can you tell if a word is misspelled onscreen? [L5]

   a. Green underline

   b. Red wavy underline

   c. Red check mark on Spelling and Grammar Status icon on the status bar

   d. Word blinks onscreen

2. What happens when you choose a menu option that displays a triangle? [L2]

   a. You see a submenu.

   b. A dialog box appears.

   c. Word immediately performs the command.

   d. The menu closes.

3. Which of the following does *not* happen when you use the Save command? [L4]

   a. Word saves an existing document with the same filename.

   b. The document closes.

   c. The Save As dialog box appears if you haven't saved the document before.

   d. You are able to use the document in the future.

4. If you want to scroll through an alphabetical list of Help topics, which Help feature do you use? [L7]

   a. Index

   b. Contents

   c. Office Assistant

   d. Answer Wizard

5. Which of the following can you do in the Print Preview window? [L6]

   a. See the amount of space for the margins.

   b. Type and edit text.

   c. Look at the overall format of the document.

   d. All of the above.

Screen ID

Label each element of the Word screen shown in Figure 1.22.

A. Ask a Question box

B. end-of-document marker

C. Formatting toolbar

D. insertion point

E. menu bar

F. mouse pointer

G. Standard toolbar

H. status bar

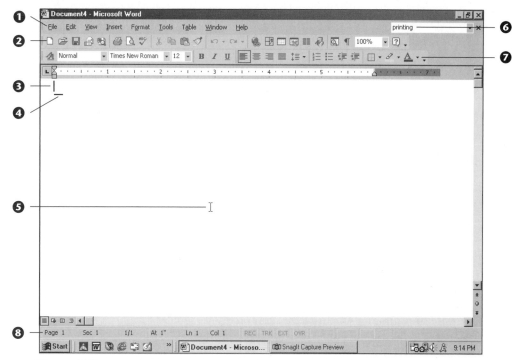

Figure 1.22

1. _____   5. _____

2. _____   6. _____

3. _____   7. _____

4. _____   8. _____

Discussion

1. Explain how the menus are adaptive. Provide an example of options on a short and long menu. [L2]

2. Explain the difference between Save and Save As. Provide an example of a situation when you would use each command. [L4]

3. Display the Microsoft Word Help window. Explore the Contents, Answer Wizard, and Index tabs. Explain how each tab of options is organized and when you would use each tab. [L7]

Skill Drill

Skill Drill exercises reinforce project skills. Each skill reinforced is the same, or nearly the same, as a skill presented in the project. Detailed instructions are provided in a step-by-step format.

1. Exploring Menus and ScreenTips

You want to study Word's menus. The more you study the screen components, the more you understand the structure and logic of using Word. Plus, you want to display shortcuts in the ScreenTips until you learn them.

1. Start Word.
2. Press Alt+A to display the Table menu. (You press A because a is underlined in Table.)
3. Click the arrows to display the full Table menu.
4. Try choosing Table Properties.
   Nothing happens because the option is grayed-out. It is available only when you perform a specific task first.
5. Press Alt once to close the Table menu without choosing any options.
6. Choose Tools from the menu bar.
7. Choose Customize from the Tools menu.
8. Click the Options tab, if needed.
9. Look at the *Show shortcut keys in ScreenTips* option. If it is selected, click Close. Otherwise, click the *Show shortcut keys in ScreenTips* check box to select it and then click Close.
10. Position the mouse pointer on the second button on the Standard toolbar to see the Screen-Tip *Open (Ctrl+O)*.
11. Position the mouse pointer on the capital B icon on the Formatting toolbar to see the Screen-Tip *Bold (Ctrl+B)*.
12. Choose File, Close to close the document. Click No if you are prompted to save the document. Choose File, Exit if you need to end your work session.

2. Displaying Different Toolbars

You want to see some of the other Word toolbars. You can display and hide toolbars, as needed.

1. Choose View and then choose Toolbars to display the Toolbars submenu.
2. Click Drawing to display the Drawing toolbar. (The toolbar appears at the bottom of the Word screen.)
3. Position the mouse pointer over the blue A button on the Drawing toolbar. (You should see the ScreenTip *Insert WordArt.*)
4. Repeat Steps 1 and 2 to hide the Drawing toolbar.
5. Click the right mouse button on any icon on the Standard toolbar.
6. Choose Word Count from the list of toolbars to display the Word Count toolbar.
7. Click the Recount button on the Word Count toolbar that appears.
   The Word Count toolbar displays that you have 0 words in the current document.
8. Right-click anywhere on the Word Count toolbar, and choose Word Count to hide that toolbar.

3. Creating, Spell-Checking, Saving, and Printing a Document

You need to compose a short note to your immediate supervisor, telling her that you need to come in later on Friday because you have a special test in the morning. You create and save the first note; then, you change the supervisor's name and save the modified document with a new filename.

1. Type `Dear Ms. Turner:`, and press `↵Enter` twice.
2. Type the following paragraph, including the errors:

   `This Friday I have a specal test in my history class at the local community college. These test is scheduled during a specific time, which is controlled by the instructer. I would appreciate being able to come in to work at 11:30 instead of my usual 8:30 time. Thank you for working around my college class scedul.`

3. Press `↵Enter` twice after the last paragraph, type `Sincerely yours,` press `↵Enter` four times, and type your name.
4. Choose File, Save As.
5. Click the *Save in* drop-down arrow, and choose the drive in which you have been instructed to save documents.
6. Type `Turner Note-WB1SD3` in the File name text box, and click Save to save the document.
7. Right-click *specal*, and choose *special* from the suggested spellings.
8. Right-click *These test*, and choose *This test* from the suggestions.
9. Right-click *is scheduled*, and choose Ignore Once to ignore the passive voice message.
   You might see wavy lines below *is controlled*. If so, you need to ignore it. If you don't see wavy lines below the phrase, skip the next step.
10. Right-click *is controlled*, and choose Ignore Once.
11. Continue right-clicking words with the wavy red or green underlines, and then choose the correct suggestions.
12. Choose File, Print, and then click OK to print the document.
13. Keep the document onscreen to continue with the next exercise.

4. Saving a Document Under a Different Name

You need to send the same message to the branch manager. Instead of typing the same text, you edit the existing document and save it with a different name.

1. In the open *Turner Note* document, click to the left of Ms. Turner on the first line, and press `Del` until you have deleted her name.
2. Type `Mr. Baxter`, the branch manager's name. Make sure that there is still a colon after the name.
3. Choose File, Save As to assign a new name to the modified document.
4. Make sure that the correct drive is displayed in the Save in option. Change it if necessary.
5. Type `Baxter Note-WB1SD4` in the File name text box, and click Save.
6. Click the Print button on the Standard toolbar to print the document without displaying the Print dialog box.
7. Choose File, Close to close the document.
8. Choose File, Exit if you need to exit Word now. Leave Word open if you are continuing with the next exercise.

5. Using the Office Assistant and the Help Index

You want to continue studying various topics in the Help Index and then print a Help topic.

1. Click the Office Assistant if it's displayed. If it's not displayed, choose Help, Show the Office Assistant, and then click it.

2. Click the <u>O</u>ptions button to display the Office Assistant dialog box.
3. Click the <u>U</u>se the Office Assistant check box to deselect it. Then, click OK.
4. Press F1 to display the Microsoft Word Help window.
5. Click the <u>I</u>ndex tab on the left side of the Microsoft Word Help window.
6. Type **save** and click the <u>S</u>earch button.
7. Click the topic, *Save a document* to display information on the right side of the window.
8. Scroll through the topic to continue reading information about saving documents.
9. Click the Close button in the top-right corner of the Microsoft Word Help window to close it.
10. Continue working in Word if you want to complete the Challenge exercises, or choose <u>F</u>ile, E<u>x</u>it to close Word.

Challenge

Challenge exercises expand on or are somewhat related to skills presented in the lessons. Each exercise provides a brief narrative introduction, followed by instructions in a numbered-step format that are not as detailed as those in the Skill Drill section.

1. Creating, Modifying, Saving, and Printing a Letter

You want to write a short note to your word processing instructor to let him or her know your goals for learning Microsoft Word.

1. In a new document window, type today's date, and press ↵Enter four times.
2. Type your instructor's name and address on separate lines. Press ↵Enter twice after the address.
3. Type the greeting, press ↵Enter twice, and type a first paragraph about yourself.
4. Save the document on your data disk as **Introduction Letter-WB1CH1**.
5. Type a second paragraph that describes why you are learning Word. Then, complete the rest of the letter with a complimentary closing and your name.
6. Check the spelling and grammar in the document by right-clicking words and phrases that have a wavy red or green underline, and choosing the correct word or phrase.
7. Save the modified document under the same name.
8. Preview, print, and close the document.

2. Creating, Saving, and Printing Two Copies of a Study Guide

You want to create a list of the terminology you studied in this project. After creating the document, you want to print two copies.

1. Create the study guide shown in Figure 1.23, pressing Tab↹ once or twice to type the definitions.

```
Jorg Carsten
Project 1 Terminology

Close          Process of removing a document from the screen.

Default        Standard setting, such as margins, determined by software.

Exit           Process of "turning off" the software.

Help           Feature that provides online assistance about tasks and commands.

ScreenTip      Little yellow box that tells name of toolbar icon.

Menu           List of commands.

Ruler          Measurements for visualizing vertical or horizontal distance.

Status Bar     Row that shows location in document, among other things.

Toolbar        Row of icons or buttons that provide quick way to execute commands.
```

Figure 1.23

2. Save the study guide with these specifications:
   ○ `Terminology List-WB1CH2` is the filename.
   ○ It should be saved to a Zip disk or personal network drive.
3. Preview the document and then print two copies of it.

3. Using Help and Printing a Help Topic

You want to print a list of keyboard shortcuts for reference. A friend told you that you can find a Help topic that provides step-by-step instructions for displaying and printing such a list.

1. Search for `keyboard shortcuts` in the Ask a Question box.
2. Choose the option that will display information about printing a list of shortcuts.
3. Print the Help topic that provides the step-by-step instructions.
4. Refer to your printout, and complete the steps to list the keyboard shortcuts.
5. Save the document that results as `Keyboard Commands-WB1CH3`, and obtain a printout of the first two pages of the keyboard shortcuts.

4. Finding Information in the Help Index

The Help Index provides an alphabetical listing of various topics. You want to find information in the Help Index to learn more about the status bar components.

1. Display the Office Assistant.
2. Click Options, deselect the option that uses the Office Assistant, and then click OK.
3. Access Microsoft Word Help without using the Office Assistant.
4. Type `status bar` as a keyword in the Index.
5. Display the topic that tells you about items on the status bar.
6. Print the topic.
7. Close the Help window.

Discovery Zone

Discovery Zone exercises require advanced knowledge of topics presented in *Essentials* lessons, application of skills from multiple lessons, or self-directed learning of new skills.

1. Saving a File with a Password

You need to create a highly confidential document. You want to save the document so that the user must enter a password to open the document. Use the Help Index or Office Assistant to find out how to save a document with a password. Print the specific step-by-step help instructions.

Compose a document that briefly discusses the difference between <u>S</u>ave and Save <u>A</u>s. Type two paragraphs. Save the document on your data disk as `Saving Documents-WB1DZ1` with the password `Secret`. Print the document.

2. Customizing Grammar Checking

Create a new blank document and type the following paragraph, including the errors and two spaces between *comitee meeting*.

```
The next comitee  meeting will be held on tusday in the conference room. Mr.
Chen will discusses the budget implications for our project. Before the meet-
ing begins you should reviewe the attached agenda, budget and polcies.
```

Display the Spelling and Grammar dialog box. Before correcting errors, select the Grammar & Style writing style, and set the *Comma required before last list item* to *always*. You may need to explore the Options and Settings buttons to find these options.

Start the Spelling and Grammar check. Correct all spelling and punctuation errors. Ignore any passive-voice detections. When you're done, type your name a double-space below the paragraph, save the document as `Committee Meeting-WB1DZ2`, and then print it.

3. Using the Language Bar

You remember reading about a new feature called the Language bar in Word Version 2002. Because you want to know more about it, use the Help feature to display information.

Specifically, find out how to show and hide the Language bar. Print the Help topic, and practice showing and hiding it. Ask your instructor if you have the devices to use this feature. If so, experiment with the Language bar and then hide it.

Working with a Document

Objectives

In this project you learn how to

- ✔ Open a Document
- ✔ Scroll in a Document
- ✔ Insert Text
- ✔ Select Text
- ✔ Delete and Change Text
- ✔ Change View Modes
- ✔ Create Envelopes
- ✔ Create Labels

Key terms in this project include

- ❑ AutoComplete
- ❑ folders
- ❑ Full Screen view
- ❑ Insert mode
- ❑ Normal view
- ❑ opening
- ❑ Overtype mode
- ❑ Print Layout view
- ❑ scrolling
- ❑ selecting
- ❑ selection bar
- ❑ Smart Tag
- ❑ zoom

Why Would I Do This?

Now that you are familiar with the Word screen and know the basics for creating, saving, and printing a document, you are ready to expand your knowledge to modify a document. In Project 1, "Getting Started with Word," you created a two-paragraph document, and corrected spelling and grammatical errors. In this project, you insert, select, and delete text to create a business letter. In addition, you create an envelope for your printed letter.

Visual Summary

Figure 2.1 shows the business letter you create.

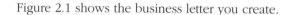

February 17, 2004

Ms. Rebecca Farnsworth
Farnsworth Advertising
5350 North Edgewood Drive
Provo, UT 84604

Dear Ms. Farnsworth:

Your proposal contains some excellent ideas for the summer advertising campaign. The theme you selected is appropriate for our new product line. We are impressed with your knowledge of the company and of our target market.

Brent Anderson, vice president of advertising, wants to set up a meeting for you to present your proposal to the board of directors. Please call me at 555-2486 to set up a meeting within the next two weeks.

Sincerely,

Ingrid Sutherland

Figure 2.1

Figure 2.2 shows the envelope you create for the business letter.

Ms. Rebecca Farnsworth
Farnsworth Advertising
5350 North Edgewood Drive
Provo, UT 84604

Figure 2.2

Lesson 1: Opening an Existing Document

One of the greatest benefits of using a computer is the capability to save documents and then use them again later. Using documents that were previously created saves valuable time in retyping and reformatting the document.

Opening is the process of displaying a previously saved document. After you open a document, you can make changes, add new text, format text, save it, and print it.

To Open an Existing Document

1 **If Word is not already running on your system, start the program, as described in Project 1.**

2 **Click the Open button on the Standard toolbar.**
The Open dialog box appears, as shown in Figure 2.3. Notice that it looks similar to the Save As dialog box you saw when you saved a document in Project 1.

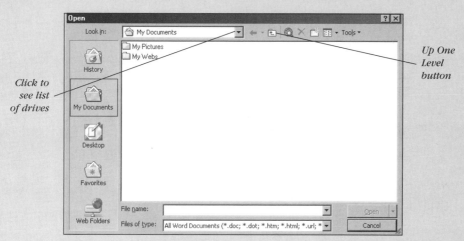

Figure 2.3

3 **Click the arrow to the right of the *Look in* box.**
The Look in list is identical to the Save in list you saw in Project 1. It lists the available storage drives, such as $3\frac{1}{2}$ Floppy (A:).

4 **Select the drive and folder containing the student files for this book.**

 If you have problems…
If you don't know where the data files are located, ask your instructor where the files are stored (for example, the hard drive or school network). You might need to download the student data files from the Prentice Hall Web site. See the Introduction of this book for more information.

5 **Double-click the folder that contains the Project 2 files.**
Data files are stored in categories called ***folders***. Each folder name correlates to a project in this book. For example, all files you need to open for this project are stored in the same folder.

(Continues)

To Open an Existing Document (Continued)

6 Click *ew1-0201* in the file list to select it.

7 Click <u>O</u>pen in the bottom-right corner of the dialog box.
Word accesses the document from its storage device and displays it in a document window. The filename *ew1-0201* appears on the title bar (see Figure 2.4).

Filename on title bar

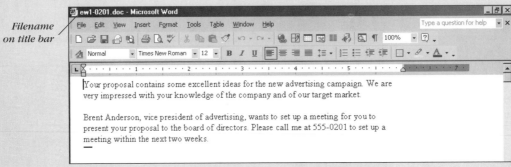

Figure 2.4

8 Choose <u>F</u>ile, Save <u>A</u>s.
The Save As dialog box displays.

9 Click the arrow to the right of the *Save <u>i</u>n* box, and choose the drive and folder where you save documents.
You need to change the *Save <u>i</u>n* location if you opened the file from a read-only network drive. You need to save files to a data disk, Zip disk, or personal network drive.

10 In the File <u>n</u>ame box, type `Proposal Letter-WB2L` and then click <u>S</u>ave.
From now on, you are instructed to open and save files without specific instructions to display the Open or Save As dialog boxes.

11 Keep the document onscreen to continue with the next lesson.

To extend your knowledge...

Displaying the Open Dialog Box

You can also display the Open dialog box by choosing <u>F</u>ile, <u>O</u>pen, or by pressing `Ctrl`+`O`.

Opening Recently Used Files

The <u>F</u>ile menu lists the last four documents that were used on your computer. If this menu lists the name of the document you want to work with, you can choose it from the menu to open that document. If the current disk does not contain the file, you see an error message.

You can customize the number of recently used files that are listed. Choose <u>T</u>ools, <u>O</u>ptions. Click the General tab. Specify how many filenames you want to list in the *Recently used file list* box and then click OK.

Opening Files from the Task Pane

If the task pane is displayed on the right side of the screen, you can click a filename to open a recently used file. You can also click *More documents* to display the Open dialog box and navigate through the storage devices to find the file you want to open.

Lesson 2: Scrolling in a Document

To make changes and corrections quickly and easily, you need to know the various ways of **scrolling**, or moving around in a document. For example, you can use either the mouse or the keyboard to move the insertion point in Word. Table 2.1 shows useful keyboard shortcuts for moving around in a document.

Table 2.1 Keyboard Shortcuts for Working in a Document	
Key(s)	**Moves the Insertion Point**
←	one character to the left
→	one character to the right
↑	up one line
↓	down one line
Home	to the beginning of the line
End	to the end of the line
PgUp	up one window or page
PgDn	down one window or page
Ctrl+Home	to the beginning of the document
Ctrl+End	to the end of the document
Ctrl+←	one word to the left
Ctrl+→	one word to the right
Ctrl+↑	up one paragraph
Ctrl+↓	down one paragraph
Ctrl+PgUp	to the top of the previous page
Ctrl+PgDn	to the top of the next page

The *Proposal Letter-WB2L* document should be open on your screen. In the next exercise, you practice scrolling through the letter using both the mouse and the keyboard.

To Scroll Through the Document

1 Press Ctrl+End to move the insertion point to the end of the document.

2 Position the mouse pointer to the immediate left of the word *proposal* on the first line in the first paragraph; then, click the left mouse button.
When the mouse pointer is shaped like an I-beam, click within the document to place the insertion point at that location. This is a fast way of positioning the insertion point when you want to add new text within an existing paragraph.

3 Press Ctrl+↓ to position the insertion point on the blank line between paragraphs.

4 Press Ctrl+↓ again to position the insertion point at the beginning of the next paragraph.
Every time you press ↵Enter, you create a paragraph. Word treats blank lines as paragraphs as well as regular text paragraphs.

(Continues)

To Scroll Through the Document (Continued)

You might see an icon called a ***Smart Tag***, which displays options when you click it. In this case, the Smart Tag might let you add Brent's name to the Microsoft Outlook Contacts folder.

5 **On the vertical scrollbar, click the down scroll arrow two times.**
Clicking items on the vertical scrollbar, such as the down scroll arrow or the up scroll arrow, does not move the insertion point. Using the vertical scrollbar merely lets you see different parts of the document. The insertion point remains where you last positioned it (see Figure 2.5).

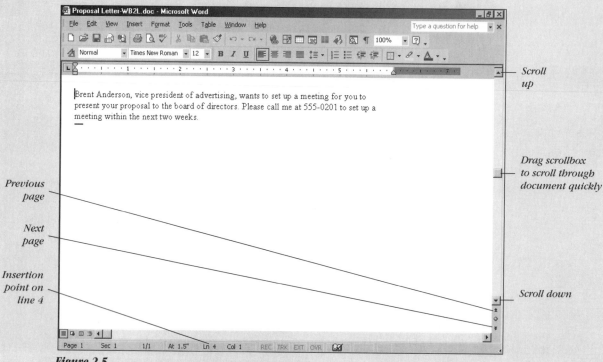

Scroll up

Drag scrollbox to scroll through document quickly

Previous page

Next page

Insertion point on line 4

Scroll down

Figure 2.5

6 **Click and drag the scrollbox to the top of the vertical scrollbar. You can now see the top of your document again.**
If your document contains more than one page, you see a ScreenTip noting the page number, such as Page: 3, as you click and drag the scrollbox.

7 **Press Ctrl+Home to move the insertion point to the top of the document.**
Take a minute now to practice some of the other keyboard shortcuts listed in Table 2.1.

In most cases, you save changes to your document before continuing to the next lesson. Because you just practiced scrolling in the document, you don't need to save the document because no changes were made.

8 **Keep the document onscreen to continue with the next lesson.**

To extend your knowledge...

Select Browse Object

Clicking the Select Browse Object button displays a palette (see Figure 2.6), so you can choose the object you want to quickly move the insertion point to.

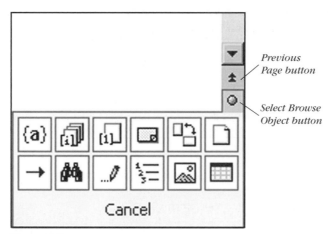

Figure 2.6

The default object is Page, which lets you move the insertion point to the top of the previous page or to the top of the next page. When you select a different browse object, such as Heading, the double arrows appear in blue. When you click the Next button, Word takes you to the next object, such as the next heading.

Click the Select Browse Object button, and choose Page to change the browse mode back to Page.

Using the Go To Option

You can move the insertion point to a specific location by using the Go To option in the Find and Replace dialog box. Click Edit, Go To, or press Ctrl+G to display the Go To options. Then type the page number in the *Enter page number* text box. See Figure 2.7 for an example of the Go To options.

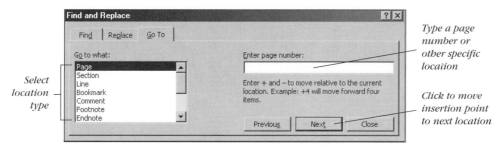

Figure 2.7

Lesson 3: Inserting Text

You can insert text within existing text when **Insert mode** is active. When you insert text, the new text is inserted at the insertion point's location. Existing text moves over to allow room for the new text. You can tell if you're in the Insert mode if OVR is grayed-out on the status bar.

In this lesson, you use Insert mode to insert text to complete the letter. You need to insert the date, inside address, salutation, and signature block to have a fully formatted letter. You will use the Auto-Complete feature to help you insert the current date. **AutoComplete** displays a ScreenTip with text, such as a date, when you type parts of certain words that are stored within Word.

To Insert the Date with AutoComplete

1 In the *Proposal Letter-WB2L* document, press Ctrl + Home to move the insertion point to the beginning of the first paragraph in the document.
You need to insert the date at the beginning of the document.

2 Start typing the name of the current month. For example, if the current month is February, type Febr.
You should see a ScreenTip that shows the rest of the month, as shown in Figure 2.8.

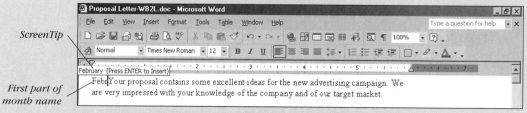

ScreenTip

First part of month name

Figure 2.8

If the current month is March, April, May, June, or July, the ScreenTip won't appear to finish the month name. After you type the full month name and press Spacebar, however, you should see a ScreenTip showing the full date.

3 Press Enter.
Word inserts the rest of the month name that was displayed in the ScreenTip instead of moving the insertion point to the next line.

4 Press Spacebar.
Now you see a ScreenTip that shows the current date, such as *February 17, 2004 (Press ENTER to Insert)*.

5 Press Enter.
Word inserts the rest of the current date.

Now you need to insert the inside address, salutation, additional words, and complimentary closing.

To Insert Text

1 Press Enter four times.
You need to add space after the date before you insert the inside address.

2 Type the following text, pressing Enter once after each line:
Ms. Rebecca Farnsworth
Farnsworth Advertising
5350 North Edgewood Drive
Provo, UT 84604

Word moves the existing paragraphs down to make room for the new lines of text you insert. Your letter should look like Figure 2.9.

To Insert Text

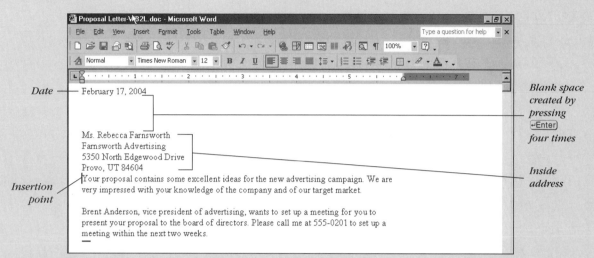

Figure 2.9

③ Press ⏎Enter again **to leave one blank line between the inside address and the salutation.**

④ Type Dear Ms. Farnsworth: **and press** ⏎Enter **twice.**
You should now have one blank line between the salutation and the first line of the first paragraph.

If you have problems...
If the Office Assistant appears to ask if you want help to create the letter, click Cancel.

You need to add a sentence between the existing sentences in the first paragraph.

⑤ **Click to the left of** *We* **in the first paragraph.**
Before inserting new text, make sure that you position the insertion point where you want the new text to appear. In this case, make sure the insertion point is to the immediate left of *We*.

⑥ **Type the following sentence, pressing** Spacebar **after the period.**
The theme you selected is appropriate for our new product line.

Because Insert mode is active, the new text appears at the insertion point. The existing text simply word-wraps differently.

⑦ Press Ctrl+End, **and press** ⏎Enter **twice to move the insertion point to the end of the letter.**
You need to type the signature block at the end of the letter.

⑧ Type Sincerely **and then press** ⏎Enter **four times to allow enough room to sign your printed letter.**

⑨ **Type your name.**
The letter is now complete. Compare your letter with the one shown in Figure 2.10.

(Continues)

To Insert Text (Continued)

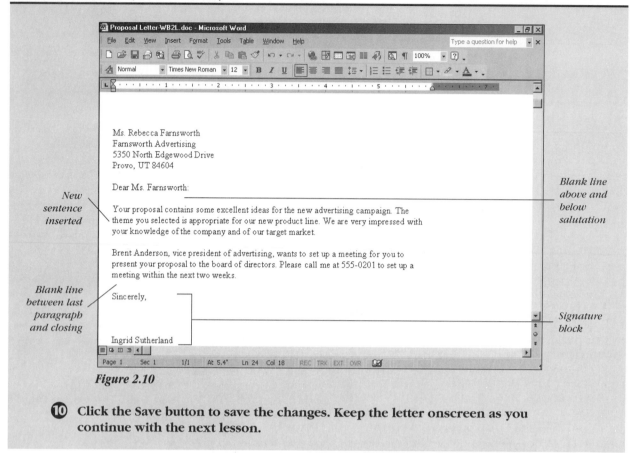

New sentence inserted

Blank line between last paragraph and closing

Blank line above and below salutation

Signature block

Figure 2.10

🔟   Click the Save button to save the changes. Keep the letter onscreen as you continue with the next lesson.

Lesson 4: Selecting Text

Making changes to a Word document is a simple process, especially when you can select text to change it. For example, you might want to delete an entire sentence or group of sentences. Instead of deleting characters one by one with (◄Backspace) or (Del), you can select and delete text.

Selecting is the action of defining an area of text so you can do something to it, such as delete or format it. When you select text, Word displays it in white with a black background. In this lesson, you learn how to select text.

To Select Text

❶   In the *Proposal Letter-WB2L* document, double-click the word *proposal* in the first paragraph to select it and the space after it.

❷   Deselect the word *proposal*, press and hold down (Ctrl), and click anywhere in the first sentence of the first paragraph.
This action selects the entire sentence, along with any additional blank spaces after the period.

❸   Triple-click anywhere inside the first paragraph.
This action selects the entire paragraph (see Figure 2.11).

To Select Text

Paragraph selected

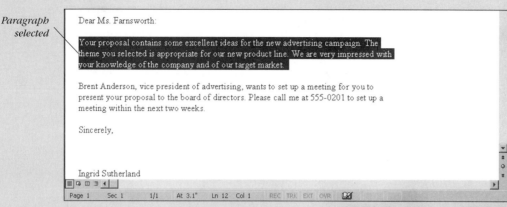

Figure 2.11

If you have problems...

If the paragraph is not selected, make sure that you click three times in quick succession, and that you don't move the mouse as you click.

4 **Click anywhere inside the document window to deselect the text.**

5 **Click at the beginning of the inside address and hold down the mouse button while you drag the mouse down to the middle of the second paragraph. Then, release the mouse button.**

Clicking and dragging is a fast way to select a specific block of text, as shown in Figure 2.12.

Start clicking and dragging here

Selection bar

Drag down to here

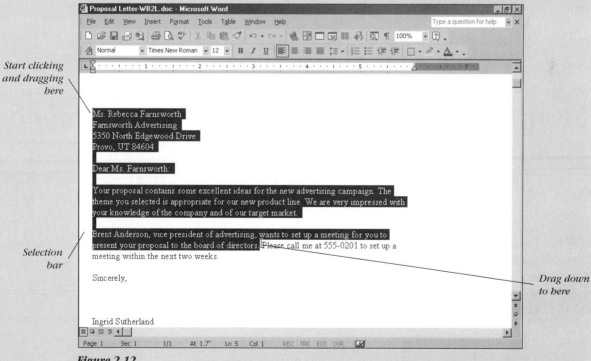

Figure 2.12

(Continues)

To Select Text (Continued)

If you have problems...

If you click and drag too fast, you might end up selecting too much text. If this happens, try this method instead of clicking and dragging: Click at the point where you want to start selecting text, press and hold down [⬆Shift], and click at the point where you want to end the selected text. This selects from the insertion point to the place where you [⬆Shift]+click.

6 Click in the document window to deselect the text.

7 Keep the document onscreen to continue with the next lesson.

To extend your knowledge...

Selecting by Clicking the Selection Bar

You can also select text by clicking the **selection bar**, the space in the left margin area where you see a right-pointing arrow (refer to Figure 2.11 in the previous exercise). Click once to select the current text line. Double-click to select the current paragraph, and triple-click to select the entire document.

Selecting Multiple Items at the Same Time

In Word Version 2002, you can now select two different areas in the document at the same time. To do this, select one area (such as a heading); press and hold down [Ctrl] as you select another area. This feature is similar to selecting nonconsecutive ranges in Excel.

Selecting Text with the Keyboard

You can also use the arrow keys on the keyboard to select text. You might find this method more convenient when selecting a small section of text, or if you prefer to keep your hands on the keyboard. First, you position the insertion point where you want to start selecting text. Press [⬆Shift] and then use the arrow keys to select text. Release [⬆Shift] to stop selecting text. Press any arrow key to deselect the text.

If you want to select the entire document, press [Ctrl]+[A].

Lesson 5: Deleting and Changing Text

As you read the first draft of your letter, you may decide that you don't like the way a particular sentence sounds, or you may find that you have simply entered the wrong information. Word lets you delete text that you don't want, enter new text, and correct existing text. In this lesson, you learn how to make basic corrections to text in a document.

To Delete and Change Text

1 In the *Proposal Letter-WB2L* document, double-click the word *new* on the first line of the first paragraph.
You want to replace the word *new* with *summer*.

2 Type summer.
When you select text and type new text, the new text replaces the selected text.

To Delete and Change Text

3 Position the insertion point at the beginning of the word *very* in the second sentence of the first paragraph.

4 Press Ctrl+Del to delete the word to the right of the insertion point.

5 Position the insertion point before the first 0 in the phone number.
This phone number is incorrect. You need to replace it with the correct phone number.

6 Double-click the OVR indicator on the status bar.
The OVR indicator appears darker. You are now in the ***Overtype mode***, which overwrites (or replaces) existing text as you type new text.

7 Type 2486 to insert the correct phone number and replace the old number, as shown in Figure 2.13.

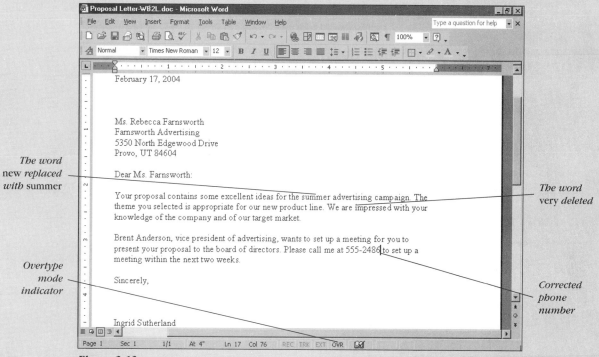

The word new replaced with summer

Overtype mode indicator

The word very deleted

Corrected phone number

Figure 2.13

If you have problems...

If you forget to turn off Overtype mode, you might accidentally delete text and replace it with other text, instead of simply inserting new text. Double-click the OVR indicator on the status bar to turn off Overtype mode.

8 Double-click the OVR indicator to return to Insert mode.

9 Save the document, and keep it onscreen to continue with the next lesson.

To extend your knowledge...

Deleting Text

You can delete the word to the left of the insertion point by pressing Ctrl+Backspace. To delete larger sections of text, select the text first and then press Del.

Insert and Overtype modes

In addition to clicking OVR on the status bar, you can press Insert on the keyboard to toggle between Insert and Overtype modes.

Lesson 6: Changing View Modes

When you work with a document, you might want to adjust the way it appears on the screen. For example, you can adjust the document to display the layout with the margins, or you can maximize the amount of screen space devoted to seeing text. In addition, you can adjust the way spacing or the size of the characters appears on your screen without changing the size of the printed characters. This lesson teaches you how to use view options to focus on particular elements of your document, such as layout or text.

Normal view shows text without displaying space for margins, page numbers, or other supplemental text. Normal view is appropriate when you are simply typing and editing text, and you want to use the screen space for displaying text without seeing the margins.

To Change View Options

1 Press Ctrl+Home to **move your insertion point to the top of the document.**

2 Click the **Print Layout View button to the left of the horizontal scrollbar.**
Print Layout view shows you what the document will look like when it's printed. This view shows margin space, graphics locations, headers, footers, and page numbers. Although your document does not contain headers, footers, or page numbers, you can look at the margins (see Figure 2.14).

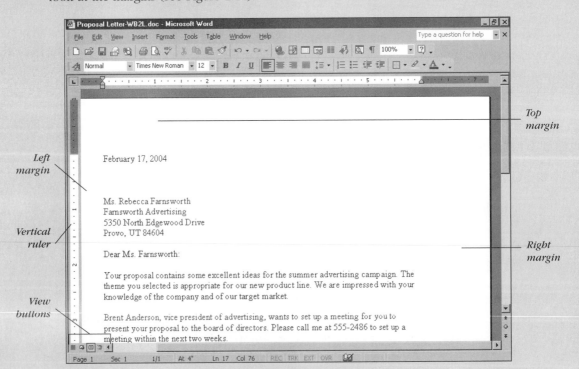

Figure 2.14

Notice that the end-of-document marker does *not* appear in Print Layout view.

3 Click the **Normal View button to change back to the regular view.**

To Change View Options

The end-of-document marker appears again in Normal view. Although you can see more text in Normal view, you still want to see more text on your screen.

4 **Choose View, and click the down arrows at the bottom of the menu to display the full View menu.**

5 **Choose Full Screen.**
Full Screen view uses the entire screen to display the document text, as shown in Figure 2.15. In this view, you do *not* see the title bar, menu bar, toolbars, or other Word elements. However, you do see the end-of-document marker.

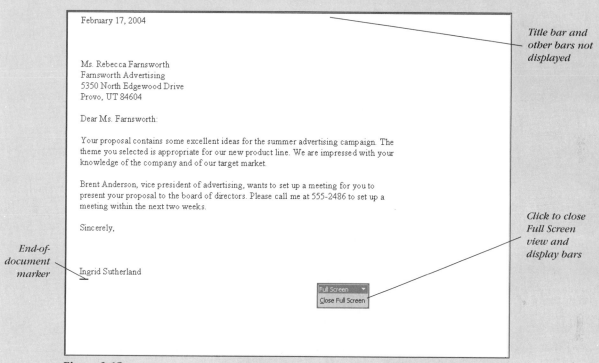

Title bar and other bars not displayed

Click to close Full Screen view and display bars

End-of-document marker

Figure 2.15

6 **Click Close Full Screen or press [Esc] to close the Full Screen view.**

7 **Click the Zoom drop-down arrow.**
You see the Zoom menu (see Figure 2.16), which lets you change the *zoom*, or magnification percentage, of your document onscreen.

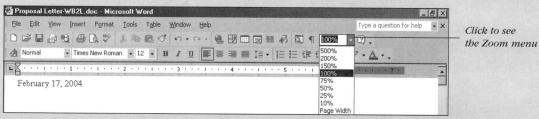

Click to see the Zoom menu

Figure 2.16

(Continues)

To Change View Options (Continued)

8 **Choose 150%.**

The document is now displayed at 150% of its regular screen size, as shown in Figure 2.17. Changing the zoom does not, however, change the size of the text when it is printed.

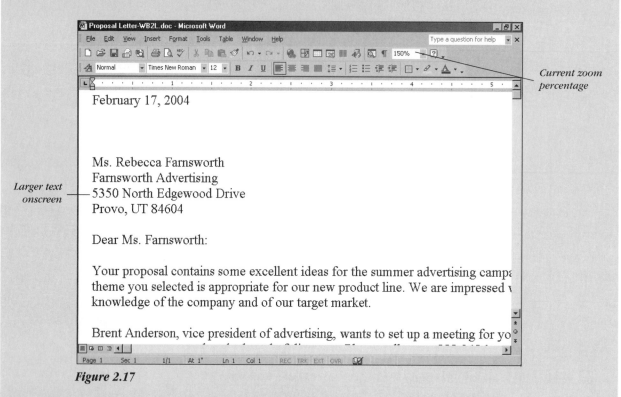

Current zoom percentage

Larger text onscreen

Figure 2.17

9 **Click the arrow to the right of the Zoom box again, and choose 100%.**

10 **Click the Print button on the Standard toolbar to print the document.**

11 **Keep the document onscreen to continue with the next lesson.**

 ## To extend your knowledge...

Setting Specific Zoom

You can click inside the Zoom box and type the exact percentage. For example, you can type **93** if you want. You don't have to type the percent sign. Press ⏎Enter after you type the zoom value.

Using the Zoom Dialog Box

Choose View, Zoom to display the Zoom dialog box, which provides preset options and a Percent option that allows you to specify the exact magnification (see Figure 2.18).

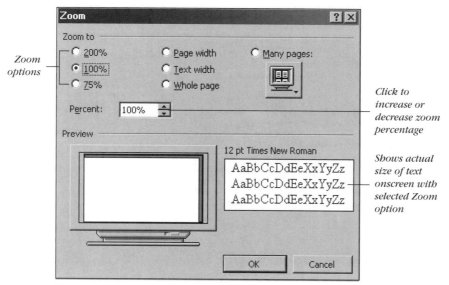

Figure 2.18

The options shown in Figure 2.18 appear when Print Layout view is active. The options will differ slightly if you have Normal view active.

Using Zoom Options

When you select the Print Layout view, you can select Whole Page, Two Pages, and Text Width from the Zoom menu. Viewing the whole page or two pages is nice because it allows you to see the overall layout, such as spacing and margins. These options are not available when you use the Normal view. Text Width displays text from the left to the right side of the monitor.

Working in Full Screen View

Although you can't see the menu bar, you can still access the menus. Simply press Alt and the hotkey to display the desired menu. For example, press Alt+V to display the View menu.

The keyboard shortcut for closing Full Screen view is Alt+C.

Lesson 7: Creating Envelopes

You have a printed copy of your letter, but you need an envelope to mail it in. Use Word's Envelope feature to quickly create and print an envelope for your letter. The Envelope feature creates the address from the existing letter, and lets you select the envelope type and other options. In this lesson, you create and print an envelope for the *Proposal Letter-WB2L* document that is displayed on your screen.

To Create an Envelope

1 **Choose Tools, Letters and Mailings.**

2 **Choose Envelopes and Labels.**
The Envelopes and Labels dialog box appears.

3 **Click the Envelopes tab if it's not already selected.**

(Continues)

To Create an Envelope (Continued)

The Envelopes and Labels dialog box shows the envelope options (see Figure 2.19). Word copies the inside address from your letter to the *Delivery address* section in the dialog box.

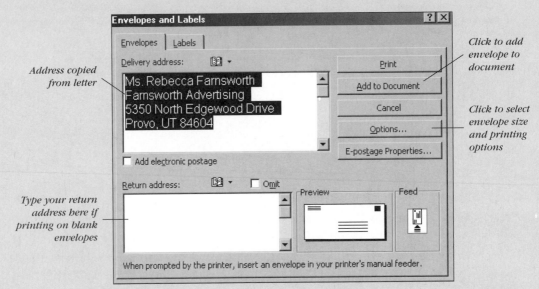

Address copied from letter

Click to add envelope to document

Click to select envelope size and printing options

Type your return address here if printing on blank envelopes

Figure 2.19

4   **Click Add to Document.**
Clicking this button inserts a new page at the beginning of the document, before the letter. The envelope is on page zero.

5   **Click the Print Layout View button.**

6   **Click the Zoom drop-down arrow and choose 75%.**
The envelope text now looks like it's placed on an envelope onscreen (see Figure 2.20).

To Create an Envelope

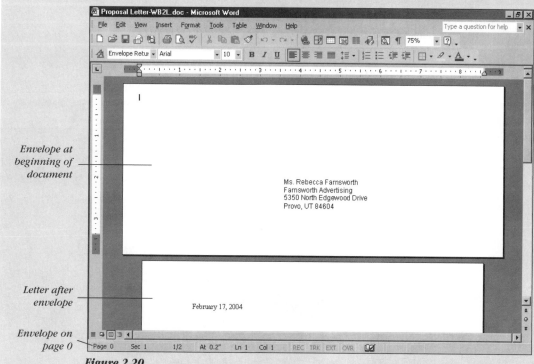

Envelope at beginning of document

Ms. Rebecca Farnsworth
Farnsworth Advertising
5350 North Edgewood Drive
Provo, UT 84604

Letter after envelope

February 17, 2004

Envelope on page 0

Figure 2.20

7 **Click the Save button on the Standard toolbar.**
You have now saved the envelope settings as part of the document.

8 **Click File, Print to display the Print dialog box.**

9 **Click the *Current page* option button; then click OK.**
You will probably see a message instructing you to manually insert the envelope into the printer. Ask your instructor for assistance, if needed. If you don't have an envelope to print on, simply insert a regular sheet of paper into the printer.

10 **Close the document.**

To extend your knowledge...

Creating Envelopes

You can select a variety of envelope options by clicking Options in the Envelopes and Labels dialog box. For example, you can select a different envelope size, add a barcode, and specify how you want to insert the envelope into the printer.

Lesson 8: Creating Labels

Instead of printing addresses on envelopes, you might want to print addresses on labels. Word's Label feature provides a variety of label formats, such as address, data disk, file folder, name badge, and video label. The label choices correspond to brand-name label product numbers, such as Avery 5160 Address labels. In this lesson, you select an address label format and enter data into some labels.

To Create Address Labels

1 **Click the New Blank Document button on the Standard toolbar to start a new document, and change the Zoom to 100%.**

2 **Choose Tools, Letters and Mailings, Envelopes and Labels.**
The Envelopes and Labels dialog box appears.

3 **Click the Labels tab.**
You can type an address into the Address text box, start a new label document, and select different label formats (see Figure 2.21).

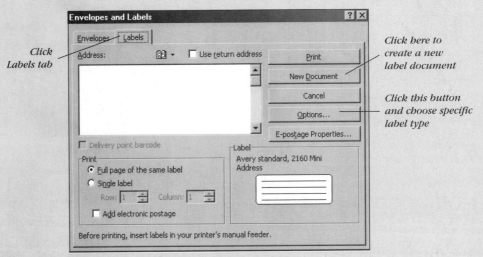

Figure 2.21

4 **Click Options.**
Before creating a label document, you should specify which label format and printer settings you want (see Figure 2.22). Most Avery-brand label products are listed.

To Create Address Labels

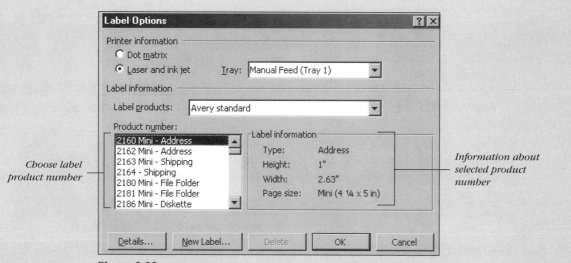

Figure 2.22

5 Scroll through the *Product number* list box and click *5160 –Address*.

6 Click OK.

7 Click New Document.
You see boxes representing the labels. You type an address in the first label and press Tab⇄ until the insertion point is in the next label. Depending on the label product number you choose, you might need to press Tab⇄ one or two times to move to the next label.

8 Type the addresses shown in Figure 2.23. Remember to press Tab⇄ twice to get from one label to the next.

Figure 2.23

9 Save the document as Address Labels-WB2L; then print and close the document.

To extend your knowledge...

Creating Return Address Labels

You can create a sheet of personal address labels for yourself quickly and easily. Simply type your name and address in the Address box, choose the label format you want, and click the *Full page of the same label* option button. When you click New Document, Word creates an entire sheet of labels for you!

Summary

In this project, you learned some very important word processing tasks. You learned how to open a document that you previously saved and how to efficiently navigate through it. You also learned how to select, insert, and delete text. In addition, you learned how to change the view options to see your document from different perspectives. Finally, you created an envelope and mailing labels.

Now you're ready to reinforce your knowledge by completing the end-of-project exercises. In addition, experiment with features. For example, create labels for videos. Furthermore, you can expand your knowledge and skills by using Help to find out more about the topics covered in this project.

Checking Concepts and Terms

Multiple Choice

Circle the letter of the correct answer for each of the following.

1. What feature would you use to adjust the percentage of a document that displays onscreen? [L6]

   a. Print Layout

   b. Zoom

   c. Full Screen

   d. Normal view

2. Which menu lists the most recently used documents? [L1]

   a. Edit

   b. Format

   c. Open

   d. File

3. Which method should you use to select one sentence within a paragraph? [L4]

   a. Double-click the sentence.

   b. Double-click the selection bar by the sentence.

   c. Press Ctrl+A.

   d. Hold Ctrl while you click in the sentence.

4. What option is the most efficient for moving the insertion point from page 3 of your document to the top of page 12? [L2]

   a. Press Ctrl+PgDn nine times.

   b. Click the Next Page button nine times.

   c. Display the Go To dialog box, type **12**, and click the Go To button.

   d. Press ↓ repeatedly until you're on page 12.

5. When you create labels, which of the following steps should you perform first? [L8]

   a. Type names and addresses.

   b. Choose the label product number.

   c. Click the New Document button in the dialog box.

   d. Press Tab to separate addresses into separate labels.

Screen ID

Label each element of the Word screen shown in Figure 2.24.

A. Normal view button

B. Overtype mode

C. Print Layout view button

D. Select Browse Object button

E. Zoom

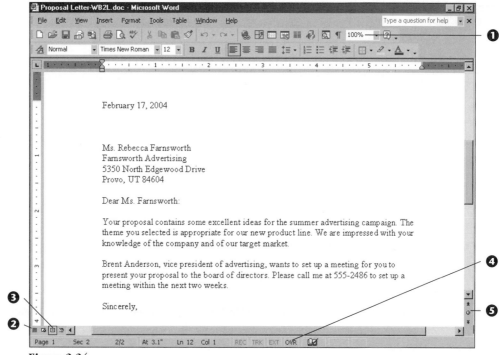

Figure 2.24

1. _____   4. _____

2. _____   5. _____

3. _____

Discussion

1. What is the advantage of knowing and using the keyboard to scroll through a document? [L2]

2. What is the difference between Normal view and Print Layout view? Provide an example of when you might use each view. [L6]

3. Explain why selecting and typing text might be preferable to using the Overtype mode to change existing text. [L5]

Skill Drill

Skill Drill exercises reinforce project skills. Each skill reinforced is the same, or nearly the same, as a skill presented in the project. Detailed instructions are provided in a step-by-step format.

1. Opening a Document

You know you can perform the same tasks with different methods. Because you want to learn the different methods and see which you like best, you decide to practice another way of opening a document.

1. In Word, press Ctrl+O to display the Open dialog box.
2. Click the *Look in* drop-down arrow, and choose the drive and folder that contains the data files for this book.
3. Click *ew1-0202*, and press ↵Enter to open the document.
4. Choose File, Save As.
5. Click the *Save in* drop-down arrow, and choose the drive that contains your data disk or Zip disk.
6. Type `Chambers Letter-WB2SD` in the *File name* box and then click Save.
7. Choose File, Close to close the document.
8. Choose File, and look at the bottom of the menu.
9. Select *1 Chambers Letter-WB2SD.doc* from the bottom of the menu.

   The menu might display the path and filename, such as *1 C:\My Documents\Chambers Letter-WB2SD.doc*.
10. Keep the document onscreen to continue with the next exercise.

2. Scrolling in the Document

To become efficient in scrolling through a document, you want to practice different methods.

1. Press Ctrl+Home to move the insertion point to the beginning of the document.
2. Click and drag the vertical scrollbox until the ScreenTip shows *Page: 1*; then release the mouse button.
3. Click the Previous Page button.
4. Click the Next Page button.
5. Press Ctrl+End to move the insertion point to the end of the document.
6. Press Ctrl+G to display the Go To option.
7. Type **0** in the *Enter page number* box, click Go To, and then click Close.
8. Drag the scroll box down to see the letter.
9. Click at the beginning of the first paragraph in the letter.
10. Press Ctrl+↓ twice to move the insertion point to the beginning of the second paragraph.
11. Leave the document onscreen to continue with the next exercise.

3. Selecting, Changing, and Deleting Text

You want to use the same letter to send to someone else. Instead of typing a new letter, you decide to select and delete the original envelope, and select and replace the inside address and salutation.

1. With the *Chambers Letter-WB2SD* document onscreen, select the entire inside address on the letter (not envelope).

2. Type the following new address while the old address is selected:

```
Mr. Aaron Chambers
McClure and Associates
305 West Main Street
Toledo, OH 43615
```

3. Make sure that you still have one blank line between the inside address and the salutation.

4. Select Ms. Farnsworth in the salutation; then type `Mr. Chambers`.

5. Click the Normal View button to the left of the horizontal scrollbar and then press Ctrl+Home.

6. Position the mouse pointer in the left margin—the selection bar area. The mouse pointer is an arrow pointing to the right.

7. Click and drag to select the envelope, including the lines that mention the section break. Press Del to delete the entire envelope page.

8. Click to the right of the hyphen in the phone number.

9. Double-click OVR on the status bar, type **7356**, and double-click OVR again.

10. Save the document, and keep it onscreen to continue with the next exercise.

4. Inserting Text

You need to insert new text within the document. Because you don't want to delete existing text, you use Insert mode.

1. Click to the left of *vice president* in the second paragraph, type **senior**, and press Spacebar.

2. Click at the beginning of the second paragraph, and type the following paragraph:

```
As you are probably aware, we are expecting sales from the summer
campaign to generate a 25 percent increase over last summer's campaign.
The economy is very favorable, and we have many new products to hit
the market.
```

3. Press Enter twice after the paragraph to have a blank line between paragraphs.

4. Click to the left of *economy*, and type **regional**. Make sure that you have a space before and after the new word.

5. Click to the left of the date, and press Ctrl+Del four times to delete the date.

6. Start typing the name of the current month. When you see the full month name in the Screen-Tip, press Enter.

7. Press Enter to see a ScreenTip showing the current date.

8. Press Enter to insert the date shown in the ScreenTip.

9. Save the document, and keep it onscreen to continue with the next exercise.

5. Viewing the Document

You want to review view options to look at the overall format and to adjust the magnification onscreen.

1. With *Chambers Letter-WB2SD* onscreen, click the Print Layout View button to the left of the horizontal scrollbar.

2. Choose View, Zoom to display the Zoom dialog box.

3. Click the Percent increment button to *125%*, and click OK.

4. Click the Normal View button to the left of the horizontal scrollbar.

5. Click the Zoom drop-down arrow, and choose 75%.

6. Keep the document onscreen to continue with the next exercise.

6. Creating an Envelope

After creating the letter, you need to create an envelope for it. You create the envelope and add it to the document window.

1. With the *Chambers Letter-WB2SD* onscreen, choose Tools, Letters and Mailing, Envelopes and Labels.

2. Click the <u>E</u>nvelopes tab, and click the <u>A</u>dd to Document button.
3. Save the document with the envelope.
4. Print the envelope and letter.
5. Close the document.

Challenge exercises expand on or are somewhat related to skills presented in the lessons. Each exercise provides a brief narrative introduction, followed by instructions in a numbered-step format that are not as detailed as those in the Skill Drill section.

1. Editing a Discount Message

You work for Mega Music, a regional retail store that sells CDs, cassettes, and movies. To promote your store to the college students, you are offering a special sale to them. A coworker created a document announcing the discount; you need to open, edit, and save the document.

1. Open *ew1-0203*, and save it as `Mega Music-WB2CH1`.
2. Use Overtype, and retype the title in capital letters.
3. Delete the text *or copy your official class schedule* from the second paragraph.
4. Change the street address number to `2286` and insert `North` between the street number and name.
5. Insert a line between the CD and VHS movies lines, and type `15% off on all cassette tapes`.
6. Select the four lines about the discount percentages, and press `Tab↹` once.
7. Insert the word `movie` between the words *your collection* in the last paragraph.
8. Save, print, and close the document.

2. Editing a Memo about Parking Rules

You composed a memo to inform employees about a new parking rule. You need to open it and make a few changes before sending it out.

1. Open *ew1-0204* and save it as `Parking Memo-WB2CH2`.
2. Select Normal view and then change the zoom to Page Width.
3. Delete the asterisk on the Date line, and use AutoComplete to enter today's date.
4. Delete the asterisk on the From line, and type your name. Make sure that the date and your name line up with the word *New* on the Subject line.
5. Press `Tab↹` to line up *All Employees* with the other items in the memorandum heading.
6. Use the most efficient method for changing *8:30* to `8:45`.
7. Select the last sentence in the memo, and replace it with `We appreciate your cooperation during this construction period.`
8. Select and change these words to all caps: *Date, To, From,* and *Subject*. If needed, adjust the second column in the heading.
9. Save, print, and close the document.

3. Editing a Memo about MOUS Certification

As the Office Manager, you are pleased to announce rewards for employees who pass MOUS certification tests. You created a memo this morning announcing the reward, but you need to edit it before sending it to your employees.

1. Open *ew1-0205*, and save it as `Certification Reward-WB2CH3`.
2. Select Robert's full name, and type your name to replace his name.
3. Use AutoComplete to insert the current date in the appropriate location in the memo heading.
4. Add the following text in the respective locations:
   - `special` before *fund* in the first paragraph
   - `by calling 555-EXAM` at the end of the first sentence in the second paragraph
   - `You are reimbursed only if you pass the exam, so be sure to study and practice!` at the end of the second paragraph
5. Delete *computer applications* in the second paragraph.
6. Select and change the following text, as indicated:
   - *test* to `measure` in the first paragraph
   - *$175* to `$200` in the third paragraph
   - *one month* to `two weeks` in the third paragraph
7. Check the current MOUS exam prices at www.mous.net on the Internet.
8. Save, print, and close the document.

4. Editing a Letter Requesting Donations

You belong to a campus organization that is sponsoring a track meet for underprivileged children in your area. As president of the organization, you are responsible for writing letters to local retail stores to solicit donations for the event. You want to receive cash and food donations. The money will help defray the cost of sponsoring the event, and the food donations will help your members prepare a cookout after the event.

1. From a blank document window, insert the date and the following inside address:
   ```
   Mr. John Davis
   Fresher Groceries, Inc.
   344 NW First
   Racine, WI 53402
   ```
2. Insert and correctly format the salutation.
3. Type a three-paragraph letter that describes what your organization is sponsoring and the type of donations you seek. End with a statement showing appreciation for any donation the retailer might provide.
4. Include an appropriate closing with your name. Type your organization name on the line below your typed name.
5. Save the document as `Donation Letter-WB2CH4`.
6. Create an envelope without a return address. Insert the envelope in the document.
7. Save the document, and print both the envelope and the letter. Then, close the document.

5. Creating Mailing Labels for Family Names

One of your family members asked you to create mailing labels for her annual holiday newsletter. She wants you to save the label document so that she can use it again next year.

1. Start a new blank document.
2. Select *Avery 5260 - Address* and start a new document.
3. Enter the names and addresses of your family members and friends. You should enter enough addresses to fill the sheet of labels. Correctly format the addresses.
4. Save the document as `Personal Address Labels-WB2CH5`.
5. Print and close the document.

iscovery Zone

Discovery Zone exercises require advanced knowledge of topics presented in *essentials* lessons, application of skills from multiple lessons, or self-directed learning of new skills.

1. Using Help to Learn About Open Options

You noticed the drop-down arrow by the Open button in the Open dialog box. Two options caught your attention: Open Read-Only and Open as Copy. Use the Help feature to find out what each option does. Print the Help topics that you find.

Create a document in which you describe Open Read-Only and Open as Copy options. Write one paragraph for each option. In each paragraph provide an example of when you might use that particular option.

Save your document as `Open Options-WB2DZ1` and then print it.

2. Creating a Sheet of Disk Labels

As an assistant for a computer consulting company, you are responsible for preparing data disks to contain documents that the clients will use during the consultations.

From a new document window, create a sheet of labels using the Avery 6460 Remove 'Em laser diskette labels. Type the following text for the label, and make sure that the same text repeats on each label. Place the labels in a new document window; don't print from within the Envelopes and Labels dialog box.

```
Introduction to Word
Computer Essentials Training
April 5, 2004
Trainer: your name
```

Save the sheet of labels as `Disk Labels-WB2DZ2`, and print the labels on a regular sheet of paper.

3. Creating a Small Envelope with a Barcode

One of your college professors said he would mail your final grade to you if you provide a self-addressed stamped envelope. You only have 6½ inch × 3⅝ inch-sized envelopes.

Create the envelope in the Envelopes and Labels dialog box. Use your name and address in the Delivery address section and your professor's name and address in the Return address section. If needed, use Help to learn how to select an envelope size and how to insert a barcode on the envelope. Make these adjustments before adding the envelope to your document. Save the document as `Instructor Envelope-WB2DZ3` and print the envelope.

Formatting Text

Objectives

In this project, you learn how to

✔ Apply and Modify Character Formats
✔ Change the Font, Size, and Color
✔ Apply Character Effects and Spacing
✔ Copy Formats with Format Painter
✔ Highlight Text
✔ Insert Symbols
✔ Display Formatting Marks
✔ Insert Nonbreaking Spaces and Hyphens

Key terms in this project include

❑ character effects
❑ character formats
❑ character spacing
❑ designer font
❑ em dash
❑ en dash
❑ font
❑ font size
❑ Format Painter
❑ formatting marks
❑ hard return
❑ headings

❑ highlight
❑ kerning
❑ nonbreaking hyphen
❑ nonbreaking space
❑ position
❑ sans serif font
❑ scale
❑ serif font
❑ spacing
❑ WYSIWYG

Why Would I Do This?

In the previous project, you used basic editing techniques such as deleting and inserting text. You are now ready to learn how to make document text look better. In this project, you learn to change the appearance of your text by adding bold, italic, and underlining. You also learn how to change the font, font size, and font color of your text to add emphasis and draw the reader's eyes to specific parts of your document. These and other features make your documents look more professional.

Visual Summary

Although the most important part of a document is accuracy of content, unformatted text doesn't entice someone to read the document. Lack of using fonts, sizes, symbols, and highlighting creates a dull image. Figure 3.1 shows unformatted text.

Microsoft Office Professional

Microsoft Office Professional contains several powerful application software programs to help people improve their professional and personal productivity. The core applications are Word, Excel, PowerPoint, and Access.

Microsoft Word is a powerful word processing program. You can use it to create a variety of documents such as letters, reports, newsletters, and fliers. Furthermore, you can create dynamic tables, drawings, and graphics. Various formatting options help you achieve a professional image. For example, you can insert a nonbreaking space in "May 15" to prevent the text from word-wrapping between the month and date.

Microsoft Excel is the leading spreadsheet software. You can use Excel to create budgets, sales forecasts, mortgage payments, and other financial spreadsheets. Excel's power lies in its "what-if" ability. After you set up formulas, you can change input data and see what type of effect the change has on a particular result.

Microsoft PowerPoint is a presentation graphics program. People around the world use this software to create dynamic, professional presentation slide shows. You can insert images, tables, and sound to enhance your slide shows. Animated transitions and specialized drawing tools help complete your presentation.

Microsoft Access is a powerful database management program. It is effective for storing, retrieving, organizing, and printing data. Companies use database software to keep track of inventory, client information, and suppliers. You can even create a database to store names, addresses, phone numbers, and e-mail addresses of your family and friends!

Figure 3.1

Formatted text, on the other hand, enhances the document. In other words, it "brings the document to life." Text formats help focus the reader's eyes and stress important aspects. Figure 3.2 shows the impact of formatted text.

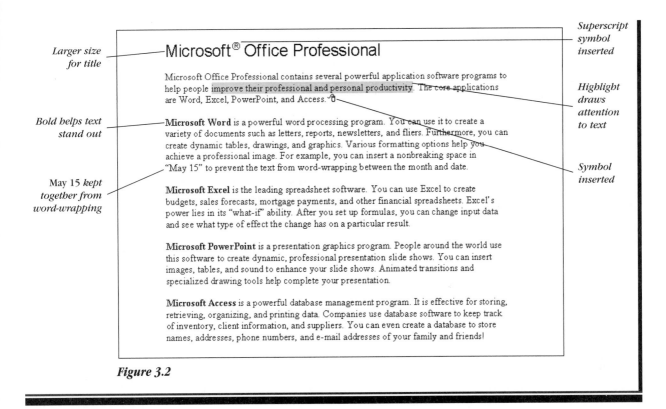

Figure 3.2

Lesson 1: Applying and Modifying Character Formats

In the last project, you learned how to select and delete text. In addition to deleting selected text, you can enhance the appearance of text by applying bold, italic, underline, or color. These text formats, known as *character formats*, emphasize ideas as well as improve readability and clarity.

Table 3.1 shows the toolbar buttons and keyboard shortcuts that you use to apply these character formats.

Table 3.1	Character Format Buttons and Keyboard Shortcuts	
Button	**Button Name**	**Keyboard Shortcut**
B	**Bold**	Ctrl + B
I	**Italic**	Ctrl + I
U	**Underline**	Ctrl + U

To Apply Character Formats

1 **Open** *ew1-0301,* **and save it as** Office Software-WB3L.
Currently, the document looks very plain. However, after you apply character formats, the document will look a lot better.

2 **Click and drag across** *Microsoft Word* **at the beginning of the second full paragraph.**
You want the software name to stand out from the rest of the paragraph.

(Continues)

To Apply Character Formats (Continued)

③ Click the Underline button on the Formatting toolbar.
The selected text, *Microsoft Word*, is now underlined, so it stands out from the regular text. After underlining the text, you need to deselect it.

④ Click inside the selected text to deselect it.
Notice how underlined text differs from regular text (see Figure 3.3).

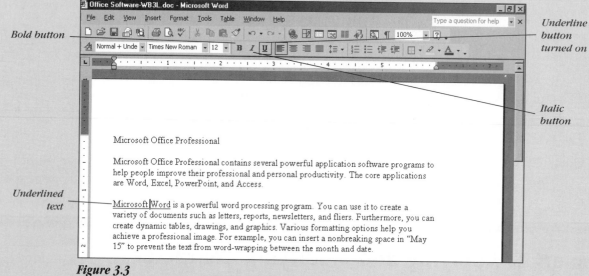

Figure 3.3

You can remove formatting if you don't want the character format after all.

⑤ Select the underlined *Microsoft Word*.
You remove formatting the same way you applied it.

⑥ Click the Underline button to remove the underline format.
If you want to apply a different character format, keep the text selected.

⑦ Click the Bold button.
The selected text, *Microsoft Word*, is now bold.

⑧ Deselect the text.

⑨ Save the document, and keep it onscreen to continue with the next lesson.

To extend your knowledge...

Using Bold, Italic, and Underline

Although both bold and italic character formats emphasize text, use bold for stronger emphasis and italic for lesser emphasis.

Some reference manuals specify that you apply bold and underline to report ***headings***—descriptive words or phrases placed between sections to help readers understand the organization of your document.

Lesson 2: Changing the Font, Size, and Color

Font refers to the overall appearance—style, weight, and typeface—of a set of characters. You can choose from literally thousands of fonts. Fonts are available from a variety of sources. For example, printers come with built-in fonts they can produce. You can also purchase font software from companies such as Adobe. Fonts range in appearance from very professional to informal fun fonts. Figure 3.4 illustrates some examples of different fonts.

Arial	KEYSTROKE
Arial Rounded MT Bold	Kids
Bauhaus Md MT	Parisian BT
Bookman Old Style	Snell BT
Broadway BT	Tango BT
Comic Sans MS	Technical
Courier New	Times New Roman
Hobo BT	Typo Upright BT
Kabel Bk BT	Westminster

Figure 3.4

When choosing a font, consider the font's readability, its suitability to the document's purpose, and its appeal to the reader. Most fonts are classified as serif or sans serif. A ***serif font***, such as Times New Roman, has tiny lines at the ends of the characters that help guide the reader's eyes across the line of text. Serif fonts should be used for text-intensive reading, such as paragraphs.

A ***sans serif font***, such as Arial, does not have the tiny lines or extensions on the characters. Although a sans serif font has a crisp, clean look, it is difficult to read in large blocks of text, such as paragraphs. Use sans serif fonts for titles, headings, and other short blocks of text.

A ***designer font*** is a special font used in creative documents, such as wedding announcements, fliers, brochures, and other special-occasion documents. Examples of designer fonts include Broadway BT, Comic Sans MS, and Keystroke.

In addition to choosing the font, you should also consider the font size. ***Font size*** is the height of the characters, which is typically measured in points. One vertical inch contains about 72 points. You should use between 10-point and 12-point size for most correspondence and reports. Point sizes below 10 are difficult to read for detailed text, and point sizes above 12 are too big for regular paragraphs. However, you might want to use a larger font size for titles and headings so that they are emphasized.

Currently, your document is formatted in 12-point Times New Roman. You want to apply 24-point Arial to the title to make it stand out. In addition, you want to apply a font color to the bold *Microsoft Word* in the second paragraph.

To Change the Font, Font Size, and Font Color

❶ **In the open** `Office Software-WB3L` **document, position the mouse pointer to the left side of the title** *Microsoft Office Professional.*

(Continues)

To Change the Font, Font Size, and Font Color (Continued)

2 **Click the mouse pointer in the selection bar area to select the title.**
You must select text to apply a different font, font size, and font color.

3 **Click the Font drop-down arrow on the Formatting toolbar.**
The Font menu displays the available fonts for the current printer (see Figure 3.5); your font list probably looks different. You can scroll through the list to see all the available fonts.

Current font selection

Most recently used fonts

List of fonts in alphabetical order

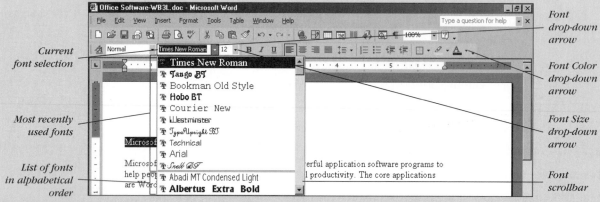

Font drop-down arrow

Font Color drop-down arrow

Font Size drop-down arrow

Font scrollbar

Figure 3.5

4 **Scroll down through the menu, and choose Arial.**
The title appears in Arial font. The Font button displays the font, *Arial*, for the currently selected text.

5 **Click the Font Size drop-down arrow.**
You see a list of different font sizes, ranging from 8 to 72.

6 **Choose *20* from the Font Size list and then click inside the text to deselect it.**
The title is now bigger at 20-point size. Notice that the Font Size button on the Formatting toolbar displays the font size, *20*, at the insertion point's location (see Figure 3.6).

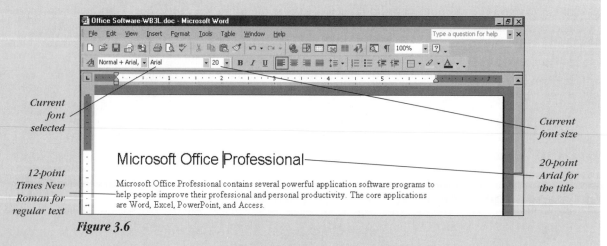

Current font selected

12-point Times New Roman for regular text

Current font size

20-point Arial for the title

Figure 3.6

To Change the Font, Font Size, and Font Color

Titles are typically printed in a larger point size, but be careful that the title isn't too over-powering compared with the regular document text.

7 **Select the bold *Microsoft Word* at the beginning of the second paragraph.**
To apply a font color, you must select the text first.

8 **Click the Font Color drop-down arrow on the Formatting toolbar.**
The Font Color palette appears, so you can choose a color for the selected text. As you move your mouse over each color, you see a ScreenTip that tells you the exact color name, such as Blue, Light Blue, and Sky Blue.

If you have problems...

If you click the Font Color button (instead of the drop-down arrow), you immediately apply the default color, which is the last color someone selected. If this happens, select your text, and make sure you click the Font Color drop-down arrow to see the palette. The new color you choose replaces the previous color.

9 **Position the mouse pointer on the blue color, the third color from the right on the second row (see Figure 3.7).**

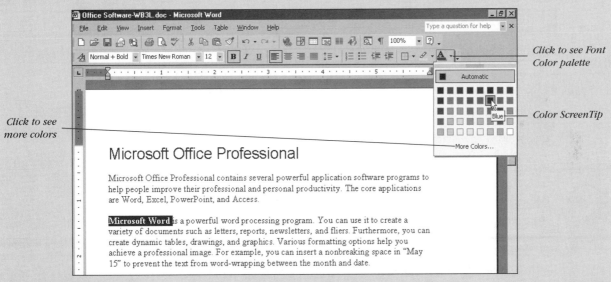

Figure 3.7

10 **Click Blue on the color palette to apply blue color to the selected text; then, deselect the text.**
Microsoft Word stands out more with the blue font color.

11 **Save the document, and keep it onscreen to continue with the next lesson.**

To extend your knowledge...

Keyboard Shortcuts for Changing Font Size

Select text and press Ctrl+[to decrease the font size one point at a time, or press Ctrl+] to increase the font size one point at a time.

Font and Font Size Keyboard Shortcuts

If your mouse isn't working, you can still access Font and Font Size on the Formatting toolbar. Press Ctrl+⇧Shift+F to activate the Font button. Press Ctrl+⇧Shift+P to activate the Font (point) Size button. For either list, press ↑ or ↓ to scroll through the list. You see only the font name or font size on the respective button as you press the scrolling keys on your keyboard. Press ⏎Enter to select the font or size you want.

Lesson 3: Applying Character Effects and Spacing

In addition to changing the font face and font size, you might want to apply other font or character attributes. **Character effects** are special formats that you apply to characters. Font effects include strikethrough, superscript, subscript, emboss, and other special effects. You can even apply onscreen text effects or specify character spacing.

You can choose some character effects by using keyboard shortcuts. Table 3.2 shows the available keyboard shortcuts.

Table 3.2 Special Effects Keyboard Shortcuts	
Keyboard Shortcut	**Effect**
Ctrl+⇧Shift+=	Superscript
Ctrl+=	Subscript
Ctrl+⇧Shift+D	Double Underline
Ctrl+⇧Shift+W	Underline Words Only
Ctrl+⇧Shift+K	Small Caps
Ctrl+⇧Shift+A	All Caps
Ctrl+⇧Shift+H	Hidden Text
Ctrl+Spacebar	Removes Character Effects

In this lesson, you insert the ® symbol, apply the superscript character effect, and set character spacing between letters in the title.

To Apply Character Effects

1 In the *Office Software-WB3L* document, type (r) immediately after *Microsoft* in the title.

When you type the closing parenthesis, Word changes *(r)* to ®, the registered trademark symbol.

2 Select only the ® symbol.

The symbol typically appears in superscript. You must select it to apply the superscript character effect.

3 Choose F**o**rmat, **F**ont to display the Font dialog box.

To Apply Character Effects

The Font dialog box (see Figure 3.8) contains options for selecting the font, font style, size, font color, underline options, and character effects.

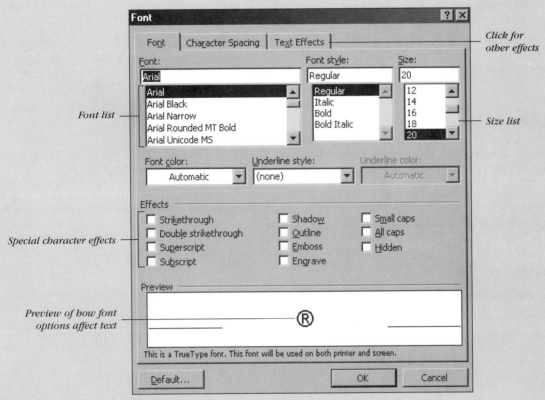

Figure 3.8

4 **Click the *Superscript* check box.**
A check mark appears in the check box to let you know the option is selected. The Preview window shows you that superscript text appears in smaller size and above the baseline.

5 **Click OK and deselect the text.**
Figure 3.9 shows the superscript symbol.

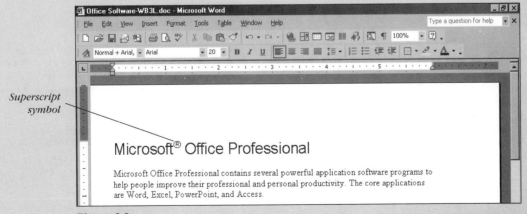

Figure 3.9

6 **Save the document, and keep it onscreen to continue with the next exercise.**

To extend your knowledge...

Font Dialog Box Keyboard Shortcut

The keyboard shortcut for accessing the Font dialog box is Ctrl + D.

Text Effects

You can select onscreen text effects to draw attention to selected text. Click the Text Effects tab in the Font dialog box. You can choose effects such as Blinking Background, Las Vegas Lights, and Marching Red Ants. These effects are for onscreen reading only; they do not appear on printouts.

The Font dialog box contains a set of options to adjust the character spacing. ***Character spacing*** is the amount of space between printed characters. Although most character spacing is acceptable, some character combinations appear too far apart or too close together in large-sized text. In the next exercise, you increase the character spacing between *f* and *t* in *Microsoft* and between *f* and *f* in *Office* so that the characters are properly spaced apart.

To Adjust Character Spacing

1 In the *Office Software-WB3L* document, select *ft* in *Microsoft* in the title.
The characters are too close together and need to be separated.

2 Choose **Format, Font** to display the Font dialog box.

3 Click the Character Spacing tab.
You have four options for adjusting the character spacing (see Figure 3.10).

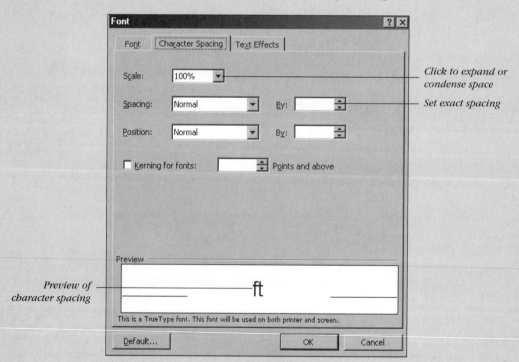

Figure 3.10

Scale increases or decreases the text horizontally as a percentage of its size. ***Spacing*** controls the amount of space between two or more characters. ***Position*** raises or lowers text from the baseline without creating superscript or subscript size. ***Kerning*** automatically adjusts spacing between characters to achieve a more evenly spaced appearance.

To Adjust Character Spacing

4 Click the <u>S</u>pacing drop-down arrow, and choose Expanded.
The *Spacing <u>B</u>y* option displays *1 pt*, which increases the amount of space between characters by 1 pt.

5 Click the Spacing <u>B</u>y spin button to display *1.5 pt* and click OK.
The selected letters have a little space between the characters now. Let's also adjust the character spacing between *f* and *f* in *Office*.

6 Select *ff* in *Office* in the title.

7 Choose F<u>o</u>rmat, <u>F</u>ont.
The Font dialog box displays the Character Spacing options.

8 Click the <u>S</u>pacing drop-down arrow, choose Expanded, click the Spacing <u>B</u>y increment button to *1.5 pt*, and click OK.

9 Deselect the text onscreen.
Figure 3.11 shows the improved character spacing between the two sets of letters.

1.5 space between f and t

1.5 space between two characters

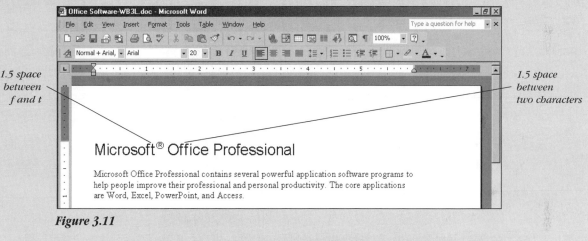

Figure 3.11

10 Save the document, and keep it onscreen to continue with the next lesson.

Lesson 4: Copying Formats with Format Painter

Similar headings and text within a document should have the same formatting. However, selecting every heading individually and clicking the desired format buttons (such as bold, underline, and font color) can be time-consuming.

By using the **Format Painter**, you can copy existing text formats to ensure consistency. As an added bonus, using the Format Painter takes fewer mouse clicks to format text than formatting each instance individually. In this lesson, you use Format Painter to copy formats (bold and blue color) from the first software name to the other software names.

To Copy Formats Using Format Painter

1 In the *Office Software-WB3L* document, click anywhere inside the bold, blue *Microsoft Word*.
You need to click inside formatted text so that Word knows what formats you want to copy.

(Continues)

To Copy Formats Using Format Painter (Continued)

② Double-click the Format Painter button on the Standard toolbar.
When you double-click the Format Painter button, the mouse pointer turns into a paint-brush next to the I-beam (see Figure 3.12).

*Double-click
to turn on
Format Painter*

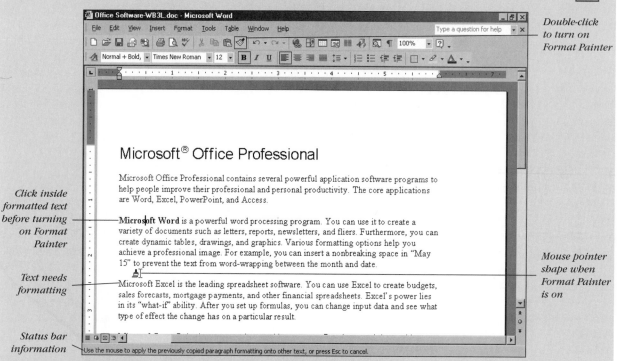

*Click inside
formatted text
before turning
on Format
Painter*

*Text needs
formatting*

*Status bar
information*

*Mouse pointer
shape when
Format Painter
is on*

Figure 3.12

 If you have problems...
Be careful where you click and drag with the Format Painter turned on; Word immediately formats any characters you select. If you accidentally format text, immediately click the Undo button to remove the format.

③ Select *Microsoft Excel* at the beginning of the next paragraph.
The second software name now has the same text enhancements as the first heading. Using Format Painter saves you from having to click two separate buttons (Bold and Font Color) to format the text.

 If you have problems...
If the insertion point was *not* in formatted text when you turned on Format Painter, it won't copy any formats. If this happens, turn off Format Painter by clicking the Format Painter button again, click inside the formatted text you wish to copy, and then use Format Painter to copy the formats.

④ Repeatedly click the scroll-down arrow on the vertical scrollbar until you see the last two paragraphs.
You need to select the software names at the beginning of these two paragraphs.

⑤ Select *Microsoft PowerPoint* and then select *Microsoft Access* to apply the text enhancements to these two software names.

To Copy Formats Using Format Painter

After formatting the last text, turn off the Format Painter.

6 **Click the Format Painter button to turn off this feature.**

7 **Click inside the text to deselect it.**
The software names at the beginning of each paragraph are now formatted consistently (see Figure 3.13).

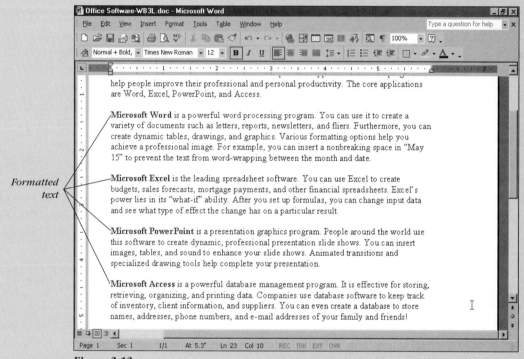

Formatted text

Figure 3.13

8 **Save the document and keep it onscreen to continue with the next lesson.**

To extend your knowledge...

Single- and Double-Clicking the Format Painter Button

If you single-click the Format Painter button, you can copy the formats only one time; then, Word turns off Format Painter.

If you double-click the Format Painter button, you can continue formatting additional text. To turn off Format Painter when you're done, click the Format Painter button once.

Formatting Headings

Instead of using Format Painter, you can create a paragraph style and apply it to your document headings. The benefit of a style over using Format Painter is that you can quickly edit the style formats, and all text formatted by that style is immediately updated. With Format Painter, you have to reapply the formats to the headings. Use the Help feature to learn how to create and apply paragraph styles.

Lesson 5: Highlighting Text

People often use a highlighting marker to highlight important parts of textbooks, magazine articles, and other documents. You can **highlight** text to draw the reader's attention to important information within the documents you create.

After reviewing the *Office Software-WB3L* document, you decide to highlight the phrase *improve their professional and personal productivity*.

To Highlight Text

1 In the *Office Software-WB3L* document, press Ctrl+Home to position the insertion point at the beginning of the document.

2 Select the phrase *improve their professional and personal productivity* in the first paragraph.

You want to highlight this phrase so it will stand out.

 ### If you have problems...

If you have trouble clicking and dragging to select text, you can use keyboard shortcuts. First, position the insertion point at the beginning of the word *improve*; press and hold down ◆Shift while you click after the *y* in *productivity*.

3 Click the Highlight button on the Formatting toolbar.

Word uses the default highlight color to highlight the text you selected. After you click the Highlight button, the text is deselected (see Figure 3.14)

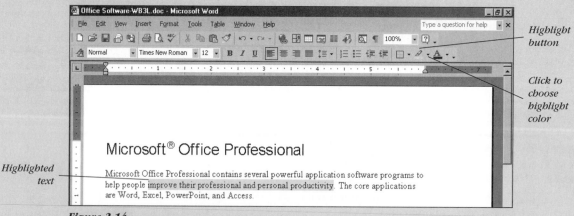

Highlight button

Click to choose highlight color

Highlighted text

Figure 3.14

4 Save the document, and keep it onscreen to continue with the next lesson.

 ## To extend your knowledge...

Using the Highlight Feature

You can click the Highlight button before selecting text. When you do this, the mouse pointer resembles a highlighting pen. You can then click and drag across text you want to highlight. The Highlight feature stays on, so you can highlight additional text. When you finish, click the Highlight button to turn it off. To remove highlight, select the highlighted text, click the Highlight drop-down arrow, and choose None.

Printing Highlighted Text

If you have a color printer, you see the highlight colors on your printout. If you're using a black-and-white printer, the highlight appears in shades of gray. Make sure that you can easily read the text with the gray highlight. If not, select a lighter highlight color, and print it again.

Lesson 6: Inserting Symbols

Although the keyboard contains some keys that produce symbols, such as the plus sign (+), hundreds of other symbols are not on the standard keyboard. For example, you might want to insert an **em dash**, a dash the width of a lowercase m, to indicate a pause or change in thought, or an **en dash**, a dash the width of a lowercase n, to indicate a series, such as pages 9–15.

You can display the Symbol dialog box to insert these special dashes, a copyright symbol, or a paragraph mark. In addition, you can select from a variety of specialized symbols such as a plane, data disk, spider web, and book. In this lesson, you insert the mouse symbol in the first paragraph.

To Insert a Symbol

1 In the *Office Software-WB3L* document, position the insertion point at the end of the first paragraph.
This is where you want to insert the symbol.

2 Choose **I**nsert, **S**ymbol.
The Symbol dialog box appears (see Figure 3.15).

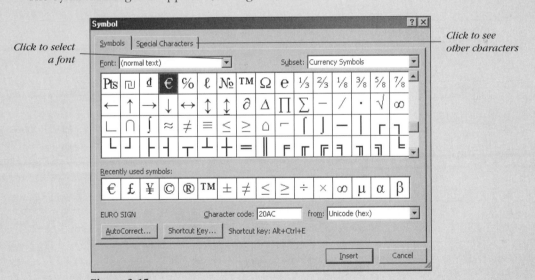

Click to select a font

Click to see other characters

Figure 3.15

The dialog box has two tabs: **S**ymbols and S**p**ecial Characters. The **S**ymbols tab provides access to hundreds of special symbols; the S**p**ecial Characters tab provides access to standard characters, such as the em dash.

3 Click the **F**ont drop-down arrow, and choose Wingdings if it is not already selected.
Some of the most interesting and diverse symbols are located in Wingdings, Wingdings 2, Wingdings 3, and Webdings. Figure 3.16 shows the Wingdings symbols.

(Continues)

To Insert a Symbol (Continued)

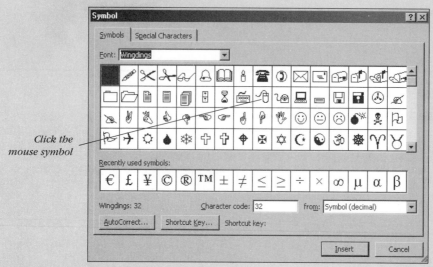

Figure 3.16

④ Click the mouse symbol in the middle of the second row.
This is the symbol that looks like an aerial view of a mouse.

⑤ Click Insert to place the symbol at the insertion point.
The Cancel button changes to the Close button after you insert a symbol.

⑥ Click Close to close the Symbol dialog box.
Figure 3.17 shows the symbol in the paragraph.

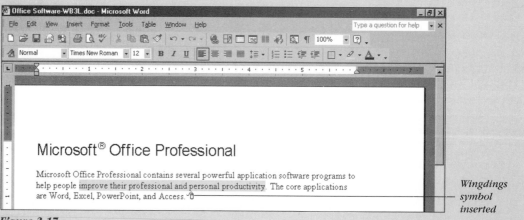

Figure 3.17

⑦ Save the document, and keep it onscreen to continue with the next lesson.

To extend your knowledge...

Using Common Symbols

If you're asked to insert a common symbol—such as an em dash, copyright symbol, or registered symbol—you can insert them from the Special Characters section of the Symbol dialog box (see Figure 3.18), or you can use the keyboard shortcuts, if available.

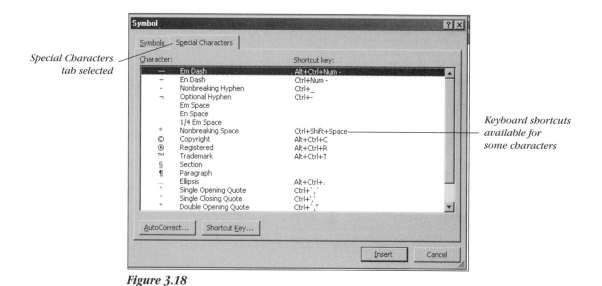

*Special Characters
tab selected*

*Keyboard shortcuts
available for
some characters*

Figure 3.18

Lesson 7: Displaying Formatting Marks

The document onscreen looks basically like what its printout looks like. This feature is known as "What You See Is What You Get" (***WYSIWYG***). Although you see most formatting, you don't see everything. For example, you might not know at a glance whether you pressed (Tab⇆) or (Spacebar) to indent text. Although either method might be acceptable in the short run, the spacing might look different if you print your document on a different system.

To help you see how your document is formatted, display formatting marks. ***Formatting marks*** are nonprinting symbols and characters that indicate spaces, tabs, hyphen types, page breaks, and hard returns. A ***hard return*** is where you press (⏎Enter) to start a new line instead of letting text word-wrap to the next line. Table 3.3 shows common formatting marks and what they indicate.

Table 3.3	Formatting Marks

Symbol	Description
·	space
°	nonbreaking space
-	hyphen
—	nonbreaking hyphen
→	tab
¶	end of paragraph

To Show and Hide Formatting Marks

❶ **Click the Show/Hide ¶ button on the Standard toolbar.**
You now see nonprinting formatting marks within your document, as shown in Figure 3.19.

(Continues)

To Show and Hide Formatting Marks (Continued)

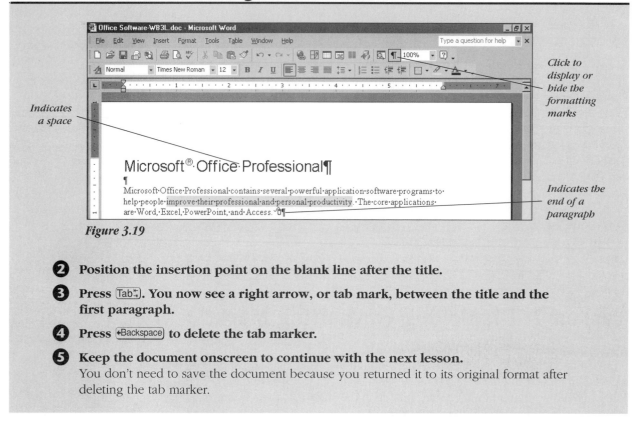

Figure 3.19

② **Position the insertion point on the blank line after the title.**

③ **Press Tab⇄. You now see a right arrow, or tab mark, between the title and the first paragraph.**

④ **Press ⇐Backspace to delete the tab marker.**

⑤ **Keep the document onscreen to continue with the next lesson.**
You don't need to save the document because you returned it to its original format after deleting the tab marker.

To extend your knowledge...

Displaying Formatting Marks

If you don't see all three types of formatting marks, you need to display the Options dialog box to change the default. To view all formatting marks, choose Tools on the menu bar and choose Options. When the Options dialog box appears, click the View tab and then click the All check box in the Formatting marks section. Click OK to close the dialog box.

Lesson 8: Inserting Nonbreaking Spaces and Hyphens

By now you know that the word-wrap feature wraps a word to the next line if it doesn't fit at the end of the current line. Occasionally, word-wrapping between certain types of words is undesirable; that is, some words should be kept together. For example, the date *March 31* should stay together instead of word-wrapping after *March*. Other items that should stay together include names, such as *Ms. Stevenson*, and page references, such as *page 15*. To prevent words from separating due to the word-wrap feature, insert a ***nonbreaking space*** or a hard space.

As you review your document, you notice that the words *May* and *15* word-wrap between the two words. You want to keep *May 15* together on the same line.

To Insert a Nonbreaking Space

1   In the *Office Software-WB3L* document, click the Show/Hide ¶ button on the Standard toolbar if the formatting marks are not already displayed.

2   Position the insertion point after *May* at the end of the fourth line in the second paragraph.

You need to delete the regular space after *May* and replace it with a nonbreaking space to keep *May 15* together (see Figure 3.20).

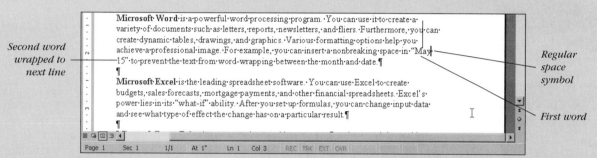

Figure 3.20

3   Press Del to delete the regular space.

This brings *May15* together without any space between the two words.

4   Press Ctrl+↑Shift+Spacebar.

Word now keeps *May 15* together. Notice the difference in the nonbreaking space symbol and the regular space symbol (see Figure 3.21).

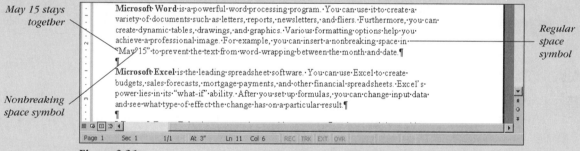

Figure 3.21

5   Click the Show/Hide ¶ button on the Standard toolbar to hide the symbols.

6   Save the document and close it.

 ## To extend your knowledge...

Nonbreaking Hyphens

Hyphens cause another word-wrap problem. Words containing hyphens can word-wrap at the hyphen location, causing undesirable results. Certain hyphenated text, such as phone numbers, should stay together.

To keep hyphenated words together, replace the regular hyphen with a nonbreaking hyphen. A ***nonbreaking hyphen*** keeps text on both sides of the hyphen together. To insert a nonbreaking hyphen, press Ctrl+↑Shift+-.

When you display the formatting symbols, a regular hyphen looks like a hyphen. A nonbreaking hyphen appears as a wider hyphen. However, the nonbreaking hyphen looks like a regular hyphen when printed.

Inserting Nonbreaking Spaces and Hyphens from the Symbols Dialog Box

Instead of using the keyboard shortcuts, you can insert nonbreaking spaces and hyphens from the Special Characters page of the Symbols dialog box.

Summary

In this project, you used character formats such as bold to emphasize text. You also selected fonts, font sizes, font colors, and character spacing to enhance the visual effectiveness of documents. By using Format Painter, you can save time by copying text formats to other text in your document. Furthermore, you can highlight text to draw attention to important ideas. You can prevent word-wrapping between words by using nonbreaking spaces and hyphens. Finally, you can display the nonprinting symbols to help you see spacing, tabs, and hard returns.

For additional information, use the Help feature to learn more about these topics. In addition, complete the following end-of-project exercises to reinforce and build on the skills you acquired in this project.

Checking Concepts and Terms

Multiple Choice

Circle the letter of the correct answer for each of the following.

1. All of the following have keyboard shortcuts except _____. [L1]

   a. underline

   b. font color

   c. bold

   d. italic

2. How many points are in a vertical inch? [L2]

   a. 10

   b. 12

   c. 24

   d. 72

3. Which effect only appears onscreen and not on a printout? [L3]

   a. Blinking background

   b. Superscript

   c. Strikethrough

   d. Emboss

4. What nonprinting format symbol represents a nonbreaking space? [L7]

   a. •

   b. ¶

   c. →

   d. °

5. Look at Figure 3.4, and identify an example of a serif font. [L2]

   a. Arial Rounded MT Bold

   b. Courier New

   c. Keystroke

   d. Westminster

Screen ID

Label each element of the Word screen shown in Figure 3.22.

A. Font Color button

B. Format Painter button

C. Highlight button

D. Nonbreaking space symbol

E. Paragraph symbol

F. Tab symbol

Figure 3.22

1. _____   4. _____

2. _____   5. _____

3. _____   6. _____

Discussion

1. Find two examples of documents (for example, the minutes of a meeting, the letter to stockholders in a company's annual report, or a magazine article) that use character formats. Identify the types of character formats and evaluate their effectiveness. If the character formats are not effective, provide suggestions for improving the document. [L1–8]

2. What is the purpose of displaying formatting marks? Provide an example when you should have the formatting marks displayed. [L7]

3. Explain how em dashes, en dashes, and nonbreaking hyphens differ. Provide an example of the use of each. [L6, 8]

Skill Drill exercises reinforce project skills. Each skill reinforced is the same, or nearly the same, as a skill presented in the project. Detailed instructions are provided in a step-by-step format.

1. Using Character Formats and Font Attributes to Enhance a Newsletter

You work for an apartment complex manager. She just finished typing the October newsletter and wants you to enhance its appearance.

1. Open *ew1-0302*, and save it as `October Newsletter-WB3SD`.
2. Click and drag across the first two lines of text.
3. Click the Font drop-down arrow; and choose Arial Rounded MT Bold, Kabel Dm BT, or Tahoma.
4. Deselect both lines and select the first line only.
5. Click the Font Size drop-down arrow, and choose 18.
6. Select the first heading, *Water Hoses*.
7. Click the Bold button.
8. Click the Font Color drop-down arrow, and choose Pink.

9. Click inside the *Water Hoses* heading to deselect it.

10. Save the document, and keep it onscreen to continue with the next exercise.

2. Using Format Painter to Format Other Headings

To save time applying character formats and font attributes to other headings, you want to use Format Painter to copy the formats from the *Water Hoses* heading to the other headings.

1. In the open *October Newsletter-WB3SD* document, make sure that the insertion point is inside the *Water Hoses* heading and then double-click the Format Painter button.

2. Scroll down to see *Thermostat Settings* at the top of the screen.

3. Click and drag across *Thermostat Settings* with the Format Painter mouse pointer.

4. Click and drag across *Sidewalk Salt* and then click and drag across *Laundry Room Hours*.

5. Click the Format Painter button to turn off this feature.

6. Save the document, and keep it onscreen to continue with the next exercise.

3. Applying Character Effects and Character Spacing

You decide to apply the Small Caps character effect to the second line to add some contrast to the headings. In addition, you notice that some characters are too close together in the main title and need to be separated.

1. In the *October Newsletter-WB3SD* document, select *October 2004 Newsletter*.

2. Choose F̲ormat, F̲ont. If needed, click the Fo̲nt tab.

3. Click the Fo̲nt tab, if necessary, to see the Fo̲nt options.

4. Click the S̲mall caps check box and then click OK.

5. Click and drag across *rt* in *Apartment* in the main title.

6. Choose F̲ormat, F̲ont.

7. Click the Chara̲cter Spacing tab.

8. Click the S̲pacing drop-down arrow, and choose Expanded.

9. Click the Spacing B̲y increment button to 1.3 and then click OK.

10. Click inside the document to deselect the text.

11. Save the document, and keep it onscreen to continue with the next exercise.

4. Highlighting Text and Inserting a Symbol in the Newsletter

You want to highlight a sentence so that it stands out for your tenants. In addition, you want to insert a thermometer symbol as a visual effect.

1. In the *October Newsletter-WB3SD* document, press and hold down Ctrl while you click the mouse button on the sentence *Please disconnect these hoses by October 15.* in the second paragraph.

2. Click the Highlight button.

3. Click on the right side of the *Thermostat Settings* heading.

4. Choose I̲nsert, S̲ymbol.

5. Click the S̲ymbols tab, if needed, to display symbol options.

6. Click the F̲ont drop-down arrow and choose Webdings.

7. Click the scroll-down arrow nine times.

8. Click the thermometer symbol, which is the second symbol from the left (fourth row down).

9. Click I̲nsert and then click Close.

10. Select the thermometer symbol, and click the Bold button to remove bold from the symbol.

11. Save the document. and keep it onscreen to continue with the next exercise.

5. Inserting a Nonbreaking Space and En Dashes

The newsletter is almost done. However, you need to insert a nonbreaking space to keep *7 a.m.* together. In addition, you want to insert en dashes in the times to look professional.

1. In the *October Newsletter-WB3SD* document, press Ctrl+End to position the insertion point at the end of the document.
2. Click the Show/Hide ¶ button to see the nonprinting symbols, if they are not already displayed.
3. Click to the immediate right of 7, and press Del to delete the regular space symbol.
4. Press Ctrl+⇧Shift+Spacebar to insert a nonbreaking space.
5. Click after *Monday* on the previous line, and press Del to delete the regular space symbol.
6. Choose Insert, Symbol.
7. Click the Special Characters tab.
8. Click En Dash, click Insert, and then click Close to insert an en dash between *Monday* and *Thursday*.
9. Click after *Friday* on the next line and press Del to delete the regular space symbol.
10. Press Ctrl+- (the minus key on the numeric keypad) to insert an en dash without having to access the Symbol dialog box.
11. Save the document, print it, and then close it.

Challenge

Challenge exercises expand on or are somewhat related to skills presented in the lessons. Each exercise provides a brief narrative introduction, followed by instructions in a numbered-step format that are not as detailed as those in the Skill Drill section.

1. Enhancing an Apartment Complex Newsletter

You need to update the apartment newsletter for December. You want to change some text, apply character formats, insert symbols, and add highlighting.

1. Open *ew1-0302*, and save it as *December Newsletter-WB3CH1*.
2. Make the following edits:
   ○ Change *October 2004* to `December 2004`.
   ○ Change *Winter will soon be* to `Winter is now`.
   ○ Select and delete the heading and paragraph about *Water Hoses*.
   ○ Select and delete the heading and paragraph about *Laundry Room Hours*.
3. Add this heading and section below the first paragraph:
   `Christmas Trees`
   `Only artificial trees are permitted in apartments. We know many residents prefer live trees, but they pose a fire hazard; therefore, our insurance company will not permit live trees in apartments. If you want the aroma of a live Christmas tree, we suggest you purchase pine-scented fragrances at the local discount store and spray your artificial tree.`
4. Make sure that you have a blank line above and below the new heading and a blank line after the new paragraph you typed.
5. Add this heading and section at the end of the document:
   `Open House`
   `Be sure to stop by the office on December 20 for the annual Holiday Party. From 5:30 p.m. to 8:00 p.m., enjoy refreshments while visiting with the management team and your neighbors.`
6. Apply 18-point Arial bold Green font color to the title, and apply 14-point Arial italic Red font color to the secondary title.

7. Select the *Christmas Trees* heading, and apply 12-point Arial bold italic. Use the Format Painter to copy these formats to the other headings.

8. Highlight in yellow the following text:
   - the first sentence of the first paragraph
   - *December 20* in the last paragraph
   - *5:30 p.m. to 8:00 p.m.* in the last paragraph

9. Insert nonbreaking spaces within *5:30 p.m.* and *8:00 p.m.*

10. Insert the symbol of a house on the right side of the heading *Open House*. The house symbol is located on the third row, ninth column in Webdings font symbols. Remove the bold and italic format from the symbol.

11. Delete the word *degrees* in the second paragraph in the *Thermostat Settings* section. Insert the degree symbol to the immediate right of *60*. This symbol is located in the normal font symbol palette.

12. Save, print, and close the document.

2. Enhancing a Letter to a Student Organization

You prepared a response to a student organization that is interested in holding a fundraiser for a charitable contribution. You work with the student organizations to inform them of the required sales tax forms for their vendors. You now want to enhance the letter to make certain points stand out.

1. Open *ew1-0303*, and save it as `Tax Letter-WB3CH2`.

2. Emphasize the subject line by making it bold and applying Arial Narrow font to *Sales Tax Forms for the Gift and Craft Fair*.

3. Use Bright Green highlight on the phrase *must return the master forms to the tax commission's office by December 15*.

4. Display the formatting marks. Insert nonbreaking spaces and hyphens in the appropriate locations. (Hint: You need at least one of each.)

5. Italicize and bold the last sentence in the third paragraph; then, apply Red font color to the sentence.

6. Save, print, and close the document.

3. Creating a Health Benefits Memo

You work in your company's Benefits Office. You need to prepare a memo to inform employees of a few changes and of upcoming seminars that further explain the changes.

1. From a new window, create the document shown in Figure 3.23, applying character formats and Arial font as shown.

2. Apply Red font color to *Changes in Benefits*.

3. Use Format Painter to copy formats from the first heading to the other heading.

4. Display the formatting marks. Make sure that you have two paragraph marks at the end of the *TO*, *FROM*, and *DATE* lines. Make sure that you have three paragraph marks after the *SUBJECT* line.

5. Correct all spelling and typographical errors.

6. Select the dates at the bottom of the memo, press Tab⇆ to indent them, and apply Red font color to them.

7. Highlight the last sentence in Turquoise.

8. Insert nonbreaking spaces and hyphens, if needed.

9. Save the document as `Health Benefits Memo-WB3CH3`; then print and close it.

> **TO:**   Full-Time Employees
>
> **FROM:**   Student Name, Benefits Office
>
> **DATE:**   March 1, 2004
>
> **SUBJECT:**   Health-Care Plan Options
>
> It's that time of year again when we update all employees' health benefit records. This memo provides some information about changes and seminars.
>
> **<u>Changes in Benefits</u>**
>
> The co-pay on prescription drugs has increased slightly. Generic prescriptions are now $5, and brand-name prescriptions are $10. We had to compromise with the service provider to keep the premiums as low as possible.
>
> We've selected another provider for dental benefits. Employees will still receive the same value and services with no out-of-pocket premiums. The deductibles are also the same. However, to receive full coverage, employees must select a dentist on the provider's list. The list will be distributed at the upcoming seminars.
>
> **<u>Seminars</u>**
>
> Additional information will be provided through seminars for all employees. At the end of each one-hour seminar, you will receive enrollment forms for the fiscal year starting on July 1. Please attend one of the following seminars:
>
>   *March 10 @ 1:15 p.m.*
>   *March 12 @ 8:30 a.m.*
>   *March 16 @ 3:30 p.m.*
>
> All seminars are held in the Lincoln Conference Room. Refreshments will be served.

Figure 3.23

4. Enhancing an Advertisement Flier

In Project 2, you created an announcement to college students about your Mega Music store's special discount. Now, you want to create and enhance a flier to go on bulletin boards around the campus.

1. Open *ew1-0304*, and save it as `Mega Music Flier-WB3CH4`.
2. Select the entire document, and apply 20-point Comic Sans MS font.
3. Select the first two lines in the document, and apply 28-point Arial Rounded MT Bold in Violet font color. (If you don't have Arial Rounded MT Bold, ask your instructor for an alternative sans serif font face.)
4. Apply an appropriate highlight color to the three lines that list the discount percentages.
5. Delete the asterisk, and insert the Webdings symbol that looks like two masks—the symbol that you often see for theatrical events. The symbol is on the ninth row of symbols. Select the symbol and apply 72-point size with Violet font color.

6. Insert the telephone symbol from the Wingdings symbols at the beginning of the phone number on the last line of the document.

7. Delete *to* between *9 a.m. to 9 p.m.* and insert an en dash. Delete any spaces before and after the en dash.

8. Save, print, and close the document.

5. Formatting Text in a Software Information Sheet

Your supervisor wants you to apply some different formatting to the information sheet about Microsoft Office Professional. He recommends using different fonts, font color, and other character formats.

1. Open *ew1-0301*, and save it as `Office Software Sheet-WB3CH5`.

2. Select the entire document, and apply Bookman Old Style font.

3. Apply these formats to the title: 16-point Albertus Medium or Arial bold font (or a font of your instructor's choice), Dark Blue font color, and Yellow highlight color.

4. Press Tab to indent the first line of each paragraph except the first paragraph.

5. Use Overtype mode to change *newsletters, and fliers* to `fliers, and newsletters` in the Microsoft Word paragraph.

6. Make the following changes:
   - *May 15* to `November 21`
   - *financial spreadsheets* to `financial statements`
   - *Excel's power lies in its* to `Business people appreciate Excel's powerful`

7. Insert a nonbreaking hyphen and a nonbreaking space in the appropriate locations.

8. Apply bold, Arial, Dark Blue font color to *Microsoft Word*. Use the Format Painter to duplicate the character formats for *Microsoft Excel*, *Microsoft PowerPoint*, and *Microsoft Access*.

9. Insert ® after *Microsoft* in the title. Make it appear in superscript.

10. Save, print, and close the document.

Discovery Zone exercises require advanced knowledge of topics presented in *essentials* lessons, application of skills from multiple lessons, or self-directed learning of new skills.

1. Enhancing a Restaurant Review Article

You are the newly appointed restaurant critic for your college newspaper. Your first article is to introduce your column and define your grading scale. Open *ew1-0305*, and save it as `Restaurant Review-WB3DZ1`. Change * to your name and ** to your e-mail address, such as `name@college.edu`.

Apply 10-point Comic Sans MS font to the entire document. Apply 14-point Arial, Plum font color, and Blinking Background text effect to the title. Use the Help feature to learn more about text effects. Use your judgment in adjusting character spacing as needed within the title. Also activate kerning for point sizes above 12. Insert any necessary nonbreaking spaces or hyphens in the correct locations.

Use Figure 3.24 to finish formatting the document. Pay close attention to detail. Use the Symbol dialog box to locate and insert é in the last sentence. Save, print, and close the document.

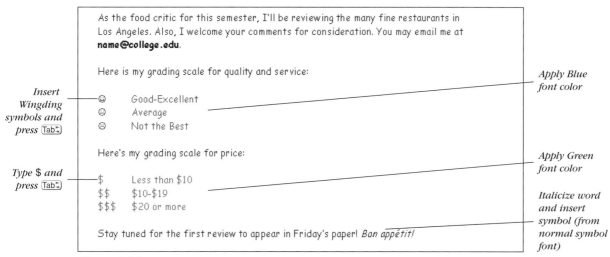

As the food critic for this semester, I'll be reviewing the many fine restaurants in Los Angeles. Also, I welcome your comments for consideration. You may email me at **name@college.edu**.

Here is my grading scale for quality and service:

Insert Wingding symbols and press [Tab⇄]

☺   Good-Excellent
☺   Average
☹   Not the Best

Apply Blue font color

Here's my grading scale for price:

Type $ and press [Tab⇄]

$ Less than $10
$$ $10-$19
$$$ $20 or more

Apply Green font color

Italicize word and insert symbol (from normal symbol font)

Stay tuned for the first review to appear in Friday's paper! *Bon appétit!*

Figure 3.24

2. Creating a Notice for a Professor's Door

You are a student worker for a department on your college campus. You were asked to create a notice to tape to a professor's door. Create the notice shown in Figure 3.25 by using the formats specified.

36-point Blippo Blk BT (or similar-looking font)

26-point Times New Roman

Yellow highlight

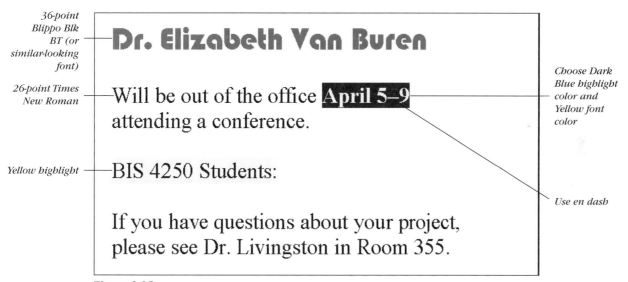

Dr. Elizabeth Van Buren

Will be out of the office April 5–9 attending a conference.

BIS 4250 Students:

If you have questions about your project, please see Dr. Livingston in Room 355.

Choose Dark Blue highlight color and Yellow font color

Use en dash

Figure 3.25

Apply a custom color to the title using these settings: Hue 238, Sat 128, Lum 133, Red 194, Green 72, and Blue 121. Use Help, if needed, to learn how to create a custom font color.

Save the document as `Office Door Notice-WB3DZ2`, and print it. Fold the note in half, just below the last text line.

3. Experimenting with the Software Announcement

You want to experiment with the *Office Software-WB3L* document you formatted within the lessons. Open the document, and save it as `Office Software-WB3DZ3`.

Experiment with different fonts for the main title. Try Outline, Emboss, and Engrave character effects (individually). Decide which effect looks the best, and apply it again.

Experiment with different highlight colors and font color combinations on the text *Microsoft Word* that is currently bold. Use Format Painter to copy the formats to the other headings.

Select the paragraphs, and choose another serif font face.

Find and insert these symbols in front of their respective paragraphs:

video camera	PowerPoint
line chart	Excel
miniature letter	Word
three computer monitors	Access

Select each symbol and remove the bold formatting. Save, print, and close the document.

Editing Documents

Objectives

In this project, you learn how to

- ✔ Insert and Modify Date and Time Fields
- ✔ Change the Case of Text
- ✔ Cut, Copy, and Paste Text
- ✔ Copy Between Document Windows
- ✔ Undo and Redo Actions
- ✔ Use AutoCorrect
- ✔ Use the Thesaurus

Key terms introduced in this project include

- ❏ action
- ❏ active document window
- ❏ AutoCorrect
- ❏ case
- ❏ copy
- ❏ cut
- ❏ date or time field
- ❏ object
- ❏ Office Clipboard
- ❏ paste
- ❏ Paste Options Smart Tag
- ❏ Redo
- ❏ synonyms
- ❏ Undo

Why Would I Do This?

Editing is an important step when preparing documents for yourself or for others. For example, you might have the perfect paragraph, but it's not in the best location. Or, you might have several documents that contain information that you need to pull together into a new document. Furthermore, you might need to change capitalization style for text without retyping it, or you might need to edit words by choosing synonyms.

In this project, you learn how to insert and modify the date and time, change capitalization style, rearrange text, and copy text from one document to another. In addition, you learn how to use Undo, AutoCorrect, and Thesaurus during the editing process.

Visual Summary

Figure 4.1 shows a document that contains a capitalized paragraph, a paragraph in the wrong location, and a word that needs to be changed.

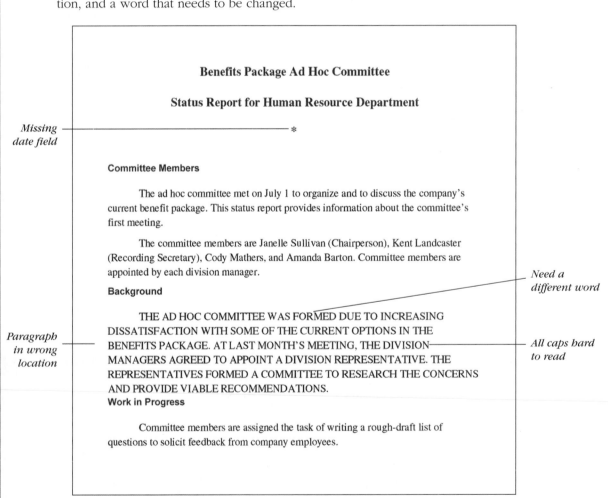

Benefits Package Ad Hoc Committee

Status Report for Human Resource Department

Missing date field — *

Committee Members

The ad hoc committee met on July 1 to organize and to discuss the company's current benefit package. This status report provides information about the committee's first meeting.

The committee members are Janelle Sullivan (Chairperson), Kent Landcaster (Recording Secretary), Cody Mathers, and Amanda Barton. Committee members are appointed by each division manager.

Need a different word

Background

Paragraph in wrong location —
THE AD HOC COMMITTEE WAS FORMED DUE TO INCREASING DISSATISFACTION WITH SOME OF THE CURRENT OPTIONS IN THE BENEFITS PACKAGE. AT LAST MONTH'S MEETING, THE DIVISION MANAGERS AGREED TO APPOINT A DIVISION REPRESENTATIVE. THE REPRESENTATIVES FORMED A COMMITTEE TO RESEARCH THE CONCERNS AND PROVIDE VIABLE RECOMMENDATIONS.

All caps hard to read

Work in Progress

Committee members are assigned the task of writing a rough-draft list of questions to solicit feedback from company employees.

Figure 4.1

Figure 4.2 shows the document after it has been edited.

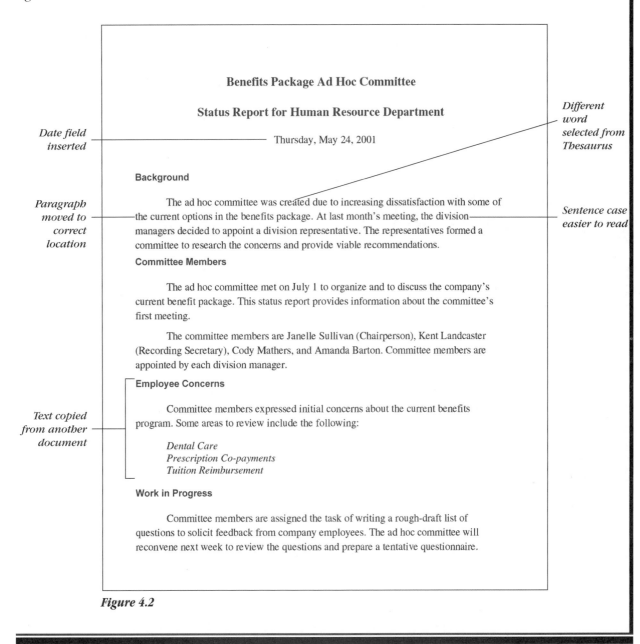

Date field inserted

Paragraph moved to correct location

Text copied from another document

Benefits Package Ad Hoc Committee

Status Report for Human Resource Department

Thursday, May 24, 2001

Background

The ad hoc committee was created due to increasing dissatisfaction with some of the current options in the benefits package. At last month's meeting, the division managers decided to appoint a division representative. The representatives formed a committee to research the concerns and provide viable recommendations.

Committee Members

The ad hoc committee met on July 1 to organize and to discuss the company's current benefit package. This status report provides information about the committee's first meeting.

The committee members are Janelle Sullivan (Chairperson), Kent Landcaster (Recording Secretary), Cody Mathers, and Amanda Barton. Committee members are appointed by each division manager.

Employee Concerns

Committee members expressed initial concerns about the current benefits program. Some areas to review include the following:

Dental Care
Prescription Co-payments
Tuition Reimbursement

Work in Progress

Committee members are assigned the task of writing a rough-draft list of questions to solicit feedback from company employees. The ad hoc committee will reconvene next week to review the questions and prepare a tentative questionnaire.

Different word selected from Thesaurus

Sentence case easier to read

Figure 4.2

Lesson 1: Inserting and Modifying Date and Time Fields

Previously, you learned that AutoComplete can help you enter some month names and the current date, such as September 24, 2004. However, you might want to use other date formats, such as 9/24/04 or 24 September 2004. In addition, you might want to insert the time in a document. In these situations, you need to use the Date and Time dialog box to insert other date or time formats.

Furthermore, you might need to insert a date or time that always displays the current date—not the date or time that you insert it. In this case, you need to insert a ***date or time field***, a placeholder for a date or time that needs to change to reflect the current date or time when opened or printed.

In this lesson, you insert and modify a date field.

To Insert Date and Time Fields

1 **Open *ew1-0401*, and save it as** `Status Report-WB4L`.
You want to delete the asterisk below the second title and replace it with a date field.

2 **Delete the asterisk, and leave the insertion point in that location.**

3 **Choose Insert, Date and Time.**
The Date and Time dialog box appears, showing you the available formats (see Figure 4.3).

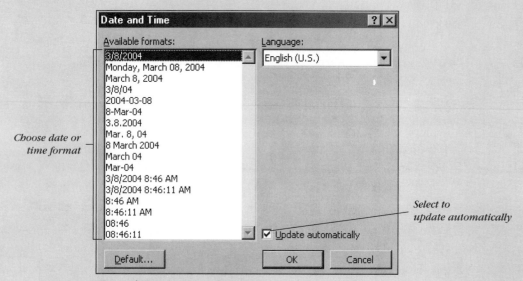

Choose date or time format

Select to update automatically

Figure 4.3

Your dates and times are different from those shown in the figures in this book. When choosing date or time options, choose the format that resembles the format specified in the instructions or in the figures.

4 **Choose format *8 March 2004* in the *Available formats* list box.**

5 **Click the *Update automatically* check box, if it's not already selected.**
If you want to create a date or time field that automatically updates the date, you must make sure that the *Update automatically* check box is selected.

6 **Click OK, and position the insertion point inside the date.**
Figure 4.4 shows the current date with a shaded background, which indicates that it is a date field.

To Insert Date and Time Fields

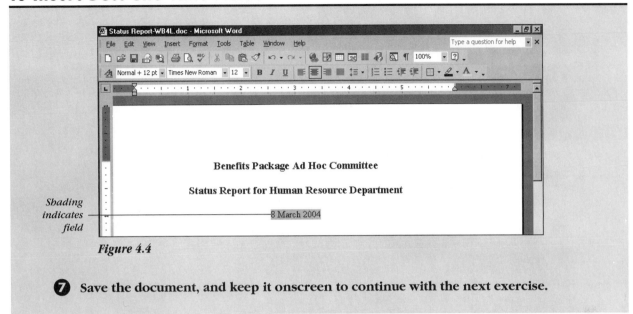

Shading indicates field

Figure 4.4

7 **Save the document, and keep it onscreen to continue with the next exercise.**

To extend your knowledge...

Updating Date and Time Fields

When you open the document on another date, the date field should reflect that particular date, not the date that you inserted the date field. If the date or time does not update automatically, click inside the field and press F9, or right-click within the field and choose *Update Field* from the shortcut menu.

After inserting a date or time field, you might want to choose a different format. You can easily modify the format of the date or time field. In addition to changing the field's characteristics, you can also change how it is formatted, such as fonts, and so on. In the next exercise, you modify the field to look like *Monday, March 08, 2004*.

To Modify a Date or Time Field

1 **In the open *Status Report-WB3L* document, right-click within the date.**
Right-clicking within the date field displays a shortcut menu (see Figure 4.5).

(Continues)

To Modify a Date or Time Field (Continued)

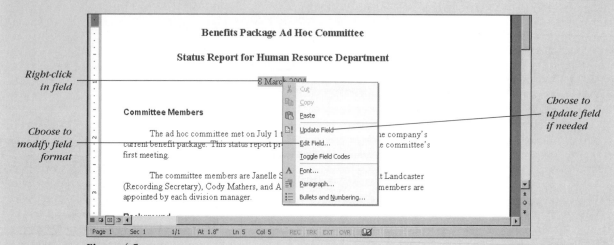

Right-click in field

Choose to modify field format

Choose to update field if needed

Figure 4.5

❷ **Choose _Edit Field_.**

The Field dialog box appears so that you can select a different date or time field format (see Figure 4.6).

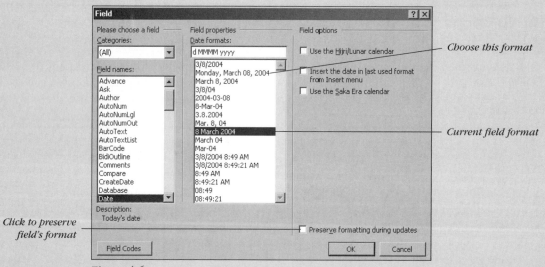

Choose this format

Current field format

Click to preserve field's format

Figure 4.6

❸ **Choose _Monday, March 08, 2004_ format.**

❹ **Click the _Preserve formatting during updates_ check box and then click OK.**

Clicking the _Preserve formatting during updates_ check box maintains any formatting you have applied to the date or time field. Otherwise, you lose the field's formats.

The date should now appear as _Monday, March 08, 2004_.

❺ **Save the document and keep it onscreen to continue with the next lesson.**

To extend your knowledge...

Creating Date and Time Field Codes

If you don't see any fields that display the date or time exactly as you want, you can create your own format from within the Field dialog box. Click the F̲ield Codes button, and enter the date or time codes exactly as you want the date or time to appear. For more information, type `Date-Time Picture field switch` in the Ask a Question text box to display Help topics to create advanced date and time fields.

Lesson 2: Changing the Case of Text

It's frustrating to discover that you typed an entire paragraph (or more) in all capital letters before realizing that you forgot to turn off Caps Lock! Instead of deleting and retyping everything you worked so hard to type, you can select the text and change its *case*. **Case** refers to the capitalization style, such as lowercase or uppercase, of text.

In this lesson, you notice that a full paragraph is capitalized. You need to change the case of the text to be consistent with the other paragraphs.

To Change the Case of Text

❶ **In the open *Status Report-WB4L* document, scroll down to see the capitalized paragraph.**
The third paragraph is formatted in all capital letters. You want to select a different case style.

❷ **Select the third paragraph, which is currently formatted in all capital letters.**
You must select the text that you want to change to a different case.

❸ **Choose Fo̲rmat, Change Cas̲e.**

If you have problems...

If you don't see the *Change Case* option, position the mouse pointer on the downward-pointing arrows at the bottom of the Fo̲rmat menu to see the full menu.

The Change Case dialog box appears (see Figure 4.7).

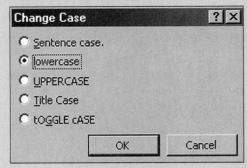

Figure 4.7

(Continues)

To Change the Case of Text (Continued)

The *Sentence case* option capitalizes only the first letter of each sentence. The *lowercase* option changes the selected text to lowercase letters. The *UPPERCASE* option changes the selected text to all capital letters. The *Title Case* option capitalizes the first letter of each word. The *tOGGLE cASE* option reverses the capitalization of selected text. For example, it changes uppercase letters to lowercase and lowercase letters to uppercase.

4 **Click *Sentence case* and click OK.**
Now, only the first letter of each sentence is capitalized. After changing the case, you should read the text and individually capitalize the first letter of proper nouns.

5 **Deselect the paragraph.**
Figure 4.8 shows how your paragraph should look after changing the case.

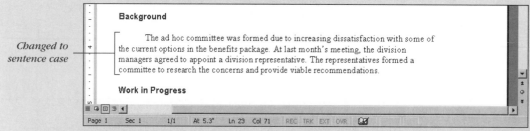

Changed to sentence case →

Background

The ad hoc committee was formed due to increasing dissatisfaction with some of the current options in the benefits package. At last month's meeting, the division managers agreed to appoint a division representative. The representatives formed a committee to research the concerns and provide viable recommendations.

Work in Progress

Page 1   Sec 1   1/1   At 5.3"   Ln 23   Col 71   REC TRK EXT OVR

Figure 4.8

6 **Save the document, and keep it onscreen to continue with the next lesson.**

To extend your knowledge...

Using Title Case

After you use the *Title Case* option from the Change Case dialog box on headings, you should change the first letter of small words to lowercase, such as *in* and *the* in the middle of the heading.

Using Keyboard Shortcuts

You can press ⬆Shift+F3 to change selected text to uppercase, lowercase, or sentence caps. Keep pressing this shortcut to cycle through the case options until the text appears in the case you want.

To quickly change selected text to all capitals, press Ctrl+⬆Shift+A.

Lesson 3: Cutting, Copying, and Pasting Text

After you create a document, you might decide to rearrange sentences and paragraphs to improve the clarity and organization of the content. You might want to move a paragraph to a different location, rearrange the sentences within a paragraph, or move sentences from different paragraphs to form one paragraph.

Here is the general process of moving text:

1. Select the text or ***object***, a non-text visual item such as an image or chart, which you want to move.
2. ***Cut*** or remove the selected item from its current location, and place it in the ***Office Clipboard***, a temporary holding place for up to 24 items you cut or copy.
3. Position the insertion point where you want the text to appear.

4. ***Paste*** the item in its new location. Pasting inserts the item that you cut or copied to the Office Clipboard.

In some cases, you need to duplicate, or ***copy***, text or an object. Instead of removing the text, you use the Copy command instead of the Cut command in Step 2. The Copy command leaves the original text or object in its location while making a duplicate in the Clipboard.

In this lesson, you move the Background section from its current location so that it's above the Committee Members section.

To Move Text

❶ In the *Status Report-WB4L* document, click the Show/Hide ¶ button to display the nonprinting symbols.

❷ Select the heading *Background*, the paragraph below it, and the paragraph symbol above *Work in Progress*, as shown in Figure 4.9.

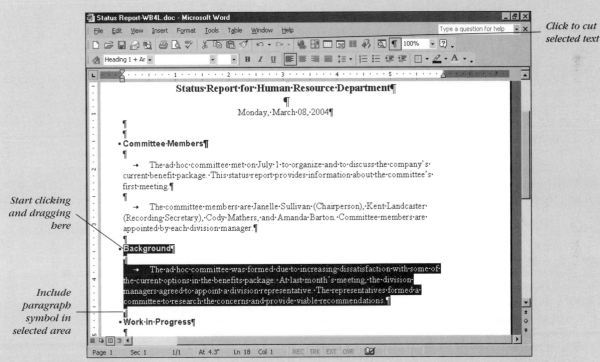

Figure 4.9

Click to cut selected text

Start clicking and dragging here

Include paragraph symbol in selected area

If you have problems...

If you're having problems selecting this text, place the insertion point at the beginning of the word *Background*, and press Ctrl+↑Shift+↓ four times.

The Background section is selected, so you can move it. You must select text and any blank lines you want to cut. Make sure that the paragraph symbol between the paragraph and the next heading is selected.

❸ Click the Cut button on the Standard toolbar.
The Background section is removed from the document. It is stored in the Office Clipboard.

(Continues)

To Move Text (Continued)

4 **Position the insertion point to the left of the letter *C* in the heading *Committee Members*.**

After cutting the text, you need to place the insertion point where you want the text to appear. In this document, you want to place the Background section before the Committee Members section.

5 **Click the Paste button on the Standard toolbar.**

When you paste the Background section in its new location, the Committee Members section moves down to accommodate it (see Figure 4.10).

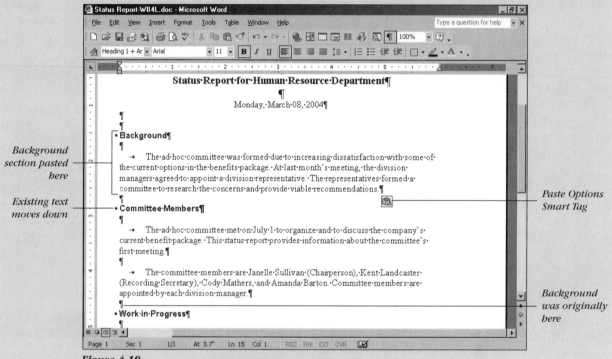

Figure 4.10

The ***Paste Options Smart Tag*** that appears lets you choose the formatting style for the text you paste. You learn more about this button in the next lesson.

6 **Save the document, and keep it onscreen to continue with the next lesson.**

Table 4.1 shows various methods for cutting, copying, and pasting items.

Table 4.1 Cut, Copy, and Paste Methods

Method	Cut	Copy	Paste
Toolbar	✂	📋	📋
Menu	Edit, Cut	Edit, Copy	Edit, Paste
Keyboard	Ctrl+X	Ctrl+C	Ctrl+V
Shortcut Menu	Right-click, Cut	Right-click, Copy	Right-click, Paste

To extend your knowledge...

Dragging and Dropping Text

You can also move text by dragging it into place. To move text, point inside the selected text, and drag it to a new location. When you release the mouse button, the text is moved from its original location to the new location. If you hold down Ctrl while dragging, you copy the selected text rather than cut it.

Using the Office Clipboard Task Pane

Choose Edit, Office Clipboard to display the Office Clipboard task pane to see the items you copy or cut (see Figure 4.11).

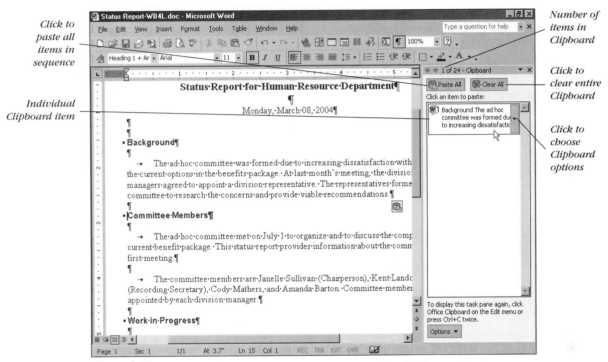

Figure 4.11

When you position the mouse pointer on a Clipboard item, a border appears around it with a down-pointing arrow on the right side. You can click the item to immediately paste it at the insertion point's location in the document. When you click the down-pointing arrow that appears when you place your mouse pointer to the right of the item, you can choose Paste to paste the item in the document, or choose Delete to remove the item from the Clipboard. Click Clear All to clear the Clipboard items.

Collecting and Pasting

You can use the Office Clipboard task pane to compile items from different sources and then paste them at one time to create a new document. The key to collecting items is to copy them in the order you want them to appear, such as first, second, and so on. When you click Paste All, the Clipboard pastes all its items in the sequence in which you copied or cut them. This is a great way to use documents obtained from team members to create a final document to submit to your supervisor.

Lesson 4: Copying Between Document Windows

In business, people often reuse information from previous reports and documents as they prepare new reports. In addition, people often work in teams, write their individual assignments, and send their documents to a team leader to collate. In these situations, you can open two or more documents and easily copy information from one document window to another. This process saves you from having to retype the information.

In this lesson, you copy some information from another document and paste it in your current document.

To Copy and Paste Between Document Windows

❶ With the *Status Report-WB4L* document onscreen, open *ew1-0402*, and make sure the formatting marks are displayed.

The *ew1-0402* document is in the *active document window*. The **active document window** is the window that contains a document with the insertion point; the title bar is blue or another color. The title bars for other document windows are a lighter color or gray.

❷ Select the heading *Employee Concerns*, the paragraph below it, and the three indented lines. Make sure that you select the paragraph mark representing the blank line below *Tuition Reimbursement*.

Figure 4.12 shows the text that you should select.

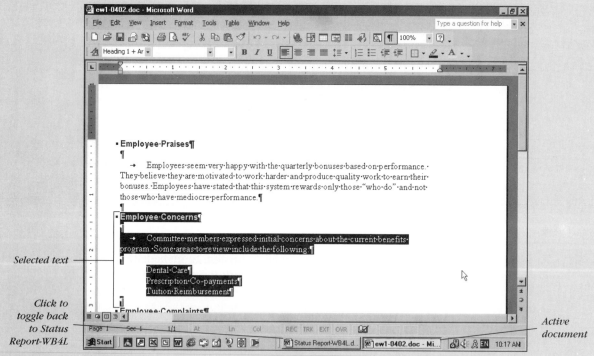

Figure 4.12

❸ Click the Copy button.
This copies the selected text to the Office Clipboard.

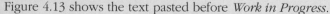

❹ Click the *Status Report-WB4L.doc* button on the Windows taskbar.
You can go back and forth between open documents by clicking their respective buttons on the taskbar. Now, *Status Report-WB4L* is the active document.

❺ Position the insertion point to the left of the *Work in Progress* heading, and click the Paste button.
Figure 4.13 shows the text pasted before *Work in Progress*.

To Copy and Paste Between Document Windows

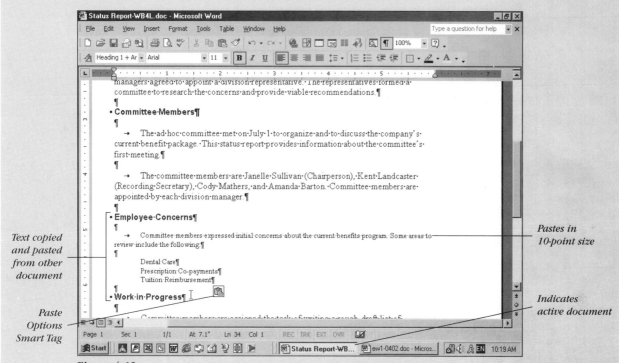

Text copied and pasted from other document

Pastes in 10-point size

Paste Options Smart Tag

Indicates active document

Figure 4.13

Notice that the paragraph and indented items appear in 10-point size, even if the original text was in 12-point size. You can use the Paste Options button to select the formatting for the pasted text.

6 **Click the Paste Options Smart Tag at the bottom-right corner of the pasted text.**
Figure 4.14 shows your options for formatting the pasted text.

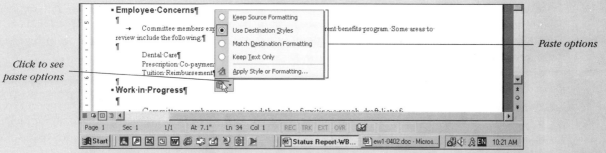

Click to see paste options

Paste options

Figure 4.14

In some instances, you want the pasted text to match the formatting in the destination document   the document in which you pasted the text. However, in this situation, the regular text would be formatted like the heading if you choose this option. Therefore, let's keep the original formatting, which was in 12-point size.

7 **Click the _Keep Source Formatting_ option.**

(Continues)

To Copy and Paste Between Document Windows (Continued)

The pasted paragraph and indented items are formatted with their original 12-point size (see Figure 4.15).

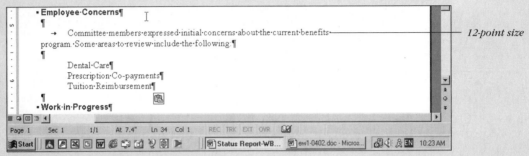

Figure 4.15

 If you have problems...

If the original formatting and the destination formatting don't format the pasted text to match the rest of the destination document's format, you might have to select the pasted text and manually apply the formats you want.

8 **Click the *ew1-0402.doc* button on the taskbar to toggle back to that document.**

9 **Choose File, Close to close *ew1-0402*.**
If you are prompted to save that document, click No. The *Status Report-WB4L* document is now the only open document.

10 **Save the document, and keep it onscreen to continue with the next lesson.**

Lesson 5: Undoing and Redoing Actions

Sometimes, you make a mistake in formatting, deleting, or typing text and then immediately realize your mistake. When this happens, use the *Undo* feature to reverse the actions you took. ***Undo*** reverses actions in sequential order—starting with the last action you performed. Using Undo again reverses the second-to-the-last action, and so on.

For example, assume that you paste a paragraph in the wrong location. Using the Undo feature removes the pasted text. If you accidentally click the Underline button, using the Undo feature removes the underline. Undo works for almost every action you perform within a document: formatting, deleting, sorting, placing graphics, and so on. Some actions cannot be reversed with Undo, however. For example, if you choose Save instead of Save As, you can't undo the saving process.

In this lesson, you delete a sentence in the first paragraph and then use Undo to restore the deleted text. In addition, you use Undo to remove italics from text.

To Undo Actions

1 **In the *Status Report-WB4L* document, press and hold Ctrl while clicking the first sentence.**
This is the sentence you want to delete.

2 **Press Del.**

To Undo Actions

The sentence is not in the Clipboard because you deleted it instead of cutting it. Figure 4.16 shows the document after deleting the sentence.

Undo button reverses actions

Tab and sentence deleted

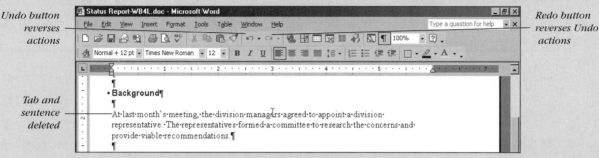

Redo button reverses Undo actions

Figure 4.16

3 **Click the Undo button on the Standard toolbar.**
The Undo feature reserves your last action. In this case, your last action deleted a sentence. Clicking the Undo button restores the deleted text.

4 **Select the three indented lines of text in the Employee Concerns section; then, click the Italic button.**

5 **Deselect the text to see the italic format.**
After italicizing the text, you realize immediately that you don't want it italicized.

6 **Click the Undo button.**
Undo reverses the last action by removing the italics from the text.

If you have problems...

If Undo doesn't undelete the text or remove the italic format, you probably performed another action on the document. Any change you make to the document, such as adding a space, is called an ***action***.

7 **Save the document, and keep the document onscreen to continue with the next exercise.**

To extend your knowledge...

Undo Keyboard Shortcut

The keyboard shortcut for undo is Ctrl+Z.

Undo List

Clicking the Undo button reverses the last action. If you need to restore previous actions, click the Undo button again. Each time you click the Undo button, you work backward—reversing the actions you took.

You can reverse a series of actions by clicking the Undo drop-down arrow. When you select an action from the list, Word reverses the most recent actions, including the one you select. Figure 4.17 shows that the last four actions will be undone.

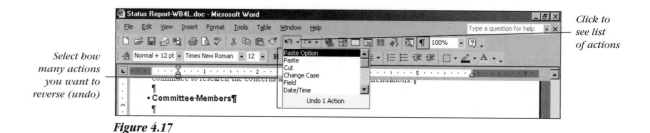

*Select how
many actions
you want to
reverse (undo)*

*Click to
see list
of actions*

Figure 4.17

If you decide that you preferred the action before undoing it, you can restore that action by using the **Redo** command to reverse the Undo command. The Redo button is grayed-out if you have not used the Undo feature in a document.

In the next exercise, you change your mind and want to reverse the last Undo action; that is, you want to restore the italic format the fastest way possible—by using Redo instead of selecting and italicizing text again.

To Redo an Action

❶ Click the Redo button.
The indented text in the Employee Concerns section is italicized again, because Redo reverses the last Undo action.

❷ Deselect the italicized items.

❸ Save the document, and keep it onscreen to continue with the next lesson.

Lesson 6: Using AutoCorrect

AutoCorrect corrects errors "on-the-fly," which means that it corrects errors as you type them. For example, it changes *teh* to *the*. It also corrects other types of errors, such as capitalization at the beginning of a sentence. It even helps you change manually typed symbols to unique symbols, such as changing :) to ☺. You can even insert AutoCorrect entries to change abbreviations to fully expanded text, such as changing *uvsc* to *Utah Valley State College*.

In this lesson, you type a sentence at the end of the document. Although you type it with errors, Auto-Correct corrects the errors for you.

To Use AutoCorrect

❶ In the *Status Report-WB4L* document, press Ctrl+End**, and click the Show/Hide ¶ button to turn off the formatting marks.**

❷ Type teh **and press** Spacebar**.**
When you press Spacebar, AutoCorrect changes *teh* to *the* and then capitalizes the first letter of the sentence.

❸ Type ad hoc comittee will reconvene next week to reveiw the questons and prepare a tenative questionaire.
Your sentence should look like the one shown in Figure 4.18.

To Use AutoCorrect

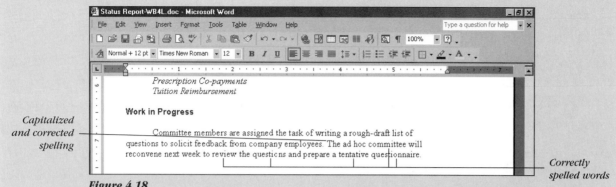

*Capitalized
and corrected
spelling*

*Correctly
spelled words*

Figure 4.18

Now let's look at AutoCorrect to see what words are detected and corrected for you.

4 **Choose Tools, AutoCorrect Options to display the AutoCorrect dialog box.**

If you have problems...

If you don't see <u>A</u>utoCorrect Options on the <u>T</u>ools menu, click the down-pointing arrows to display the full <u>T</u>ools menu.

5 **Click the scroll-down arrow on the right side of the dialog box to scroll through the list until you see the word *committee* in the second column.**

The first column shows misspelled words, and the second column shows the correct spellings, as shown in Figure 4.19.

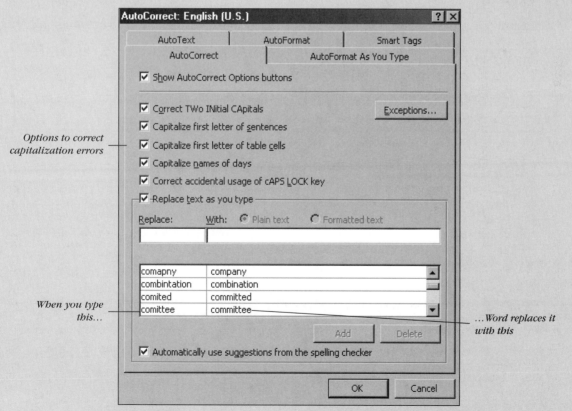

*Options to correct
capitalization errors*

*When you type
this...*

*...Word replaces it
with this*

Figure 4.19

(Continues)

To Use AutoCorrect (Continued)

6 **Click the AutoText tab.**
The AutoText section of the AutoCorrect dialog box contains frequently used text. When you start to type text that matches one of the AutoText entries, you see a ScreenTip that prompts you to press ⏎Enter to complete the text automatically so you don't have to type the rest of it.

7 **Click the scroll down arrow to see *Ladies and Gentlemen:*.**
When you start to type text stored as AutoText, you see a prompt to press ⏎Enter to complete the text for you.

8 **Click Cancel to close the dialog box.**

9 **Press ⏎Enter twice and type** Ladi.
You should see the following ScreenTip: *Ladies and Gentlemen: (Press ENTER to Insert)*.

10 **Press ⏎Enter.**
Ladies and Gentlemen: appears automatically without your having to type the rest of it.

11 **Click the Undo button twice to remove the *Ladies and Gentlemen:* text.**

12 **Save the document and keep it onscreen to continue with the next lesson.**

To extend your knowledge...

Adding AutoCorrect Entries

You can add words you typically misspell or abbreviations in AutoCorrect. Assume that you typically misspell *business* as *busenes*. With the AutoCorrect dialog box, type **busenes** in the *Replace* text box, and type **business** in the *With* text box. After entering the two words, click *Add* to add the entry.

Learning More About AutoText

Use the Help feature to learn more about AutoText. After reading the Help information, you can experiment with adding AutoText entries.

Lesson 7: Using the Thesaurus

Finding the perfect word to communicate your ideas clearly is sometimes difficult. You might type a word, but you then realize that it doesn't quite describe what you're thinking. It might not have the impact for which you were searching. The Thesaurus tool helps you choose words to improve the clarity of your documents. You can select **synonyms** (words with similar meanings) from Word's Thesaurus feature and get your point across with greater ease.

To Use Thesaurus

1 **In the *Status Report-WB4L* document, click in the word *formed* on the first line in the first paragraph.**
You should click within the word that you want to look up in Thesaurus.

2 **Choose Tools, Language, Thesaurus.**
The thesaurus appears with a list of possible replacement words (see Figure 4.20).

To Use Thesaurus

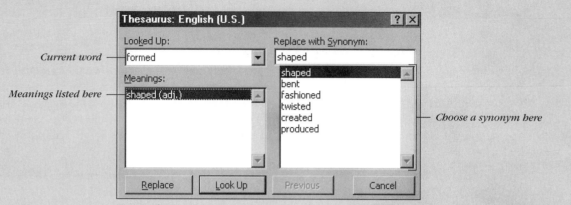

Current word ——— **Looked Up:** formed

Meanings listed here ——— **Meanings:**

Choose a synonym here ———

Figure 4.20

If a word has multiple meanings, you can click a meaning and then see different synonyms on the right side of the dialog box.

If you have problems...

You see an error message if Thesaurus is not loaded on your computer. If you have the Microsoft Office installation CD, insert it and follow the prompts to install Thesaurus.

③ **Click *created* in the Replace with Synonym box and then click Replace.**
Word replaces *formed* with *created*, the synonym you select.

④ **Right-click *agreed* in the first paragraph.**
A shortcut menu appears with a Synonyms option. Choosing a synonym from this menu might be preferable to using the Thesaurus dialog box.

⑤ **Choose Synonyms.**
Figure 4.21 shows a list of synonyms for the current word.

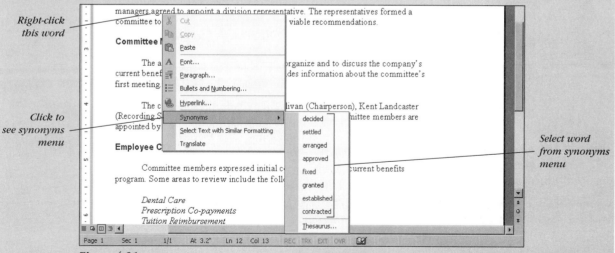

Right-click this word

Click to see synonyms menu

Select word from synonyms menu

Figure 4.21

⑥ **Choose *decided*.**
Word replaces *agreed* with *decided*.

⑦ **Save the document and close it.**

Summary

You now know how to perform several essential tasks to enhance text and improve the clarity of your document. You learned how to quickly change the case of selected text instead of retyping it. In addition, you moved text to a different location and copied text from one document to another. You'll probably find the Undo and Redo features handy to reverse actions you made in a document. Furthermore, you inserted a date field, saw first-hand how AutoCorrect corrects some commonly misspelled words, and used Thesaurus to find a synonym.

You can extend your learning by exploring some of the other Date and Time field options, AutoCorrect options, and the Office Clipboard task pane. For more information, refer to the online Help feature and complete the end-of-projects tasks assigned by your instructor.

Checking Concepts and Terms

Multiple Choice

Circle the letter of the correct answer for each of the following.

1. What Change Case option capitalizes the first letter after a punctuation mark, such as the period, question mark, or exclamation mark? [L2]

   a. Sentence case

   b. Title Case

   c. tOGGLE cASE

   d. UPPERCASE

2. What is the keyboard shortcut for cutting text? [L3]

   a. Ctrl+C

   b. Ctrl+X

   c. Ctrl+Z

   d. Shift+F3

3. What feature reverses the last action you performed on the document? [L5]

   a. Redo

   b. Paste

   c. Undo

   d. Format Painter

4. AutoCorrect does all of the following tasks except which one? [L6]

   a. Corrects some misspelled words as you type.

   b. Capitalizes the first letter of a sentence if you don't.

   c. Changes some keyboard symbols to other symbols, such as a smiley face.

   d. Places red wavy lines below grammatical errors.

5. What is the first step for duplicating text? [L4]

   a. Click the Paste button.

   b. Click the Copy button.

   c. Position the insertion point where you want the duplicate text to appear.

   d. Select the original text that you want to duplicate.

Screen ID

Label each element of the Word screen shown in Figure 4.22.

A. Clipboard item

B. Copy button

C. Cut button

D. Paste button

E. Pastes entire Clipboard contents in sequence

F. Redo button

G. Removes items from Clipboard

H. Undo button

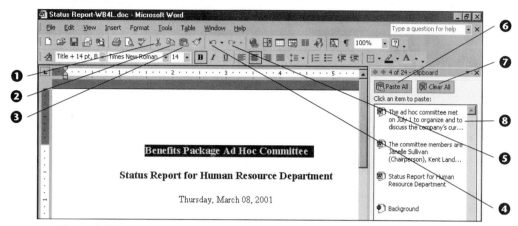

Figure 4.22

1. _____   5. _____

2. _____   6. _____

3. _____   7. _____

4. _____   8. _____

Discussion

1. What is the purpose of AutoCorrect? How does it improve your efficiency? [L6]

2. Practice using the drag-and-drop method for moving text. Explain how it might be helpful to use this feature. Discuss any disadvantages you experience in using the drag-and-drop feature

compared to using the Cut and Paste commands. [L3]

3. What is the purpose of a date or time field? Discuss situations in which you should insert a date or time field instead of typing it yourself. [L1]

Skill Drill exercises reinforce project skills. Each skill reinforced is the same, or nearly the same, as a skill presented in the project. Detailed instructions are provided in a step-by-step format.

1. Inserting Date and Time Fields

You are working on a memo to send to a colleague. However, you're not sure if you have time to finish it today. Because you are worried that you might forget to change the date if you finish it a few days from now, you insert a date field.

    1. Open *ew1-0403*, and save it as `Newsletter Memo-WB4SD`.

    2. Select the date in the memo (but don't select the paragraph symbol), and press Del.

    3. Choose Insert, Date and Time.

4. Click the *March 4, 2004* format. (The exact date will differ on your computer.)

5. If the *Update automatically* check box is not selected, click it.

6. Click OK.

7. Right-click within the date field and choose *Edit Field*.

8. Click the *3/4/2004 2:50 PM* format and then click OK. (The exact date and time will differ, but choose the same format.)

9. Save the document and keep it onscreen to continue with the next exercise.

2. Changing the Case

You just finished composing a status report memo to your manager. After proofreading the memo, you decide to change the case of some text to either uppercase or sentence case.

1. In the open *Newsletter Memo-WB4SD* document, change Andy Barton's name to your name.

2. Double-click the word *Subject*.

3. Choose F*o*rmat, Change Cas*e*.

4. Click the *U*PPERCASE option and then click OK.

5. Select the first heading, *News articles*.

6. Press ⌖Shift+F3 three times to choose the Title Case capitalization style.

7. Use the same process to apply the Title Case style to the other two headings.

8. Save the document and keep it onscreen to continue with the next exercise.

3. Using Undo and Redo

As you continue editing your memo, you realize that you want to undo some actions you take. Therefore, you use Undo and Redo, as needed.

1. In the open *Newsletter Memo-WB4SD* document, select and bold *Winter Newsletter* on the fourth line of the document.

2. Click the Undo button to remove bold from *Winter Newsletter*.

3. Click the Undo button again to change the case style of the last heading that you formatted in Skill Drill 2.

You realize that you "accidentally" clicked Undo too many times and did not want to reverse the case action.

4. Click the Redo button to reverse the last Undo action. In other words, you are restoring the Title Case capitalization style to the last heading.

5. Save the document and keep it onscreen to continue with the next exercise.

4. Moving Text to a Different Location

As you read through the memo, you decide to move the Art Work section below the News Articles section. In addition, you notice that a sentence should also be moved to a different location.

1. In the *Newsletter Memo-WB4SD* document, click at the beginning of the heading *Art Work*.

2. Click the Show/Hide ¶ button to see the nonprinting symbols if they are not already displayed.

3. Select the *Art Work* heading and the paragraph below it. Make sure that you include the ¶ symbol below the paragraph.

4. Click the Cut button to remove the selected text from its location.

5. Position the insertion point to the left of the *Classified Advertisements* heading.

6. Click the Paste button to paste the text between the News Articles and Classified Advertisement sections.

7. Select the sentence that begins with *The residents have expressed…*, which is the last sentence in the Classified Advertisement section.

8. Press Ctrl+X to cut the sentence.

9. Position the insertion point at the beginning of the sentence that begins with *We are currently accepting...* in the same paragraph, and press Ctrl+V to paste it as the second sentence in the paragraph.

10. Press Spacebar, if necessary, to have a space between sentences.

11. Save the document, and keep it onscreen to continue with the next exercise.

5. Copying Text from One Document to Another

Your assistant sent you a document that contains some information you need in your current document. Therefore, you want to copy it so that you don't have to type the data yourself.

1. Leave the *Newsletter Memo-WB4SD* document open.

2. Open *ew1-0404*, the document that contains text you want to duplicate in your newsletter memo.

3. Select the second paragraph and the blank line below it.

4. Press Ctrl+C to copy it to the Clipboard.

5. Close *ew1-0404*.

6. Position the insertion point below the paragraph in the Classified Advertisement section.

7. Press ↵Enter, and click the Paste button to paste the text you had copied from the other document.

8. Make sure that you have one blank line above the pasted paragraph. Make adjustments as needed.

9. If the pasted paragraph appears in 10-point size, click the Paste Options Smart Tag and choose *Keep Source Formatting* to maintain its 12-point size.

10. Save the document, and keep it onscreen to continue with the next exercise.

6. Using AutoCorrect and Thesaurus

You need to add a sentence to the document. As you quickly type it, you make some mistakes. Auto-Correct will correct them for you. Furthermore, you want to find an appropriate synonym for a word in the document.

1. In the *Newsletter Memo-WB4SD* document, position the insertion point at the end of the first paragraph in the News Articles section.

2. Type the following sentence exactly as shown with mistakes:

   `some topiks for artecles include informing residents ofthe new recycling program and trafic issues during home football games in september and october.`

3. Check to make sure that AutoCorrect corrected the misspelled words as you typed them.

4. Right-click *currently* in the first paragraph in the Classified Advertisements section, choose Synonyms, and choose *presently*.

5. Save the document, print it, and close it.

Challenge

Challenge exercises expand on or are somewhat related to skills presented in the lessons. Each exercise provides a brief narrative introduction, followed by instructions in a numbered-step format that are not as detailed as those in the Skill Drill section.

1. Correcting Errors in a Letter

You work as an assistant for a real estate company. One of the agents wrote a letter to condominium owners who expressed interest in selling their condominiums. The agent asked you to make the necessary corrections.

1. Open *ew1-0405*, and save it as `Condominium Letter-WB4CH1`.
2. Insert the date as a field in this format: *April 15, 2004* at the top of the document.
3. Double-click the Spelling and Grammar Status button on the status bar to display the first spelling or grammatical error, and correct it. Continue doing this until you correct all errors.
4. Choose an appropriate synonym for *maximum* in the last paragraph.
5. Select the appropriate case for the third paragraph. Manually capitalize any letters that should remain capitalized.
6. Select the four items below the third paragraph, press `Tab⇵`, and italicize them.
7. Apply bold to the first paragraph.
8. Select *Sincerely*, and capitalize it.
9. Delete the first sentence in the first paragraph.
10. Click the drop-down arrow to the right of the Undo button. Select Undo actions, starting with bolding text to the latest action.
11. Save, print, and close the document.

2. Enhancing and Editing a Welcome Letter

You live in a townhouse condominium complex in Amarillo, Texas. You are also on the welcome committee that greets new residents as they buy a townhouse. You have prepared a welcome letter, and you need to enhance and correct it.

1. Open *ew1-0406* and save it as `Welcome New Owners-WB4CH2`.
2. Insert today's date as a field in this format: *January 15, 2004.*
3. Select Title Case for each of these headings: lawn care, snow removal, and workout room.
4. Select *Lawn Care*, and make it bold and underlined. Use Format Painter to copy these formats to the other two headings.
5. Open *ew1-0407*, and copy the *Swimming Pool* paragraph and the blank line below it. Paste the text at the beginning of the Lawn Care paragraph in the *Welcome New Owners-WB4CH2* document. (The paragraphs should remain separate with one blank line between them.) Close *ew1-0407*.
6. Use the Paste Options Smart Tag to format the pasted text consistently with the original text. If these options don't provide the format you want, manually format the paragraph.
7. Apply Arial Narrow, bold, and Green font color to the first occurrence of Madison Village. Use Format Painter to apply these formats to the other Madison Village occurrences.
8. Move the *Snow Removal* paragraph below the *Workout Room* paragraph.
9. Check the spacing between paragraphs, and make the necessary adjustments.
10. Delete the *Snow Removal* paragraph; then undo the action.
11. Save, print, and close the document.

3. Correcting Errors and Enhancing Minutes from a Meeting

You are the secretary for a condominium association. You need to enhance the minutes and correct errors in them.

1. Open *ew1-0408*, and save it as `Association Minutes-WB4CH3`.
2. Type the following sentence *exactly* as shown at the end of the *Minutes* paragraph, and let AutoCorrect correct errors for you: `teh minutes were aproved as corected.`
3. Enhance the title by applying boldface, Arial, and Violet font color to it.

4. Enhance the headings by applying 11-point Arial, bold, and Violet font color. Use Format Painter to help copy the formats from one heading to the other headings.

5. Use the appropriate Change Case option on the headings, as you did in the lesson; make sure that they are consistently formatted. You need to manually change prepositions, such as *to,* to lowercase.

6. Move the Condominium Dues section above the Parking Regulations section. You should have one blank line between paragraphs.

7. Choose an appropriate synonym for the word *additional* in the *Condominium Dues* paragraph.

8. Save, print, and close the document.

4. Editing an Author Guideline Document

You are an assistant to a project manager for a textbook series. The project manager gave you a rough-draft document that will be e-mailed to the authors so that they will know what to include in their projects.

1. Open *ew1-0409,* and save it as `Author Guidelines-WB4CH4`.

2. Use the Change Case feature to change the paragraph headings to Title Case format.

3. Rearrange the paragraphs based on the order in which items are mentioned in the first sentence of the first paragraph. Make sure that you have one blank line between paragraphs after rearranging them.

4. Use Thesaurus to find a synonym for *useful* in the first sentence in the *Project Overview* paragraph.

5. At the end of the document, modify the date field to display the date and time in this format: *4/30/2004 9:15 PM.*

6. Move the first sentence in the first paragraph so that it's the last sentence in the first paragraph.

7. Save, print, and close the document.

Discovery Zone exercises require advanced knowledge of topics presented in *essentials* lessons, application of skills from multiple lessons, or self-directed learning of new skills.

1. Creating AutoCorrect Entries

You really like the way AutoCorrect can correct some errors as you type. Because you find yourself typing your name and a club name several times a day, you want to create AutoCorrect entries that allow you to type an abbreviation and automatically expand it to the full text.

Use onscreen Help to learn how to create and use AutoCorrect entries. Then, create the following two entries:

- ccc for College Computer Club
- your initials for your full name

Be careful when creating the entry for your name. Some names may expand state abbreviations or simple words, which you don't want to do. For example, a person named *Ingrid Smith* should not create an AutoCorrect entry named *is.*

Create the document shown in Figure 4.23, using your initials for Vice President and Activities Director instead of *zxy*.

---

ccc Officers

The ccc officers for the 2003-04 academic year are listed below:

President   Vicki Kamoreaux

Vice President   xyz

Secretary   Tyler Jorgenson

Treasurer   Gloria Rokovitz

Activities Director   zxy

Figure 4.23

Word should automatically expand the abbreviations as you type them. Select the title, and use the keyboard shortcut for changing the case to uppercase. Make two more copies of the list, so you have three copies of the list on one piece of paper. Save the document as `Club Officers-WB4DZ1` and print it.

2. Compiling an Information Sheet by Using the Office Clipboard

You have a master file of workshop descriptions that your training company provides to business people in the area. You need to prepare a custom workshop program for one of your clients. In a new document window, type the title in 16-point Arial font, bold, and Small Caps effect. Triple-space after the title, select 12-point, Bookman Old Style font; and type the paragraph shown in Figure 4.24.

COMPUTER WORKSHOPS FOR BRADSHAW AND ASSOCIATES

We are pleased to provide the workshops you requested for individuals in your organization. According to our agreement, you may send up to 15 individuals to each session listed below. The workshops are scheduled for May 18 in your conference room. If you have additional questions, please call Taralyn VanBuren at 555-7843.

Figure 4.24

Save the document as `Workshops for Bradshaw-WB4DZ2`. Open *ew1-0410*. Refer to Lesson 3, "Cutting, Copying, and Pasting Text," and onscreen Help to learn about the Office Clipboard and how to use it to collect and paste several items at once.

Display the Office Clipboard task pane. Clear any existing items in the Clipboard, and copy the paragraphs to the Clipboard in this order: *Upgrade to Word 2002, Automating Your Work,* and *Collaborating on Documents.* Paste the entire Clipboard contents below the introductory paragraph in *Workshops for Bradshaw-WB4DZ2.* Make sure that you have one blank line between paragraphs, and ensure that the pasted paragraphs have the same font and font size as the introductory paragraph. Save the document, and print it.

Change *Bradshaw and Associates* to `The Rowley Group`. Save the modified document as `Workshops for Rowley-WB4DZ2`. Delete the paragraphs about the workshops. Clear the Office Clipboard. Click *ew1-0410* on the taskbar to go back to this document, and copy these paragraphs in this order to the Clipboard: *Basic Formatting with Word, Graphics Jamboree, Integrating Excel Data into Word,* and *Organizing Items in Tables.* Paste the entire Office Clipboard contents at the bottom of The Rowley Group document. Adjust the font and font size, if necessary, to be consistent with the first paragraph. Save the document and print it. Close all open documents.

Formatting Paragraphs

Objectives

In this project, you learn how to

- ✔ Set Line and Paragraph Spacing
- ✔ Select Text Alignment
- ✔ Indent Text
- ✔ Insert Bulleted and Numbered Lists
- ✔ Create an Outline Numbered List
- ✔ Add Borders and Shading
- ✔ Set and Modify Tabs
- ✔ Reveal and Clear Formats

Key terms introduced in this project include

- ❑ alignment
- ❑ bar tab
- ❑ border
- ❑ bullet
- ❑ bulleted list
- ❑ double indent
- ❑ double-spaced
- ❑ first line indent
- ❑ hanging indent
- ❑ leader
- ❑ left indent
- ❑ line break
- ❑ line spacing
- ❑ outline numbered list
- ❑ paragraph spacing
- ❑ Reveal Formatting task pane
- ❑ reverse text effect
- ❑ right indent
- ❑ shading
- ❑ single-spaced
- ❑ soft return
- ❑ tabs

Why Would I Do This?

So far, you created documents using the default settings. Although these settings are acceptable for some basic documents, you probably want to have control over the format settings used for different types of documents. In this project, you learn a lot of common paragraph-formatting techniques that can make your documents look professional. You can use these formats to control a single paragraph or groups of paragraphs.

Visual Summary

In this project, you format paragraphs and text in an annual report. Figure 5.1 shows the paragraph formats applied to text on the first page of the report.

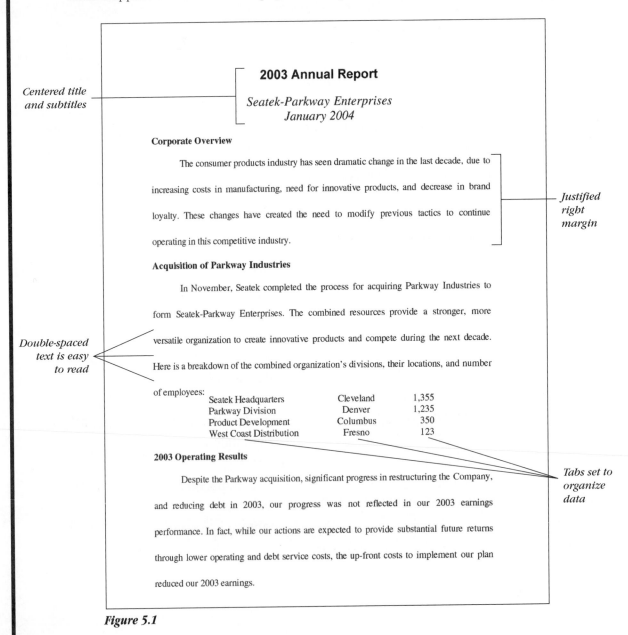

Centered title and subtitles

Double-spaced text is easy to read

Justified right margin

Tabs set to organize data

2003 Annual Report

Seatek-Parkway Enterprises
January 2004

Corporate Overview

The consumer products industry has seen dramatic change in the last decade, due to increasing costs in manufacturing, need for innovative products, and decrease in brand loyalty. These changes have created the need to modify previous tactics to continue operating in this competitive industry.

Acquisition of Parkway Industries

In November, Seatek completed the process for acquiring Parkway Industries to form Seatek-Parkway Enterprises. The combined resources provide a stronger, more versatile organization to create innovative products and compete during the next decade. Here is a breakdown of the combined organization's divisions, their locations, and number of employees:

Seatek Headquarters	Cleveland	1,355
Parkway Division	Denver	1,235
Product Development	Columbus	350
West Coast Distribution	Fresno	123

2003 Operating Results

Despite the Parkway acquisition, significant progress in restructuring the Company, and reducing debt in 2003, our progress was not reflected in our 2003 earnings performance. In fact, while our actions are expected to provide substantial future returns through lower operating and debt service costs, the up-front costs to implement our plan reduced our 2003 earnings.

Figure 5.1

Figure 5.2 shows the last part of the document with additional paragraph formats.

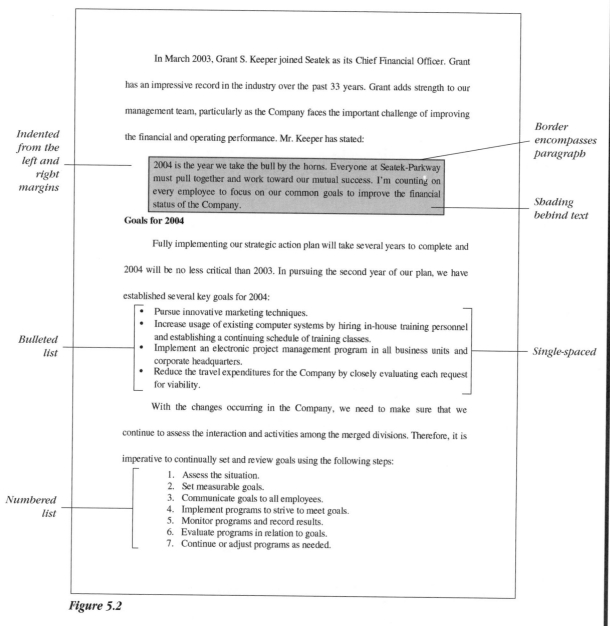

Figure 5.2

Lesson 1: Setting Line and Paragraph Spacing

Line spacing is the amount of vertical space from the bottom of one text line to the bottom of another. You use line spacing to control the amount of space between text lines in Word.

When you create a new document, Word makes the document text *single-spaced*, which means that text lines are close together with a small space to separate the lines. Although some documents, such as letters, should be single-spaced, other documents look better ***double-spaced***. For example, a long report is typically easier to read if it is double-spaced.

If you click inside a paragraph and change the line spacing, only that paragraph is affected. To change line spacing for multiple paragraphs, you must select them first. In this lesson, you change the line spacing to double for most of the document.

To Change Line Spacing

1 Open *ew1-0501*, and save it as `Annual Report-WB5L`.

2 Position the insertion point at the beginning of the *Corporate Overview* heading.
Before setting the line spacing, you must select the paragraphs that you want to format. In this document, you want to double-space most paragraphs, except the titles and some text at the end of the document.

3 Leaving the insertion point in that location, click and drag the vertical scroll box down to see the second page.

4 Press and hold down ⬆Shift and click after the colon that ends the first paragraph below the *Goals for 2004* heading.
The paragraphs that you want to format are selected.

5 Click the Line Spacing button.
Figure 5.3 shows the Line Spacing menu.

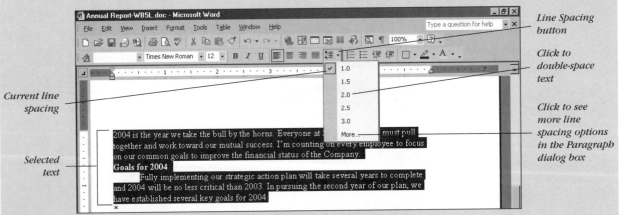

Figure 5.3

6 Click *2.0* on the Line Spacing menu.
The text is now double-spaced. When you double-space text, Word leaves one blank line between lines within a paragraph. Each soft return and each hard return in the selected area are doubled. A ***soft return*** occurs when Word word-wraps text to the next line within a paragraph as you type it.

7 Press Ctrl+Home to return the insertion point to the beginning of the document, and deselect the text.

8 Click the Show/Hide ¶ button on the Standard toolbar.
Although hard returns create blank lines between the titles, the blank lines within and between paragraphs are caused by the double-spacing (see Figure 5.4).

To Change Line Spacing

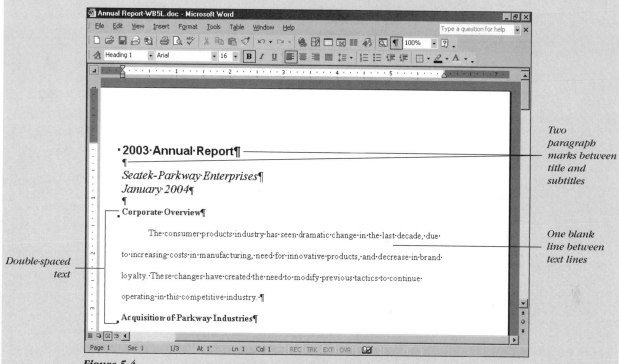

Figure 5.4

Now, you want to single-space the quoted paragraph to set it off from the regular paragraphs. The quoted text is probably the last paragraph on page 2 of your document.

⑨ Scroll down, and click inside the paragraph that starts with *2004 is the year we take the bull by the horns.*
Instead of selecting single-line spacing from the Line Spacing menu, you use a keyboard shortcut to save time.

⑩ Press Ctrl+1.
This keyboard shortcut single-spaces the current paragraph or group of selected paragraphs.

⑪ Save the document, and keep it onscreen to continue with the next exercise.

 ## To extend your knowledge...

The Paragraph Dialog Box

The Paragraph dialog box also contains an option for choosing the line spacing. To display the Paragraph dialog box, choose Format, Paragraph or right-click within a paragraph and choose Paragraph.

Line Spacing Keyboard Shortcuts

Use the following keyboard shortcuts to change line spacing for selected text: Ctrl+1 for single-spacing, Ctrl+2 for double-spacing, and Ctrl+5 for 1.5 spacing.

Table 5.1 lists and describes the line-spacing options available in the Paragraph dialog box.

Table 5.1 **Line-Spacing Options**	
Spacing Option	**Description**
Single	Places a text line immediately beneath the previous line.
1.5 lines	Leaves one-and-one-half the amount of space of single-spacing.
Double	Doubles the amount of space between lines.
At least	Specifies the minimum amount of spacing between lines. Word adjusts the spacing as needed to make room for larger fonts or graphics.
Exactly	Specifies an exact spacing measurement. Word cannot adjust the line spacing to make room for larger elements.
Multiple	Specifies how much Word can adjust the line spacing (up or down) by a particular percentage. For example, 1.25 increases the space by 25 percent; .75 decreases the space by 25 percent. You can also enter full values, such as **3** to triple-space text.

You might want to keep text single-spaced by adjusting the spacing between paragraphs (that is, change the space created by paragraph marks each time you press `↵Enter`). For example, you might want to have single-spaced paragraphs with the equivalent of double-spacing between paragraphs.

You can achieve this effect by setting the ***paragraph spacing***, which controls the amount of space before or after the paragraph. Access the Paragraph dialog box, and change the <u>B</u>efore or Aft<u>e</u>r spacing. For example, changing the Aft<u>e</u>r spacing to 12 points creates a double-space after the paragraph. In the next exercise, you choose 12-point paragraph spacing for the single-spaced paragraph to leave space after it.

To Change Paragraph Spacing

1 In the open *Annual Report-WB5L* document, make sure that the insertion point is inside the single-spaced paragraph that begins with *2004 is the year....*
You need space between this paragraph and the following heading. Depending on your screen display and current printer, you might see *Goals for 2004* at the top of page 3. Nevertheless, you need a blank space in case you add or delete text later.

2 Choose F<u>o</u>rmat, <u>P</u>aragraph.
The Paragraph dialog box contains the options for changing paragraph formats, such as paragraph spacing (see Figure 5.5).

To Change Paragraph Spacing

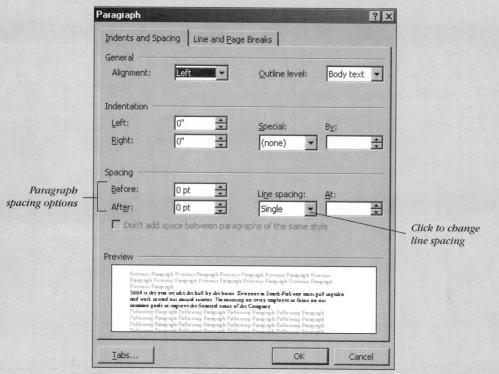

Paragraph
spacing options

Click to change
line spacing

Figure 5.5

❸ In the Spacing section, click the *After* spin button to increase the spacing to *12 pt*.
Choosing *12 pt* spacing after paragraph is the equivalent of one blank line after the paragraph.

❹ Click OK.
The blank line above the paragraph is due to the double-space setting, and the space after the paragraph is due to the 12-pt after-paragraph spacing (see Figure 5.6).

(Continues)

To Change Paragraph Spacing (Continued)

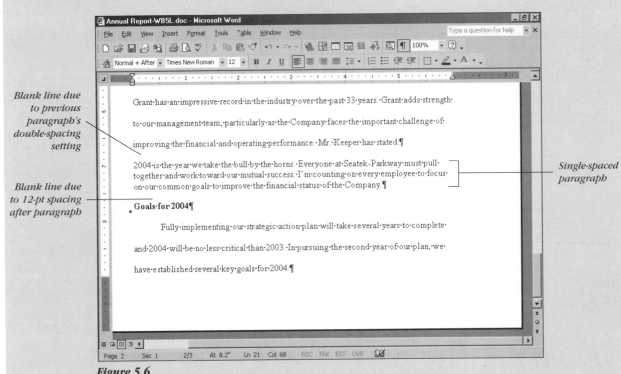

Blank line due to previous paragraph's double-spacing setting

Blank line due to 12-pt spacing after paragraph

Single-spaced paragraph

Grant·has·an·impressive·record·in·the·industry·over·the·past·33·years.·Grant·adds·strength·
to·our·management·team,·particularly·as·the·Company·faces·the·important·challenge·of·
improving·the·financial·and·operating·performance.·Mr.·Keeper·has·stated:¶

2004·is·the·year·we·take·the·bull·by·the·horns.·Everyone·at·Seatek·Parkway·must·pull·
together·and·work·toward·our·mutual·success.·I'm·counting·on·every·employee·to·focus·
on·our·common·goals·to·improve·the·financial·status·of·the·Company.¶

Goals·for·2004¶

Fully·implementing·our·strategic·action·plan·will·take·several·years·to·complete·
and·2004·will·be·no·less·critical·than·2003.·In·pursuing·the·second·year·of·our·plan,·we·
have·established·several·key·goals·for·2004.¶

Figure 5.6

You need only one hard return *before* the quoted text because double-spacing is in effect until the beginning of the quoted paragraph. You need either two hard returns or a 12-point spacing after paragraph for the quoted paragraph because single-spacing is in effect until you reach the beginning of the following paragraph.

⑤ Save the document, and keep it onscreen to continue with the next lesson.

Lesson 2: Selecting Text Alignment

Alignment refers to the placement of text between the left and right margins. The default alignment is Align Left, which aligns text with the left margin. Table 5.2 lists and describes the four alignment options.

Table 5.2 Alignment Options			
Button	**Option**	**Keyboard Shortcut**	**Description**
	Align Left	Ctrl+L	Aligns text on the left margin only. The left side is perfectly aligned, and the right side is ragged.
	Center	Ctrl+E	Centers text between the left and right margins.
	Align Right	Ctrl+R	Aligns text at the right margin only. The right side is perfectly aligned, and the left side is ragged.
	Justify	Ctrl+J	Aligns text along the left and right margins, so both sides are perfectly aligned. Inserts extra space between words to justify text.

In this lesson, you justify the paragraphs to make them look more formal. The smooth edges on the left and right sides provide a cleaner look for the document. Also, you need to center the title between the margins.

To Change the Alignment

❶ In the *Annual Report-WB5L* document, choose Edit, Select All.
Because you want to justify the text in the whole document, you must first select the entire document.

❷ Click the Justify button on the Formatting toolbar.
When you justify text, Word inserts a small amount of space between the characters, so the text aligns at both the left and right margins. Notice, however, that you see one space symbol between words, even in justified text. Justified text creates a more formal appearance than left-aligned text.

❸ Press Ctrl+Home to deselect the text, and position the insertion point at the top of the document within the main title.
Now, you need to center the title between the margins. To change the alignment for a single paragraph, click within that paragraph (such as a title followed by a hard return), and click the alignment button. Only that paragraph's alignment changes.

❹ Click the Center button on the Formatting toolbar to center the title between the left and right margins.

❺ Select the two-line italicized subtitles and then click the Center button on the Formatting toolbar to center them.

❻ Deselect the text.
Figure 5.7 shows the centered titles and justified paragraphs.

(Continues)

To Change the Alignment (Continued)

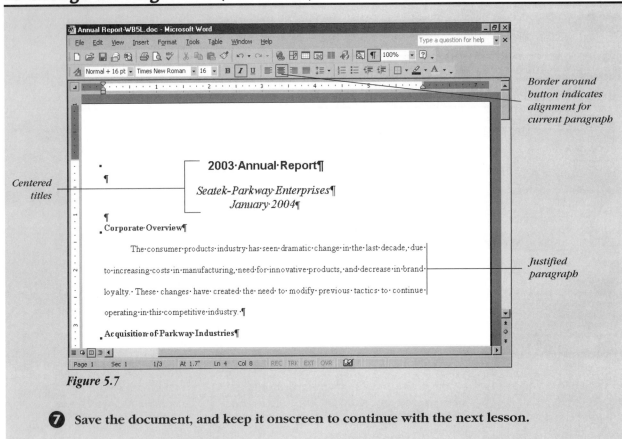

Border around button indicates alignment for current paragraph

Centered titles

Justified paragraph

Figure 5.7

7 Save the document, and keep it onscreen to continue with the next lesson.

To extend your knowledge...

Aligning New Text

In the previous exercise, you changed the alignment for existing text by selecting it first. You can also select alignment before typing a document. For example, you can select Center alignment, type a document title, press ⏎Enter two or three times, and select Justify alignment. All new text from that point forward is automatically justified without selecting it first.

Lesson 3: Indenting Text

By now, you know to press (Tab⭾) to indent the first line of a paragraph. This format is typical in formal reports, letters, and legal documents. Sometimes, however, you might want to indent an entire paragraph from the left margin, right margin, or both margins. A *left indent* indents a paragraph a specified amount of space from the left margin, whereas a *right indent* indents a paragraph a specified amount of space from the right margin.

As you review the annual report, you see a quotation from the Chief Financial Officer, Grant Keeper, at the top of the third page. Often, you see a paragraph of quoted text indented from both margins, which is called a *double indent*. In this lesson, you indent the paragraph from both margins.

To Indent Text

1 **In the *Annual Report-WB5L* document, position the insertion point within the single-spaced paragraph that begins with *2004 is the year....***

This quotation needs to be indented from both margins. Because you are formatting a single paragraph, you don't need to select it first. Simply position the insertion point within the paragraph that you want to format.

2 **Choose F_ormat, _Paragraph to display the Paragraph dialog box.**

You need to change the settings in the Indentation section.

3 **In the Indentation section, click the *Left* spin button until you see *0.5"* in the *Left* text box.**

4 **Click the *Right* spin button until you see *0.5"* in the *Right* text box, and click OK.**

The quotation paragraph is indented from the left and right margins (see Figure 5.8).

Indented 0.5 inches from left margin ———

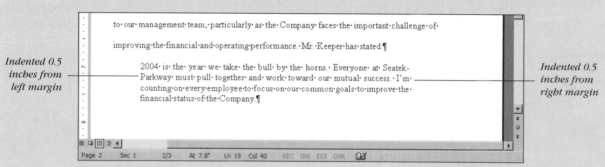

——— *Indented 0.5 inches from right margin*

Figure 5.8

5 **Click the Show/Hide ¶ button to turn off the formatting marks.**

6 **Save the document and keep it onscreen to continue with the next lesson.**

 ## To extend your knowledge...

Indent Markers on the Ruler

The ruler contains markers that you can also use to indent text. Figure 5.9 shows the ruler indent markers as well as indent buttons on the Formatting toolbar.

First Line Indent marker

Hanging Indent marker

Left Indent marker

Decrease Indent button

Increase Indent button

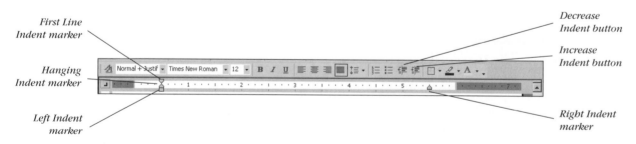

Right Indent marker

Figure 5.9

Indent and Decrease Indents

Click the Decrease Indent button to decrease (bring text to the left) indented text one-half inch. The keyboard shortcut for decreasing indented text is Ctrl+⇧Shift+M.

Click the Increase Indent button to increase the indent one-half inch. The keyboard shortcut for indenting text from the left side is Ctrl+M.

You can also set indents on the ruler. Click and drag the Left Indent marker to set the amount of space to indent text from the left margin.

Click and drag the Right Indent marker to set the amount of space to indent from the right margin.

First Line Indent

A *first line indent* automatically indents the first line of each paragraph. You can specify how much to indent the text. To set a first line indent, click the *Special* drop-down arrow in the Paragraph dialog box, and choose *First line*. Set the amount of space for the indent, such as 0.5", in the *By* text box. Alternatively, you can click and drag the First Line Indent marker on the ruler.

Hanging Indent

A *hanging indent* keeps the first line of a paragraph at the left margin and indents the rest of the lines of that paragraph from the left margin. Bibliographic entries are typically formatted with a hanging indent.

You can create a hanging indent by choosing *Hanging* from the *Special* drop-down list in the Paragraph dialog box, by clicking and dragging the Hanging Indent marker on the ruler, or by pressing Ctrl+T. If you accidentally indent a hanging indent too far, press Ctrl+Shift+T to reduce the hanging indent.

Sorting Paragraphs

You might need to sort indenting paragraphs in a document. For example, if the bibliographic entries are not alphabetized by authors' last names, you need to sort them. Select the paragraphs you want to sort; choose T̲able, S̲ort; and then click OK.

Lesson 4: Inserting Bulleted and Numbered Lists

In word processing, a *bullet* is a special symbol used to attract attention to something on the page. People often use a *bulleted list* to itemize a series to make it stand out and be easy to read. For example, the objectives and terminology appear in bulleted lists on the first page of each project in this book. Use bulleted lists for listing items that can go in any order; use a numbered list for a list of items that must be in sequential order.

In this lesson, you create a bulleted list of goals for the coming year, and a numbered list to indicate sequence for setting and evaluating goals.

To Create a Bulleted List

1 **In the *Annual Report-WB5L* document, go to the top of the third page.**

2 **Scroll down and delete the asterisk (*) after the first paragraph; keep the insertion point on the blank line.**
This location is where you want to create a bulleted list that itemizes the company's goals for the upcoming year.

3 **Click the Bullets button on the Formatting toolbar.**
Word indents the bullet, which is a round dot, and then indents from the bullet for you to type text.

To Create a Bulleted List

If you have problems...

Word creates a bulleted list based on the last bullet type selected. If you see a different bullet shape, such as a check mark, choose Format, Bullets and Numbering, click the rounded bullet list from the palette, and click OK.

4 **Type** Pursue innovative marketing techniques. **and press** ⏎Enter.
When you press ⏎Enter, Word inserts another bullet, followed by an indent (see Figure 5.10).

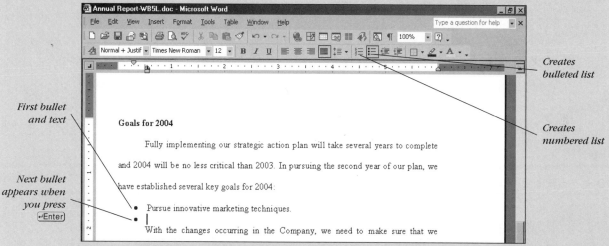

First bullet and text

Next bullet appears when you press ⏎Enter

Creates bulleted list

Creates numbered list

Figure 5.10

The bulleted list is single-spaced because you didn't select the asterisk when you selected other paragraphs to double-space in Lesson 1. The paragraph following the asterisk was already double-spaced for you.

5 **Type the following paragraphs, pressing** ⏎Enter **after each one.**

Increase usage of existing computer systems by hiring in-house training personnel and establishing a continuing schedule of training classes.

Implement an electronic project management program in all business units and corporate headquarters.

Reduce the travel expenditures for the Company by closely evaluating each request for viability.

Your document should look like Figure 5.11.

(Continues)

To Create a Bulleted List (Continued)

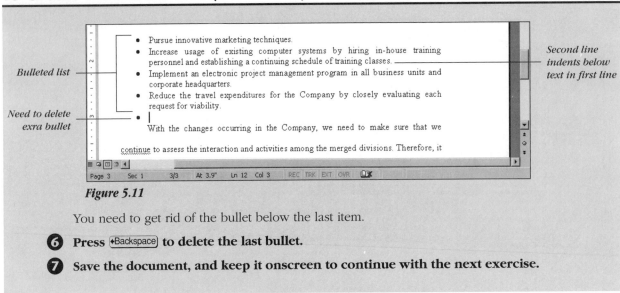

Bulleted list

Need to delete exra bullet

Second line indents below text in first line

Figure 5.11

You need to get rid of the bullet below the last item.

6 Press ⌫Backspace **to delete the last bullet.**

7 **Save the document, and keep it onscreen to continue with the next exercise.**

In the next exercise, you want to create a numbered list from the items at the end of the document.

To Create a Numbered List

1 **In the *Annual Report-WB5L* document, select the single-spaced items at the end of the document.**
There are six single-spaced items that need to be formatted as a numbered list.

2 **Click the Numbering button on the Formatting toolbar and then deselect the text.**
Word inserts numbers for each selected paragraph (see Figure 5.12).

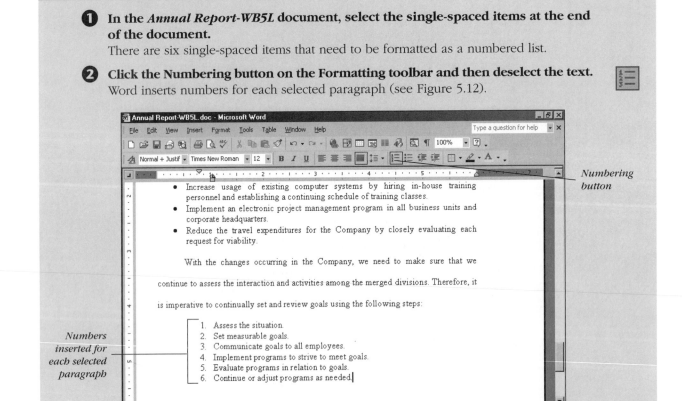

Numbering button

Numbers inserted for each selected paragraph

Figure 5.12

To Create a Numbered List

While reviewing the list, you notice that a step is missing.

3 **Click at the end of the fourth numbered paragraph, and press** ⏎Enter.
Word inserts a blank line and number to type a new numbered paragraph. The remaining numbered paragraphs are renumbered to accommodate the new numbered paragraph.

4 **Type** Monitor programs and record results.
Figure 5.13 shows the updated numbered list.

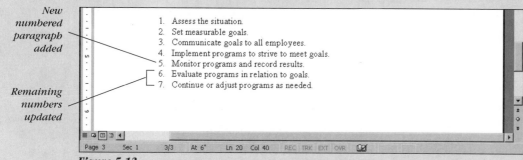

New numbered paragraph added

Remaining numbers updated

1. Assess the situation.
2. Set measurable goals.
3. Communicate goals to all employees.
4. Implement programs to strive to meet goals.
5. Monitor programs and record results.
6. Evaluate programs in relation to goals.
7. Continue or adjust programs as needed.

Figure 5.13

5 **Save and close the document.**

To extend your knowledge...

Creating Numbered Lists from Scratch

You can create a numbered list from scratch. To do this, click the Numbering button, and type the text for the first numbered paragraph; press ⏎Enter to continue creating a numbered list, similar to creating a bulleted list from scratch.

Bullet and Numbering Styles

You can choose other bullet and number styles for new or existing lists. For existing lists, select the items; then, choose F_ormat, Bullets and _Numbering. When the Bullets and Numbering dialog box appears (see Figure 5.14), click the style you want and then click OK.

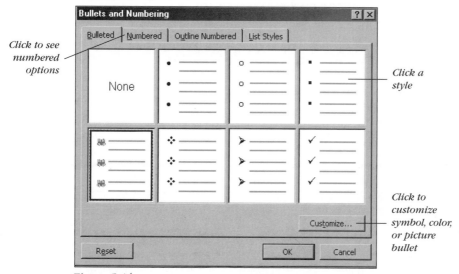

Click to see numbered options

Click a style

Click to customize symbol, color, or picture bullet

Figure 5.14

You can customize your bulleted list or choose another symbol. To do this, click an existing bullet in the Bullets and Numbering dialog box and then click the Customize button. The Customize Bulleted List dialog box contains options for customizing your bulleted list (see Figure 5.15).

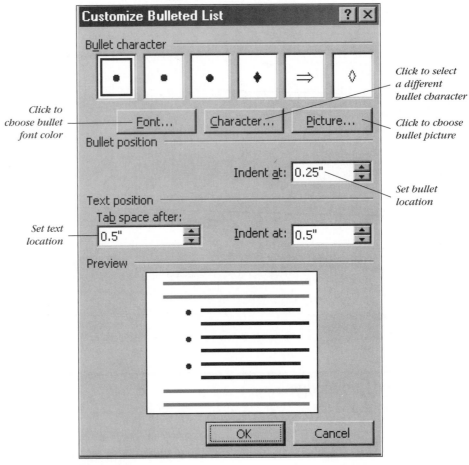

Figure 5.15

By default, bullets are indented 0.25″ from the left margin; however, you can place bullets at the left margin by changing the indent to 0″. You can also set the amount of space for indenting text after the bullet.

Click Font to select a font color for the bullets. Click Character to choose a bullet character from the Symbols dialog box as you did in Lesson 6, "Inserting Symbols," of Project 3, "Formatting Text."

Lesson 5: Creating an Outline Numbered List

Numbered lists are appropriate for formatting a sequence of steps or procedures. However, you might need an *outline numbered list*, which is a numbered list with subcategories like an outline. In this lesson, you create an outline numbered list to show key administrators for selected divisions of Seatek-Parkway Enterprises.

To Create an Outline Numbered List

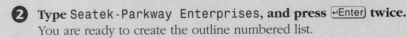

1 **Click the New Blank Document button to create a new document.**

2 **Type** Seatek-Parkway Enterprises, **and press** ⏎Enter **twice.**
You are ready to create the outline numbered list.

To Create an Outline Numbered List

③ Choose F̲ormat, Bullets and N̲umbering.
The Bullets and Numbering dialog box contains options for starting a numbered outline.

④ Click the Ou̲tline Numbered tab at the top of the dialog box.
The Ou̲tline Numbered tab provides various outline styles to choose from (see Figure 5.16).

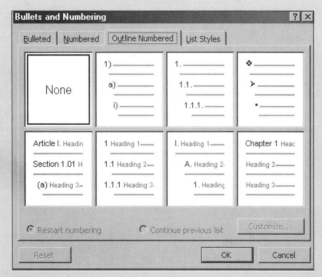

Figure 5.16

⑤ Click the first style to the right of None and then click OK.
Word starts the numbered outline similar to a regular numbered list.

⑥ Type Manufacturing, **and press** ⏎Enter.
Word inserts the next number, but you want to have subdivisions within the first number.

⑦ Press Tab↹ **to create a lower-level entry.**
Pressing Tab↹ creates a lower-level entry within an outline.

⑧ Type East Coast Plant, **and press** ⏎Enter.

⑨ Press Tab↹, **type** Fred Barton, **and press** ⏎Enter.

⑩ Type Liz Keone, **press** ⏎Enter, **and press** ⬆Shift+Tab↹.
Pressing ⬆Shift+Tab↹ creates a higher-level entry.

⑪ Type the rest of the entries shown in Figure 5.17 to complete the outline. Press Tab↹ **and** ⬆Shift+Tab↹ **as needed to create higher-level or lower-level entries.**

(Continues)

To Create an Outline Numbered List (Continued)

```
               Seatek-Parkway Enterprises

          1)  Manufacturing
               a)  East Coast Plant
                    i)   Fred Barton
                    ii)  Liz Keone
               b)  West Coast Plant
                    i)   Betty Ann Bartley
                    ii)  Paul Knaphus
          2)  Advertising
               a)  Benjamin Womble
               b)  Iris Eccles
```

Figure 5.17

12 **Save the document as** `Company Outline-WB5L`, **and close it.**

To extend your knowledge...

Viewing Outlines

You can click the Outline View button or choose <u>V</u>iew, <u>O</u>utline to display the Outline toolbar. The Outline toolbar contains buttons for promoting or demoting entries, moving entries up or down within the outline, and showing certain outline levels. Figure 5.18 shows the Outline toolbar.

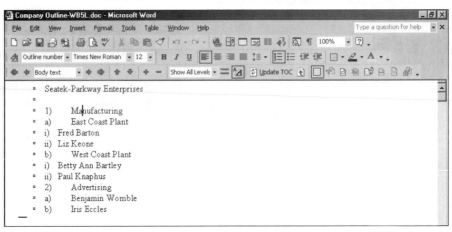

Figure 5.18

Refer to online Help to learn more about working with outlines.

Lesson 6: Adding Borders and Shading

You can draw attention to an entire paragraph by putting a border around it. A **border** is a line that surrounds a paragraph or group of paragraphs. You can select the setting, line style, color, and width. To further enhance a border, you can also apply **shading**, a background color behind the text. Unlike a highlight color that places a color behind the text only, shading fills in the space between lines also.

In this lesson, you add a border with shading for the double-indented paragraph.

To Add a Border and Shading

1 Open *Annual Report-WB5L*, and click inside the double-indented paragraph on page 2.

2 Choose F**o**rmat, **B**orders and Shading; and click the **B**orders tab, if needed.
The Borders and Shading dialog box appears so that you can select the border's characteristics (see Figure 5.19).

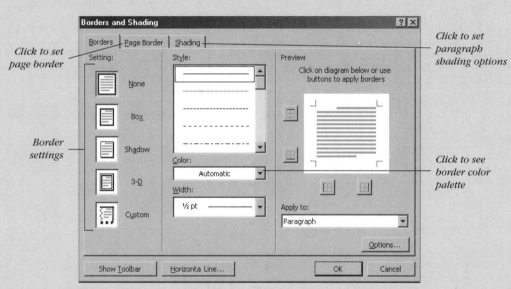

Figure 5.19

3 Click Bo**x** in the Setting section to select the primary format of the border.

4 Click the **C**olor drop-down arrow.
A color palette appears, so you can choose the color you want for the border.

5 Click Blue (the third color from the right on the second row).
The color palette closes, and you see the blue color displayed.

6 Click the **S**hading tab at the top of the dialog box.
You see shading options (see Figure 5.20).

(Continues)

To Add a Border and Shading (Continued)

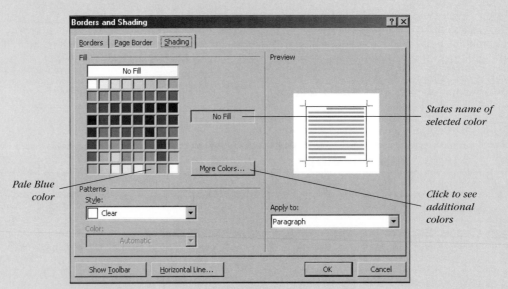

Figure 5.20

❼ Click Pale Blue, the third color from the right on the last row, and then click OK.
Word applies a blue shadow border with Pale Blue shading around the selected paragraph, as shown in Figure 5.21.

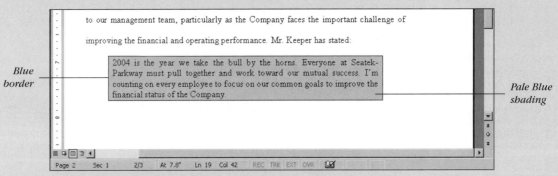

Figure 5.21

❽ Save the document, and keep it onscreen to continue with the next lesson.

To extend your knowledge...

Choosing Border and Shading Colors

Choose complementary colors for the border and shading. Typically, you should choose a darker border color and a lighter shading color. If the shading color is too dark, the text will be difficult to read.

You can create a ***reverse text effect***, which is an appearance that uses a dark background with a lighter colored font. For example, choose Blue shading color and Yellow font color.

Choosing a Page Border

You can also create a border for the entire page. Click the Page Border tab at the top of the Borders and Shading dialog box, and choose the options you want. Instead of using line page borders, you might want to select a creative page border. Click the Art drop-down arrow to display fun image borders, such as hearts and stars (see Figure 5.22).

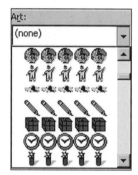

Figure 5.22

You might get an error message, saying that the art borders are not installed. If this happens, insert the Microsoft Office XP installation CD, and perform a custom installation to install the art borders.

With page borders, you can choose the pages you want to place the border on. Click the *Apply to* drop-down arrow and choose from *Whole document, This section, This section—First page only*, or *This section—All except first page*. If your document contains section breaks, which you'll learn about in Project 6, you can apply different page borders to each section.

In addition, click Options to customize the page border. For example, you can set the page border margins.

Lesson 7: Setting and Modifying Tabs

You can set *tabs*—markers that specify the position for aligning text—to create organized lists. You can set left, center, right, and decimal tabs. In addition, you can set a *bar tab*, a marker that produces a vertical bar between two columns when you press Tab⇄.

When you start a new document, Word uses the default tab settings. Every time you press Tab⇄, the insertion point moves over one-half inch. You can use the Ruler to set tabs at any location. Table 5.3 shows the different tab and indent alignments you can set on the ruler.

Table 5.3	Tab Alignment Buttons	
Symbol	**Type**	**Description**
L	Left Tab	Aligns text at the left side of the tab setting, and continues to the right—similar to Left alignment.
⊥	Center Tab	Centers text on the tab setting; half of the characters appear on the left side and half of the characters appear on the right side of the tab setting.
⌐	Right Tab	Aligns text at the right side of the tab setting—similar to Right alignment.
⊥	Decimal Tab	Aligns text at the decimal point.
∣	Bar Tab	Inserts a vertical line at the tab setting; useful for separating tabular columns.
▽	First Line Indent	Sets the amount of space for indenting the first line of a paragraph.
△	Hanging Indent	Sets the indent for all lines of a paragraph except the first line.

In this lesson, you set tabs to create a list of the organization's divisions, locations, and employees.

To Set Tabs on the Ruler

① **In the open *Annual Report-WB5L* document, delete the asterisk (*) that is above the *2003 Operating Results* heading on the first page.**
This is where you want to create a tabulated list.

If you have problems...
If you don't see the Ruler below the Formatting toolbar, choose View, Ruler.

Each mark on the Ruler is one-eighth of an inch.

② **Click below the 1″ marker on the Ruler.**
You should see a symbol that looks like an L, indicating a left tab setting (see Figure 5.23).

To Set Tabs on the Ruler

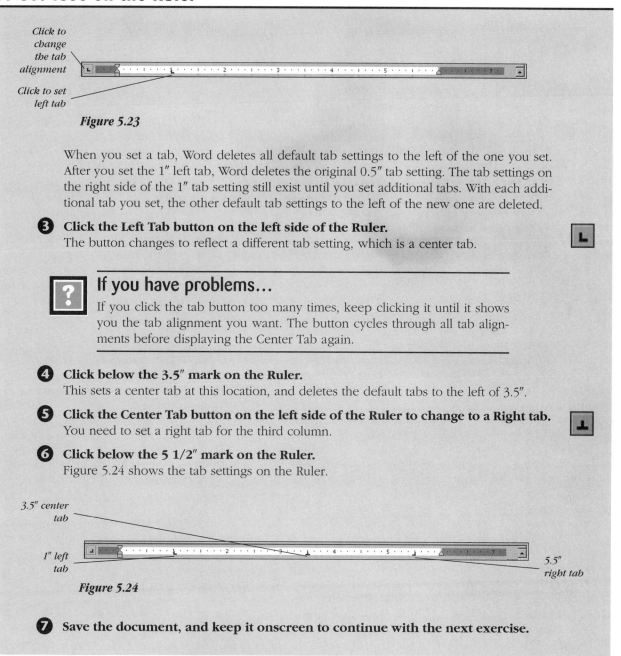

Click to change the tab alignment

Click to set left tab

Figure 5.23

When you set a tab, Word deletes all default tab settings to the left of the one you set. After you set the 1″ left tab, Word deletes the original 0.5″ tab setting. The tab settings on the right side of the 1″ tab setting still exist until you set additional tabs. With each additional tab you set, the other default tab settings to the left of the new one are deleted.

3 **Click the Left Tab button on the left side of the Ruler.**
The button changes to reflect a different tab setting, which is a center tab.

? If you have problems...

If you click the tab button too many times, keep clicking it until it shows you the tab alignment you want. The button cycles through all tab alignments before displaying the Center Tab again.

4 **Click below the 3.5″ mark on the Ruler.**
This sets a center tab at this location, and deletes the default tabs to the left of 3.5″.

5 **Click the Center Tab button on the left side of the Ruler to change to a Right tab.**
You need to set a right tab for the third column.

6 **Click below the 5 1/2″ mark on the Ruler.**
Figure 5.24 shows the tab settings on the Ruler.

3.5″ center tab

1″ left tab

5.5″ right tab

Figure 5.24

7 **Save the document, and keep it onscreen to continue with the next exercise.**

You are ready to type the tabulated text. When you press ⏎Enter, you create a hard return, which is treated as a new paragraph. However, you might want to change the tab settings for the entire list after typing it. With hard returns, you'd have to select the tabulated text before adjusting tabs.

Instead of pressing ⏎Enter to insert additional lines of tabulated text, you can insert a *line break* between lines. A ***line break*** continues text on the next line, but treats the text as a continuation of the previous paragraph instead of a separate paragraph. You insert a line break by pressing ⬆Shift+⏎Enter.

In the next exercise, you type the tabulated text with a line break between lines.

To Type Tabulated Text with Line Breaks

1 **In the *Annual Report-WB5L* document, click the Show/Hide ¶ button.**

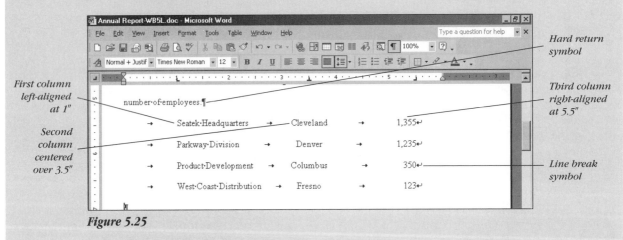

2 **Press** Tab⇄**, and type** Seatek Headquarters.
Typically, you press Tab⇄ before typing text in the first column.

3 **Press** Tab⇄**, and type** Cleveland.
Cleveland appears in the second column.

4 **Press** Tab⇄**, and type** 1,355.
The value appears in the third column.

5 **Press** ⇧Shift+⏎Enter.
Word inserts a line break symbol and positions the insertion point on the next line. The new line is treated as part of the same paragraph.

6 **Type the rest of the tabulated list, pressing** ⇧Shift+⏎Enter **after each line.**

Parkway Division	Denver	1,235
Product Development	Columbus	350
West Coast Distribution	Fresno	123

Figure 5.25 shows how the tabulated text appears.

Figure 5.25

7 **Save the document, and keep it onscreen to continue with the next exercise.**

After typing tabulated text, make sure that the tabulated columns are balanced. You should have the same amount of space before the first column and after the last column. Furthermore, you should balance the space between the columns. Currently, the third column is too far to the right. In this lesson, you move the third tab marker to 5″ to balance the tabulated text.

To Move Tab Settings

1 **In the *Annual Report-WB5L* document, click inside the tabulated text.**
You want to single-space the tabulated text.

2 **Click the Line Spacing button on the Formatting toolbar and choose *1.0*.**
Because you inserted line breaks instead of hard returns within the tabulated text, the tabulated text is treated as one paragraph and is now single-spaced.

To Move Tab Settings

If you have problems...

If the entire list is not single-spaced, you probably have hard returns within the tabulated text instead of line breaks. If so, press `Del` to delete the ¶ symbols, and press `Shift`+`Enter` to insert line breaks.

3 **Click the 5.5″ tab marker, and drag it to the left to the 5″ position.**
When you release the mouse, the entire third column moves to the left. Aligning the third column at 5″ provides a one-inch space on the right side, which balances the one-inch space before the first column. Now, you need to move the second column to balance the internal space.

4 **Click the 3.5″ tab marker to 3 5/8″ position.**
The internal space between columns is balanced (see Figure 5.26).

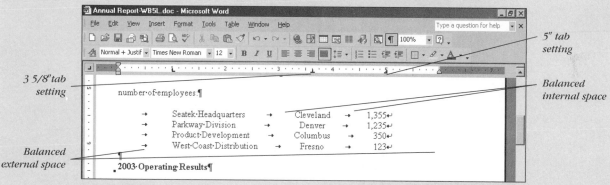

Figure 5.26

5 **Click the Show/Hide ¶ button to hide the nonprinting symbols.**

6 **Save the document, and keep it onscreen to continue with the next lesson.**

To extend your knowledge...

Setting Exact Measurements

You can set a more precise measurement by pressing `Alt` as you click and drag the tab marker along the Ruler. When you do this, Word displays the amount of space between the left margin and the tab setting and the amount of space between the tab setting and the right margin (see Figure 5.27).

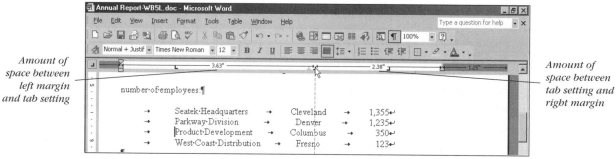

Figure 5.27

The Tabs dialog box is another way to clear and set tabs. Using the Tabs dialog box has an advantage in that you can set *leader* options that produce dots, a dashed line, or a solid line between the current column and the next column. Leaders guide the reader's eyes from one column to the next. Figure 5.28 shows the Tabs dialog box.

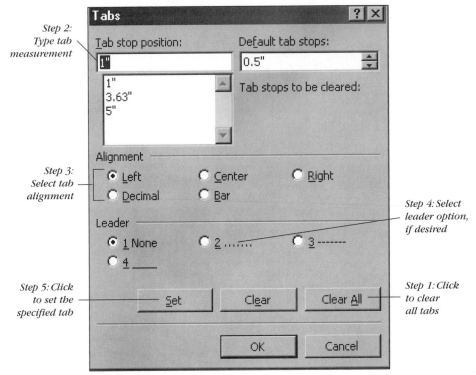

Figure 5.28

Using Line Breaks in Numbered Lists

If you want a blank line between items in a numbered list, you can't press ⏎Enter twice because Word removes the number when you press ⏎Enter the second time. Therefore, you can use paragraph spacing or insert line breaks to create blank lines between numbered items.

Lesson 8: Revealing and Clearing Formats

While double-checking a printed document, you might notice a formatting problem. However, identifying the exact problem might not be obvious. For example, did you double-space text, press ⏎Enter an extra time, or set paragraph spacing? You can detect the exact format of text by displaying the *Reveal Formatting task pane* that shows the font characteristics, alignment, indentation, spacing, and tabs.

In this lesson, you reveal formatting to see how you formatted different text.

To Reveal Formatting

❶ In the *Annual Report-WB5L* document, make sure the insertion point is inside the tabulated text.

❷ Choose F**o**rmat, Re**v**eal Formatting.
The Reveal Formatting task pane appears (see Figure 5.29).

To Reveal Formatting

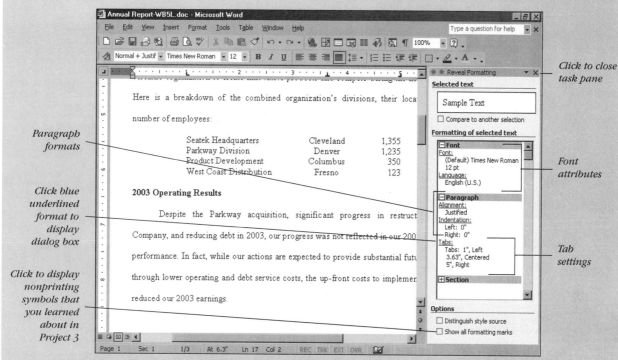

Figure 5.29

The task pane window shows character formats, paragraph formats, and tab settings. It does not show nonprinting symbols, such as hard returns, nonbreaking spaces, and regular spaces. Clicking the *Show all formatting marks* check box displays the nonprinting symbols in the document window, not the task pane.

3 **Click the blue underlined *Tabs* link in the Reveal Formatting task pane.**
The Tabs dialog box appears so that you can change the tab settings.

4 **Click Cancel to close the dialog box without changing any formats.**
Next, view the formats for the paragraph with the border and shading.

5 **Scroll to the bottom of page 2, and click inside the paragraph that contains the pale blue shading.**
The Reveal Formatting task pane shows that the paragraph is justified with 0.5″ left and right indentation, 12 pt spacing after the paragraph, single solid blue line, and a pale blue shading.

6 **Click the task pane's Close button.**

You can remove formats if you want to return text to its original unformatted condition. That way, you can start fresh by reformatting it. In the next exercise, you see how the Clear Formats option works.

To Clear Formats

1 **In the *Annual Report-WB5L* document, make sure that the insertion point is in the shaded paragraph.**

2 **Choose Edit, Clear, Formats.**

(Continues)

To Clear Formats (Continued)

All formatting is removed from the paragraph. It is no longer indented, justified, shaded, or enclosed in a border (see Figure 5.30).

Formats removed from paragraph

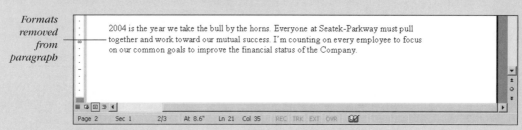

2004 is the year we take the bull by the horns. Everyone at Seatek-Parkway must pull together and work toward our mutual success. I'm counting on every employee to focus on our common goals to improve the financial status of the Company.

| Page 2 | Sec 1 | 2/3 | At 8.6" | Ln 21 | Col 35 | REC | TRK | EXT | OVR |

Figure 5.30

If the paragraph had character formats, such as bold, the bold would not have cleared. Character formats are cleared if you *select* text before using the Clear option.

3 **Click the Undo button to restore the formats to the paragraph.**

4 **Save, print, and close the document.**

Summary

In this project, you learned some exciting methods to format paragraphs. You made text easier to read by using double-spacing and paragraph spacing, inserting bulleted and numbered lists, and adding a border with shading. You also learned how to set tabs, change the alignment, and indent text. All of these formatting techniques dramatically improve the professionalism of the document you create.

Although these features are a great way to start improving your documents, Word offers a lot more enhancements. Use the Help feature to learn more about formatting options, especially those found in the Paragraph, Borders and Shading, and Tabs dialog boxes. There are no limits to what you can do with these features!

Checking Concepts and Terms

Multiple Choice

Circle the letter of the correct answer for each of the following.

1. What term refers to the way text lines up at the left and right margins? [L2]

   a. line spacing

   b. margins

   c. justified text

   d. alignment

2. What feature keeps the first line of a paragraph at the left margin and indents the rest of the paragraph? [L3]

   a. indent

   b. double indent

   c. hanging indent

   d. double-spacing

3. What format is most appropriate for emphasizing a list of items in sequential order? [L4]

a. bulleted list

b. numbered list

c. border

d. highlight

4. What type of tab produces a vertical line between columns? [L7]

a. left

b. dot leader

c. bar

d. hanging indent

5. Which type of formatting does not appear in the Reveal Formatting task pane? [L8]

a. Nonbreaking Space

b. Indentation

c. Font

d. Alignment

Screen ID

Label each element of the Word screen shown in Figure 5.31.

A. center-aligned text

B. Decrease Indent

C. double-spaced text

D. Increase Indent

E. justified text

F. numbered list

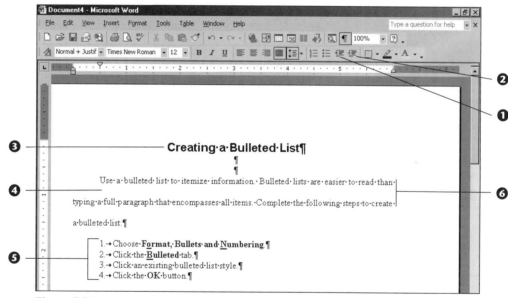

Figure 5.31

1. _____

2. _____

3. _____

4. _____

5. _____

6. _____

Discussion

1. What is the difference between line spacing and paragraph spacing? [L1]

2. Why would you clear formats from a paragraph? [L8]

3. What is the purpose of displaying the Reveal Formatting task pane? [L8]

Skill Drill exercises reinforce project skills. Each skill reinforced is the same, or nearly the same, as a skill presented in the project. Detailed instructions are provided in a step-by-step format.

1. Setting Text Alignment

You created a short report for a class. After creating the text, you decide to center the title and justify the rest of the document.

1. Open *ew1-0502*, and save it as `Internet Report-WB5SD`.
2. Choose Edit, Select All.
3. Click the Justify button on the Formatting toolbar.
4. Click in the document window to deselect text.
5. Position the insertion point within the title *Using the Internet,* and click the Center button on the Formatting toolbar.
6. Select the subtitle *Internet Protocol*; then click the Center button on the Formatting toolbar.
7. Repeat step 6 for these two subtitles: *Domain Names* and *Problems.*
8. Save the document and keep it onscreen to continue with the next exercise.

2. Changing Line Spacing and Paragraph Spacing

You decide to change the line spacing in your document to double-spacing to improve its readability. Then, you want to single-space a list of domain names. Finally, you want to add a little space above the centered headings by increasing the spacing before paragraph.

1. In the *Internet Report-WB5SD* document, position the insertion point at the beginning of the first paragraph.
2. Select the paragraphs you want to format by pressing Ctrl+⬆Shift+End.
3. Press Ctrl+2 to double-space the selected paragraphs.
4. Position the insertion point before the text *.edu* on page 2.
5. Hold down ⬆Shift and click at the end of the *.org* paragraph to select the paragraphs about domain names.
6. Click the Line Spacing button on the Formatting toolbar, and choose *1.0.*
7. Position the insertion point in the centered heading, *Internet Protocol.*
8. Choose Format, Paragraph.
9. Click the Spacing Before spin button to *6 pt,* and click OK.
10. Click in the heading *Domain Names*; then, repeat steps 8 and 9 to increase spacing before paragraph.
11. Click in the *Problems* heading.

12. Choose F̲ormat, P̲aragraph; click the Spacing B̲efore spin button to *18 pt*; and click OK. When you changed the line spacing for the *org* paragraph, you eliminated the blank space between that paragraph and the following heading. Therefore, setting 18 pt paragraph spacing before the heading creates the visual space of one blank line plus the other 6 pt space you used for the other headings.

13. Save the document, and keep it onscreen to continue with the next exercise.

3. Creating a Bulleted List and Indenting Text

The list of domain conventions is difficult to read. You determine that including a bullet before each convention will improve both the appearance and readability of the list. In addition, you want to indent the left side of the bulleted list so that the bullets are indented the same amount of space as the paragraphs. Finally, you want to double-indent the last paragraph.

1. With the *Internet Report-WB5SD* onscreen, position the insertion point before the text *.edu* on page 2.
2. Select the list of domains.
3. Click the Bullets button on the Formatting toolbar.
4. Click the Increase Indent button on the Formatting toolbar to indent the bulleted lists from the left side.
5. Press Ctrl+End to position the insertion point in the last paragraph.
6. Choose F̲ormat, P̲aragraph.
7. Click the L̲eft spin button until you see *0.5"*.
8. Click the R̲ight spin button until you see *0.5"*.
9. Click the *Li̲ne spacing* drop-down arrow, and choose *Single*.
10. Click OK.
11. Save the document, and keep it onscreen to continue with the next exercise.

4. Applying Borders and Shading

You believe the bulleted list would look nicer with a border and paragraph shading.

1. In the *Internet Report-WB5SD* document, select the bulleted list.
2. Choose F̲ormat, B̲orders and Shading.
3. Click the B̲orders tab, if needed, and click the Sh̲adow setting.
4. Click the C̲olor drop-down arrow, and click Orange.
5. Click the S̲hading tab.
6. Click Tan, the second color from the left on the last row.
7. Click OK, and deselect the bulleted list.
8. Save the document, and keep it onscreen to continue with the next exercise.

5. Revealing and Clearing Formats

You want to study the formats that you applied to various paragraphs. Therefore, you display the Reveal Formatting task pane. In addition, you clear formats from a paragraph.

1. In the *Internet Report-WB5SD* document, select the bulleted list.
2. Choose F̲ormat, Re̲veal Formatting to see the Reveal Formatting task pane.
3. Click the task pane's scroll-down arrow to display the Bullets and Numbering section.
4. Click *List* in the task pane to display the Bullets and Numbering dialog box.
5. Click the arrowhead-shaped bulleted list style and then click OK.
6. Click *Alignment* in the task pane to display the Paragraph dialog box.
7. Click the *Alignment* drop-down arrow, choose *Left*, and click OK.
8. Click in the *Problems* heading to see the information shown in the task pane.
9. Click the *Show all formatting marks* check box at the bottom of the task pane to see non-printing symbols such as the ¶ marks.

10. Click the task pane's Close button.

11. With the insertion point still in the *Problems* heading, choose Edit, Clear, Formats to remove formats from that heading.

12. Click the Undo button to restore the heading's formats.

13. Save, print, and close the document.

Challenge

Challenge exercises expand on or are somewhat related to skills presented in the lessons. Each exercise provides a brief narrative introduction, followed by instructions in a numbered-step format that are not as detailed as those in the Skill Drill section.

1. Editing a Welcome Letter

You composed a letter to welcome new members to an organization of which you are president. You use several of the formatting techniques you learned in this project to improve the appearance of the letter.

1. Open *ew1-0503*, and save it as `Welcome Letter-WB5CH1`.

2. Change Ken's name to your name in the signature block.

3. Select the entire document, and choose Justify alignment.

4. Delete the asterisk, and create the following bulleted list:
   - `Having administrative professionals be guest speakers at meetings.`
   - `Participating in the regional and national conferences.`
   - `Shadowing an administrative professional for a day.`
   - `Finding internships for members of the organization.`

5. Select the bulleted list, display the Bullets and Numbering dialog box, and choose the check mark bulleted list.

6. Select the salutation through the last paragraph. Set 12-point spacing after paragraph.

7. Select the Date, Time, and three Where lines. Set 1.5″ left and right indents, 0 pt spacing after paragraph, and a blue paragraph border. Click on the last Where line, and set a 12 pt after paragraph spacing. Indent all text after the colons so they align at 2.5″.

8. Select the entire document, and display the Reveal Formatting task pane.

9. Click *Font* on the task pane to display the Font dialog box.

10. Select Bookman Old Style and 12 point size.

11. Save, print, and close the document.

2. Formatting an Invitation to a Halloween Party

You are having a Halloween party at your home, and decide to create your own invitations. You create the text first and then want to improve it by changing fonts, changing text alignment, creating a fun bulleted list, and adding a page border.

1. Open *ew1-0504*, and save it as `Halloween Party-WB5CH2`.

2. Apply triple-spacing to the entire document.

3. Make the first line of the invitation (`Hey! It's a Halloween Party!`) larger (at least 30-point) and bolder by using the Font dialog box. Because this is a fun invitation, try a different font—such as Chiller, Dauphin, Desdemona, or Copperplate Gothic Bold. Ask your instructor for an alternative font if you don't have any of the fonts specified previously. Adjust the font size if the title takes up two lines.

4. Apply your font choice to the last line of the invitation so both lines have the same appearance. Apply 16-point size to the last line.

5. Pick another font for the body of the invitation. Select one that coordinates with the one you used for the title.

6. Select the When, Where, Why, and RSVP lines. Display the Bullets and Numbering dialog box. Customize the bulleted list by choosing a Halloween-type symbol, such as the spider or spider web, from the Webdings font. Select orange font for the bullets. Also set 1.5″ left indent for the bulleted list.

7. Center the first line of the invitation. Left-align the body of the invitation and the bulleted list. Center the last line of the invitation.

8. Select a Halloween theme page border from the A̲rt drop-down list. Select an appropriate page border color.

9. Make adjustments in internal spacing (line or paragraph) and font sizes to spread the text out, so it's not all clustered together.

10. Save, print, and close the document.

3. Creating and Formatting a Reference Page (Bibliography)

Your supervisor gave you a rough-draft sheet of references. She asked you to correctly format the reference page.

1. In a new document window, type the title `Works Cited`, centered between the left and right margins. Triple-space after the title. Then, change to left alignment.

2. Create the following references using hanging indents and italicize the book titles. Keep the entire list single-spaced for now (no blank lines between reference entries).

   Boettcher, David. "Motivating Customer Service Associates." *Contemporary Managerial Report* 25 Jan. 2003: 86.

   Reudter, Rodolph. *Managerial Failures in the Food Services Industry.* Proc. of the Regional Managerial Professionals Conference, Oct. 2003, State University. Las Vegas, 2004.

   Faamausili, Jon. "Practical Tips for Managing Employees." *City Daily Times* 15 Jan. 2004: B15.

   Corrado, Vicente. *The Performance Appraisal: More Than a Critical Review.* Boston: Book Group Publishing Company, 2002.

3. Insert nonbreaking spaces if needed to keep appropriate words together.

4. Select the four reference entries, and set 16-point spacing after paragraph.

5. Use the Sort command to sort the selected paragraphs in alphabetical order.

6. Adjust spacing after the title if needed to maintain the triple-space. (Check the paragraph spacing for the blank lines to make sure that it is 0 points before the first reference entry.)

7. Select the title, apply Small Caps effect, and choose 14-point Arial Rounded MT Bold (or Arial with bold).

8. Save the document as `Works Cited-WB5CH3`, print it, and close the document.

4. Creating a Memo with Tabulated Text

You want to send a memo to your company's employees about upcoming Word workshops. You want to align the colons in the heading, so you plan to set appropriate tabs. In addition, you create a tabulated list of workshops, dates, and times.

1. In a new document window, press ⏎Enter three times, and save the document as `Word Workshops-WB5CH4`.

2. In the Tabs dialog box, clear existing tabs, and set a 0.81″ right tab and a 0.95″ left tab.

3. Type the following heading with these specifications:
   - Press Tab⇥ before typing the first column for each line.
   - Type the bold capitalized words. Turn off bold after typing the colon, press Tab⇥, and type the second column.

○ Press ⏎Enter twice after typing each of the first three lines of the heading; press ⏎Enter three times after typing the subject line.

```
    TO:      All Employees
  FROM:      your name
  DATE:      February 2, 2004
SUBJECT:     Word Workshops
```

4. Type the following paragraph:

   The Computer Services Department has completed the installation of the new computer systems and Microsoft Office XP software. We are offering the following training sessions to help you become more proficient in Word 2002. All sessions will be held in Room 415. Please call Extension 5840 to register for workshops you'd like to attend.

5. Double-space, clear existing tabs, and set the following tabs: 1″ left, 3.38″ center, and 5″ right.

6. Type the following tabulated text, inserting line breaks between lines:

```
New Features          February 9       3:30 p.m.
Section Formats       February 23      9:00 a.m.
Table Formats         March 8          12:00 p.m.
Excel Integration     March 22         10:00 a.m.
Styles & Templates    April 5          3:30 p.m.
Advanced Formats      April 19         10:30 a.m.
```

7. Select the tabulated text and move the second tab to the left about 1/8″.

8. Save, print, and close the document.

5. Setting Tabs to Create a Table of Contents

You recently completed a report, and now want to create a table of contents that provides leaders between the headings in the first column and the page numbers.

1. In a new document window, type **Table of Contents**.

2. Triple-space, set tabs, and type the table of contents with hard returns instead of line breaks, as shown in Figure 5.32.

TABLE OF CONTENTS

The Personal Interview 1

Introduction...1

Pre-interview Impression Effects...1
    Pre-interview Impressions...1
    Self-Fulfilling Prophecy...2
    The Bias of Information Processing 2

Perception of the Interview..3
    The Unfavorable Information Effect...3
    Interviewer Decision Styles 3
    The Attribution Theory and Attribution Bias 3
    Stereotypes...4
    Non-Verbal Communications 4
    Physical Characteristics 5

Figure 5.32

3. Center the title, and apply 14-point Arial bold to the title.

4. Save the document as `Table of Contents-WB5CH5`.

5. Print and close the document.

6. Balancing Tabulated Text in a Letter

You work as an assistant to a product manager at a major publishing company. Your supervisor typed a letter to a new author, and asked you to type in contact data as tabulated text within the letter. You must use your own judgment to perfectly balance the tabulated text between the left and right margins, and to balance the internal space between columns.

1. Open *ew1-0505*, and save it as `Author Letter-WB5CH6`.

2. Select the first three full paragraphs, and apply 12-point spacing after paragraph.

3. Delete the asterisk, and set tabs for the following data. Set a center tab for the second column and a right tab for the last column to help you balance the tabulated text when you are through. Type the following single-spaced tabulated text with line breaks between lines:

```
Esther Israelsen      Acquisitions Editor    (201) 555-9040
Sunther Chaney        Product Manager        (201) 555-9050
Gaylen Sainsbury      Developmental Editor   (435) 555-4321
Tiffany Truong        Technical Editor       (419) 555-6742
Ira Wesemann          Production Manager     (201) 555-9187
```

4. Modify the tab settings for the first and last columns to balance the tabulated text between the left and right margins.

5. Modify the middle tab setting to balance space between the tabulated columns.

6. Make sure that there is one blank line after the last tabulated line.

7. Insert a nonbreaking space and a nonbreaking hyphen with the phone number in the last paragraph.

8. Save, print, and close the document.

Discovery Zone

Discovery Zone exercises require advanced knowledge of topics presented in *essentials* lessons, application of skills from multiple lessons, or self-directed learning of new skills.

1. Creating a Health Information Sheet

As part of an assignment in a health class, you create an information sheet on osteoarthritis to share with your classmates.

Open *ew1-0506*, and save it as `Osteoarthritis-WB5DZ1`. Use one of these sans serif fonts for the title and two headings: Arial Rounded MT Bold, AvantGarde with bold font style, Kabel Dm BT, or Arial with bold. Use Bookman Old Style font for the paragraph and bulleted items. When creating the page border, select the fourth style from the bottom of the Style list. Use a Pale Blue shading and other formats, as indicated in Figure 5.33.

16-point; centered

Shading color and line spacing

Picture bulleted list with adjusted special indent

12-point; 6-point space above and below paragraph

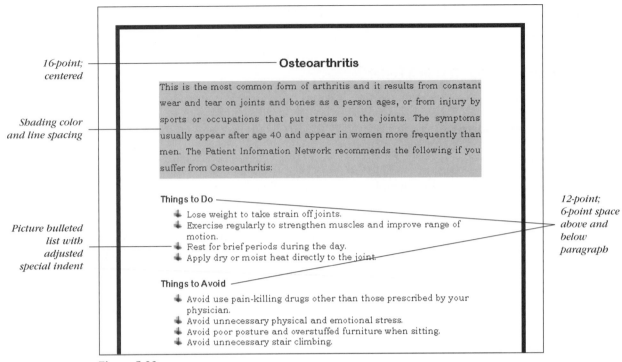

Figure 5.33

Save, print, and close the document.

2. Formatting a Course Description Document

Refer to Figure 5.34 to create a course description document. Create the customized bulleted list using the disk symbol found in the Wingdings font. Save the document as `Course Descriptions-WB5DZ2` and print it.

Sans serif font such as Antique Olive

Black 3-pt width border, Orange shading, and sans serif font

6-point spacing after paragraph

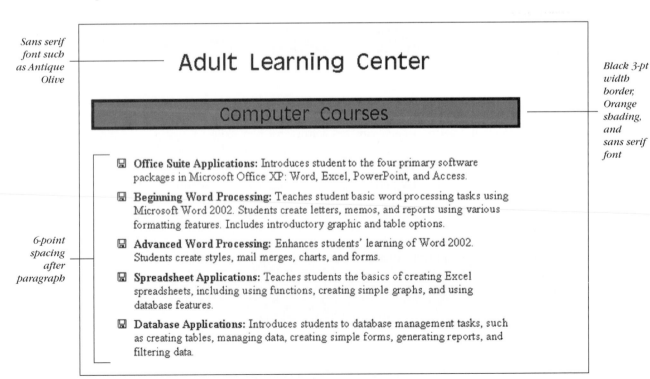

Figure 5.34

3. Preparing an Outline Numbered List for Teachers

As a student assistant in your college's administration office, you have been asked to type an outline numbered list of teaching responsibilities. In a new document window, type `Teaching Responsibilities` centered, boldface, and in 14-point Arial. Make sure that the rest of the document is left-aligned.

Create the outline numbered list using the style and format shown in Figure 5.35.

```
1.  RESPONSIBILITY TO SELF AND PROFESSION
    1.1.  Seek the truth of subject matter.
    1.2.  Stay informed by reading journals in respective field
2.  RESPONSIBILITY TO STUDENTS
    2.1.  Demonstrate minimum competencies for teaching.
          2.1.1.  Develop a lesson plan.
          2.1.2.  Select student instructional materials (e.g., textbooks, supplemental
                  reading, etc.)
          2.1.3.  Provide appropriate student laboratory experience.
          2.1.4.  Introduce each lesson.
          2.1.5.  Provide opportunities for student participation and feedback.
          2.1.6.  Summarize the lesson at the conclusion of each lecture.
          2.1.7.  Assess student performance.
    2.2.  Prepare each course.
          2.2.1.  Determine course content based on official objectives.
          2.2.2.  Prepare and distribute a detailed course syllabus.
                  2.2.2.1.  List major course objectives.
                  2.2.2.2.  Include instructor's name, office, phone, and e-mail address.
                  2.2.2.3.  Describe attendance policy.
                  2.2.2.4.  Outline assignments and deadlines.
                  2.2.2.5.  Discuss testing procedures.
                  2.2.2.6.  Inform students of grading scale and weighted categories.
          2.2.3.  Create appropriate testing materials.
    2.3.  Determine teaching methods.
```

Figure 5.35

After you select the appropriate outline style, customize it to adjust the formats based on the following specifications:

Level 1:	Aligned at 0″	Indent at 0.25″
Level 2:	Aligned at 0.25″	Indent at 0.65″
Level 3:	Aligned at 0.65″	Indent at 1.15″
Level 4:	Aligned at 1.15″	Indent at 1.75″

Type the outline list shown in the figure; choose the Outline view mode; and then demote the last entry, *Determine teaching methods*. Move down *List major course objectives*.

For the first first-level entry, set a 12-pt spacing after paragraph. For the second first-level entry, set a 12-pt before and 12-pt after paragraph spacing.

Save the document as `Teaching Responsibilities-WB5DZ3`. Print and close the document.

Formatting Documents

Objectives

In this project, you learn how to

- ✔ Set Margins
- ✔ Insert Section and Page Breaks
- ✔ Center Text Vertically
- ✔ Insert Page Numbers
- ✔ Prevent Text from Separating Between Pages
- ✔ Create Headers and Footers
- ✔ Navigate with the Document Map

Key terms introduced in this project include

- ❏ automatic page break
- ❏ Document Map
- ❏ footer
- ❏ header
- ❏ manual page break
- ❏ margins
- ❏ orphan
- ❏ section break
- ❏ suppress
- ❏ vertical alignment
- ❏ widow

Why Would I Do This?

By now you know how to format paragraphs or small sections of text. Now you are ready to format entire documents and control pagination. In this project, you set margins, insert section and page breaks, center text vertically, insert page numbers, and create headers and footers. Finally, you keep bulleted text from spanning page breaks and use navigation features to get around a long document.

Visual Summary

Figure 6.1 shows a title page that is centered vertically and horizontally.

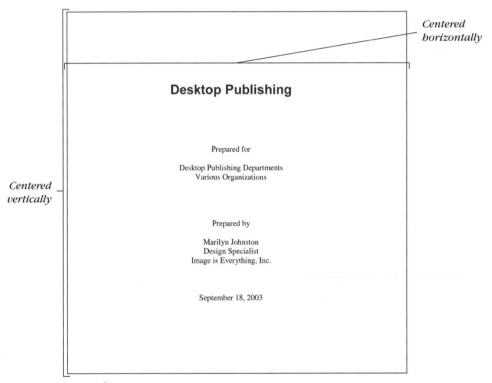

Centered horizontally

Desktop Publishing

Prepared for

Desktop Publishing Departments
Various Organizations

Prepared by

Marilyn Johnston
Design Specialist
Image is Everything, Inc.

September 18, 2003

Centered vertically

Figure 6.1

Figure 6.2 shows the second page in a report that contains a header, different margins, a bulleted list, and a page number.

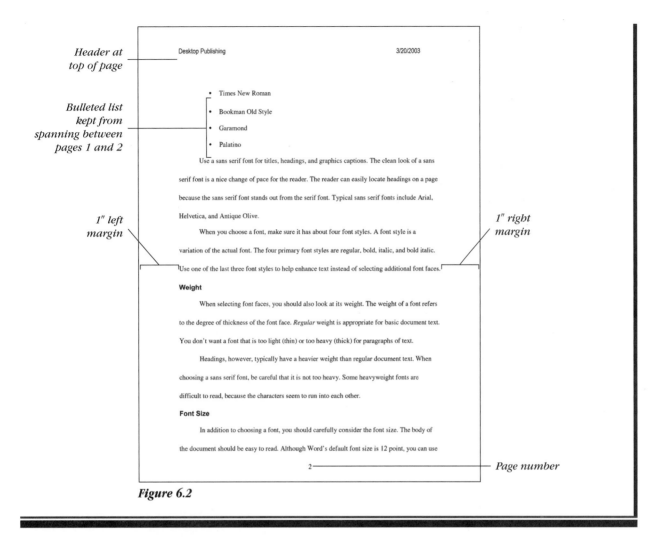

Header at top of page

Bulleted list kept from spanning between pages 1 and 2

1" left margin

1" right margin

Page number

Figure 6.2

Lesson 1: Setting Margins

A document's ***margins*** determine the amount of white space around the text. New documents have 1″ top and bottom margins and 1.25″ left and right margins. These margin settings are acceptable for many documents. However, you should change margins when doing so improves the appearance of your document. General or company reference manuals specify certain margin settings for particular documents.

In this lesson, you set a larger top margin and smaller left and right margins in a document.

To Set Margins

❶ **Open *ew1-0601*, and save it as** `Desktop Publishing-WB6L`.
The report is currently formatted by the default margins.

❷ **Press** `PgDn` **twice to see paragraphs in the document.**
You want to see how the current margins affect line endings.

❸ **Choose File, Page Setup; click the *Margins* tab if needed to see the margin options.**
The Page Setup dialog box appears with options for setting the margins, selecting paper sizes, and specifying the layout (see Figure 6.3).

(Continues)

To Set Margins (Continued)

Click the
Margins tab

Margin
settings

Choose the
document
part for
applying
the settings

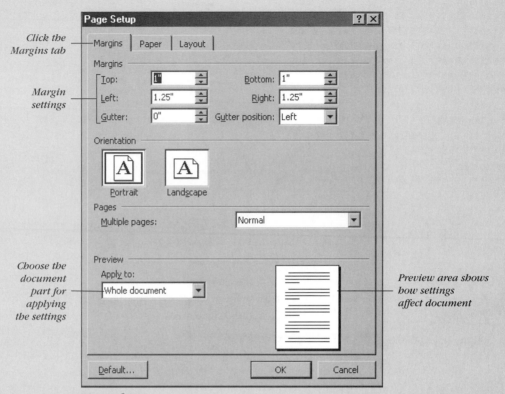

Preview area shows
how settings
affect document

Figure 6.3

4 Type 1.5 in the *Top* text box.
Because the *Top* text box is selected when you first open the Page Setup dialog box, you can type the margin setting; the number you type replaces the original setting. You don't have to type the inch mark ("); Word assumes that you are setting margins in inches.

5 Click the *Left* spin button to decrease the left margin to 1".
The left margin setting is now smaller.

6 Click the *Right* spin button to decrease the right margin to 1".
The right margin setting is now smaller. Notice that the margin settings will be applied to the entire document because the default *Apply to* option is *Whole document*. This is why the insertion point can be anywhere in the document when you change margins.

7 Click OK.
Each line in the paragraph contains more text because decreasing the left and right margins increases the space for text (see Figure 6.4).

To Set Margins

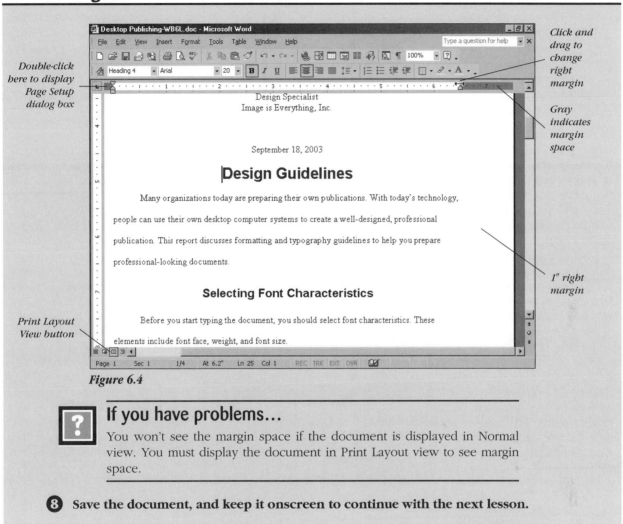

Double-click here to display Page Setup dialog box

Print Layout View button

Click and drag to change right margin

Gray indicates margin space

1" right margin

Figure 6.4

If you have problems...

You won't see the margin space if the document is displayed in Normal view. You must display the document in Print Layout view to see margin space.

8 **Save the document, and keep it onscreen to continue with the next lesson.**

To extend your knowledge...

Displaying the Page Setup Dialog Box

Double-click the empty gray space on the far left or far right side of the ruler to display the Page Setup dialog box.

Setting Margins on the Ruler

When you display the document in Print Layout view, you can set the margins on the ruler. You can set the left and right margins on the horizontal ruler and the top and bottom margins on the vertical ruler.

As shown in Figure 6.4, the white area on the ruler displays the typing area between the margins, and the dark gray area represents the margins. To change the margins, click and drag the margin markers on the ruler. You see a two-headed arrow as you click and drag the margin markers.

Lesson 2: Inserting Section and Page Breaks

When you set some formats, such as margins, Word applies those formats to the *entire* document. However, you might need to apply different formats throughout the document. Therefore, you need to insert **section breaks**, which are markers that divide the document into sections that you can format separately.

In this lesson, you insert a section break so that you can format the title page differently from the rest of the document.

To Insert a Section Break

1 **In the *Desktop Publishing-WB6L* document, click the Normal View button.**
The first page contains information for a title page and regular document text. You need to start the document text on a new page. More importantly, you need to be able to format the title page differently from the document text.

2 **Position the insertion point to the left of *Design Guidelines*, which is below the date on the first page.**
You want the document title to start a new section.

3 **Choose Insert, Break.**
The Break dialog box contains options for inserting page and section breaks (see Figure 6.5).

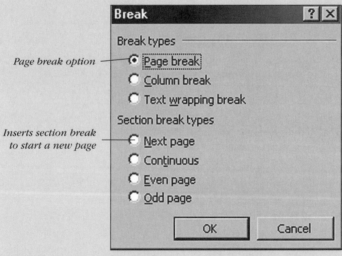

Page break option —

Inserts section break to start a new page —

Figure 6.5

4 **Click the *Next page* option, and click OK.**
Figure 6.6 shows the section break, indicated by a double-dotted line and *Section Break (Next Page)*.

To Insert a Section Break

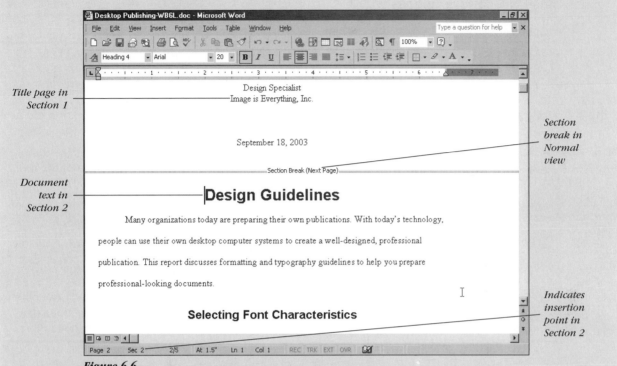

Title page in Section 1

Document text in Section 2

Section break in Normal view

Indicates insertion point in Section 2

Figure 6.6

If you have problems...

You won't see *Section Break (Next Page)* in Print Layout view unless you display the nonprinting symbols.

The title page is Section 1, and the document text is Section 2. Now, you can format each section separately.

5 **Save the document, and keep it onscreen to continue with the next exercise.**

Table 6.1 lists and describes the options in the Break dialog box.

Table 6.1 | Break Options

Option	Description
Page break	Inserts a hard page break (starts a new page) within the same section.
Column break	Starts a new column within columnar text.
Text wrapping break	Stops entering text on the current line and continues text on the next blank line; treats next line as part of paragraph. Useful for positioning text below a picture or table.
Next page	Inserts a section break by starting a new page. Allows you to apply different formats to different sections.
Continuous	Starts a new section on the *same* page. Useful for creating different formats, such as margins, on the same page of a newsletter.
Even page	Starts a new section by forcing text to appear on the next available even-numbered page. If the next page is an odd-numbered page, Word leaves that page blank.
Odd page	Starts a new section by forcing text to appear on the next available odd-numbered page. Useful for making sure all new sections or chapters start on the right-hand side of a double-sided document.

When a page is full and cannot contain any more data, Word inserts an ***automatic page break***, which ends the current page and starts the next page. Automatic page breaks change when you add or delete data on a page. You can create a ***manual page break*** to start a new page instead of continuing to enter data until Word inserts an automatic page break. Manual page breaks, which are appropriate for ensuring the start of a new page, stay where you insert them unless you specifically delete them.

In the previous exercise, you created a new section page break so that you can apply different formats to each section—title page section and document section. However, in some cases, you might want to create a page break within the same section and continue the same formats. Therefore, you insert a manual page break instead of a section break.

In this lesson, you insert a manual page break to start *Setting the Spacing* on a new page within the same section as the previous text.

To Insert a Manual Page Break

❶ In the *Desktop Publishing-WB6L* document, click to the left of *Setting the Spacing*, which is near the top of page 4.
You want the heading *Setting the Spacing* to start at the top of a new page.

❷ Choose Insert, Break.

❸ Make sure that the *Page break* option is selected and then click OK.
Word inserts a manual page break, designed by a dotted line and the words *Page Break* in Normal view. *Setting the Spacing* is now positioned at the top of a new page (see Figure 6.7) within the same section—Section 2.

To Insert a Manual Page Break

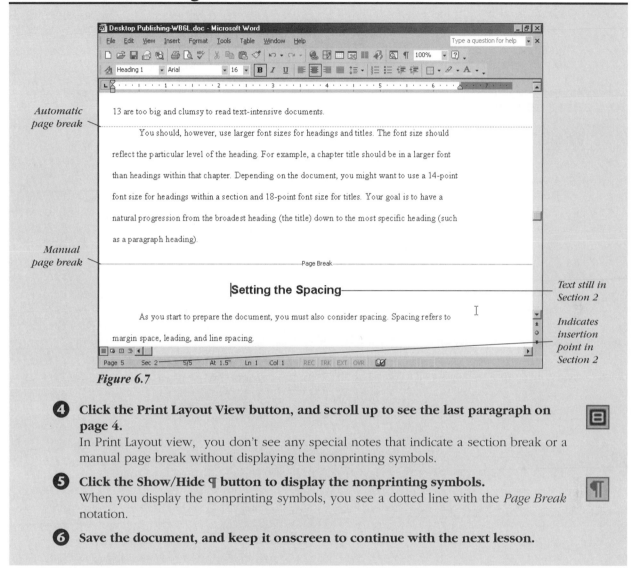

Automatic page break

Manual page break

Text still in Section 2

Indicates insertion point in Section 2

Figure 6.7

❹ **Click the Print Layout View button, and scroll up to see the last paragraph on page 4.**
In Print Layout view, you don't see any special notes that indicate a section break or a manual page break without displaying the nonprinting symbols.

❺ **Click the Show/Hide ¶ button to display the nonprinting symbols.**
When you display the nonprinting symbols, you see a dotted line with the *Page Break* notation.

❻ **Save the document, and keep it onscreen to continue with the next lesson.**

To extend your knowledge...

Manual Page Break Keyboard Shortcut

You can insert a manual page break quickly by pressing Ctrl+⏎Enter.

Lesson 3: Centering Text Vertically on a Page

Typically, the first page in a document or research paper is the title page. The standard format is to center it horizontally and vertically. In Project 5, "Formatting Paragraphs," you applied Center alignment to center text horizontally (left to right).

In addition to aligning text horizontally, you might need to select *vertical alignment*, which controls how text aligns between the top and bottom margins. The default vertical alignment is Top, which starts text at the top margin and continues down a page. When formatting a title page, you should choose Center vertical alignment to center the text between the top and bottom margins.

In this lesson, you vertically center text on the title page in your document.

To Center Text Vertically on a Page

❶ In the *Desktop Publishing-WB6L* document, click the Show/Hide ¶ button to hide the nonprinting symbols.

❷ Press Ctrl+Home to position the insertion point at the beginning of the document.

❸ Choose File, Page Setup.
The Page Setup dialog box appears with the margin options displayed. You need to display the layout options.

❹ Click the *Layout* tab.
The layout options appear. Notice that the default *Vertical alignment* option is *Top* (see Figure 6.8)

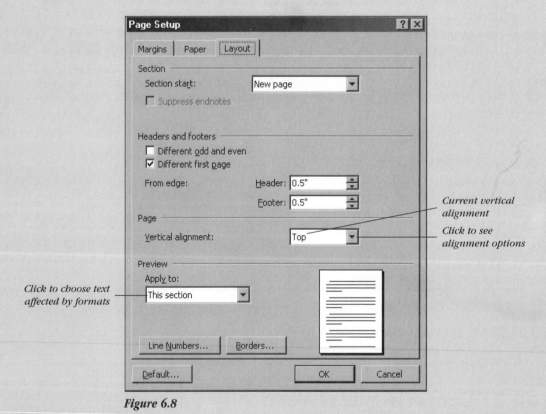

Figure 6.8

❺ Click the *Vertical alignment* drop-down arrow.

❻ Choose *Center*.
The *Vertical alignment* option now displays *Center*. The center vertical alignment format applies to the current section only, indicated by *This section* as the *Apply to* option.

To Center Text Vertically on a Page

If you have problems...

If the *Apply to* options are only *Whole document* and *This point forward*, you need to make sure you have a section break—not a hard page break—after the title page. Using a hard page break does not let you vertically center the title page only; Word would vertically center the entire document.

7 **Click OK.**

8 **Click the Zoom drop-down arrow on the Standard toolbar, and choose *Two Pages*.**   `100%  ▼`

The title page is now centered vertically on the page within Section 1, whereas the rest of the document text in Section 2 is aligned at the top margin (see Figure 6.9).

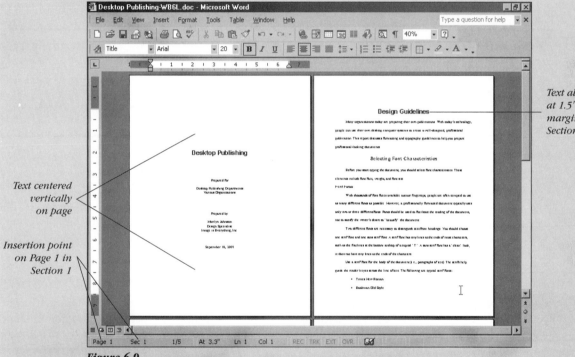

Text aligned at 1.5" top margin in Section 2

Text centered vertically on page

Insertion point on Page 1 in Section 1

Figure 6.9

9 **Press** `Ctrl`+`PgDn` **two times to see pages 3 and 4.**

Text in this section has a top vertical alignment, which you can easily see on page 4.

10 **Save the document, and keep it onscreen to continue with the next lesson.**

When you select options in the Page Setup dialog box, you specify the amount of text to which you wish to apply the formats. Table 6.2 lists and describes the *Apply to* options.

Table 6.2	**Page Setup Apply to Options**	
Option	**Description**
Whole document	Applies formats to the entire document, regardless of where the insertion point is when you access the dialog box.
This point forward	Applies formats from the current page to the end of the document.
This section	Applies formats to the current section only; other sections retain their formats.
Selected text	Applies formats to only the text you selected prior to accessing the Page Setup dialog box.
Selected sections	Applies formats to the sections you selected in the document.

To extend your knowledge...

Page Setup Options for Different Sections

You might be instructed to specify different page setup options for different sections of a document. Make sure that you click in the specified section before accessing the Page Setup dialog box. Then, ensure that the *Apply to* option is *This section*.

Lesson 4: Inserting Page Numbers

Page numbers are essential in long documents. They serve as a convenient reference point for the writer and the reader. Without page numbers in a long document, you would have difficulty trying to find text on a particular page or trying to tell someone else where to locate a particular passage in the document.

Use the Page Numbers feature to automatically insert page numbers throughout your document. You select the page-number position (top or bottom of the page) and the alignment (left, center, right, inside, or outside). Word not only inserts page numbers but also updates the numbers when you add or delete pages. In this lesson, you insert page numbers in your report.

To Insert Page Numbers

❶ In the *Desktop Publishing-WB6L* document, press Ctrl+Home, and make sure that you are displaying the document in Print Layout View with the Two Pages zoom option.

Although your document is divided into two sections, Word applies page numbering to the *entire* document, continuing page numbers from one section to the next. To prevent a page number from appearing on the title page, you must position the insertion point on that page before you access the Page Numbers feature so that you can instruct Word *not* to number the first page of each section.

❷ Choose Insert, Page Numbers.

The Page Numbers dialog box appears so you can choose the position and alignment of the page numbers (see Figure 6.10).

To Insert Page Numbers

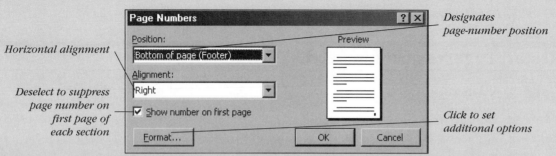

Horizontal alignment

Deselect to suppress page number on first page of each section

Designates page-number position

Click to set additional options

Figure 6.10

③ **Click the _Alignment_ drop-down arrow, and choose _Center_.**

This option centers the page numbers between the left and right margins, similar to the Center alignment you used in Project 5 to center text horizontally between the margins.

④ **If the _Show number on first page_ check box is checked, click the check box to deselect this option.**

By deselecting _Show number on first page_, you **suppress**, or "hide" the page number on the first page of each section in the document. The page is still counted as page 1, but the page number does not appear.

⑤ **Click OK.**

Word does not show a page number on the title page or the next page because each page is the first page in its respective section.

If you were displaying the document in Normal view, Word automatically switches to Print Layout view so that you can see page numbers. Normal view does not display page numbers.

⑥ **Click the Zoom drop-down arrow, and choose 100%.**

⑦ **Scroll to the bottom of page 3.**

In Print Layout view, you see the page number at the bottom of the third page. It is centered between the left and right margins, as shown in Figure 6.11.

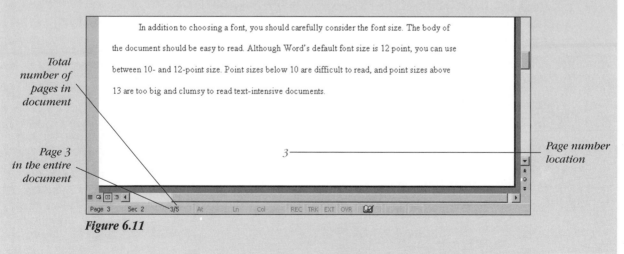

Total number of pages in document

Page 3 in the entire document

Page number location

Figure 6.11

The page numbers actually appear, starting with the second page within Section 2. Word, however, counts the title page as page 1 and the first page of Section 2 as page 2. Typically, you should count the first page of the body of the report as page 1. Therefore, in the next exercise, you position the insertion point at the beginning of Section 2 and restart the section page numbers at 1 again.

To Restart Page Numbers in Section 2

1 **Position the insertion point at the top of page 2, the first page of the body of the document.**

The first page of the body of the report—not the title page—should count as page 1. Therefore, you must change the page number value back to 1 on this page.

2 **Choose Insert, Page Numbers.**

The alignment should still be *Center*, and the *Show number on first page* is still deselected.

3 **Click the *Format* button to display additional options.**

The Page Number Format dialog box appears. The default *Page numbering* option is *Continue from previous section* (see Figure 6.12).

Continues numbering pages from previous section

Click to change format, such as lowercase Roman numerals

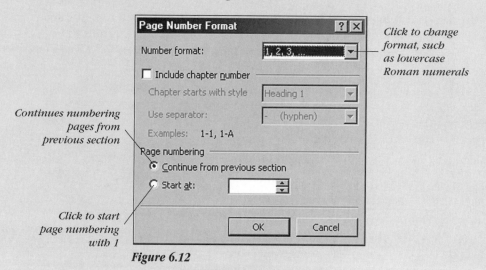

Click to start page numbering with 1

Figure 6.12

4 **Click the *Start at* option, and make sure that it displays 1.**

Changing the *Start at* option to **1** starts counting the first page of the current section as page 1, instead of continuing page numbering from the previous (title page) section.

5 **Click OK to close the Page Number Format dialog box; then click OK in the Page Numbers dialog box.**

The first page in Section 2 is counted as page 1 within its section (see Figure 6.13).

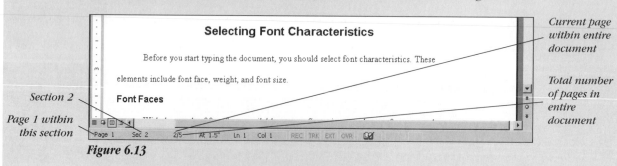

Current page within entire document

Total number of pages in entire document

Section 2

Page 1 within this section

Figure 6.13

To Restart Page Numbers in Section 2

6 **Scroll to the bottom of page 2 within Section 2.**
The page number is page 2 in Section 2. It is the third page in the entire document, as indicated by *Page 2 Sec 2 3/5*.

7 **Save the document, and keep it onscreen to continue with the next lesson.**

 ## To extend your knowledge...

Modifying Page Numbering

You might decide to change one or more page-numbering options. For example, you might want to choose a different page number alignment, start at a different page number, or use a different numbering format such as lowercase Roman numerals.

To change page-numbering, position the insertion point at the beginning of the section you want to change, and access the Page Numbers dialog box. Make the changes you want, and click OK.

Lesson 5: Preventing Text from Separating Across Page Breaks

To achieve a professional appearance, certain types of text should not separate between pages. For example, your document should not contain widows or orphans. A ***widow*** is the last line of a paragraph that appears by itself at the top of a page. An ***orphan*** is the first line of a paragraph that appears by itself at the bottom of a page. However, you don't have to worry about widows and orphans because Word's Widow/Orphan Control feature is a default option. Word also typically keeps a heading from being the last line on a page with the following paragraph on the next page.

However, Word lets other text separate between pages. For example, it does not keep bulleted lists or tabulated text together on a page. Your document has a bulleted list that spans across the bottom of page 1 and the top of page 2 in Section 2.

Word can identify widows and orphans because lines within a paragraph end in a soft return. The Widow/Orphan Control can't keep bulleted list items together, however, because each line ends with a hard return instead of a soft return.

In this lesson, you select the bulleted list and use the *Keep with ne*x*t* option in the Paragraph dialog box.

To Keep Text from Separating Across Page Breaks

1 **In the *Desktop Publishing-WB6L* document, click the Normal View button and change the zoom to 100%, if needed.**
Because the bottom and top margin spaces don't appear in Normal View, you can more easily select text that spans across page breaks.

2 **Scroll through the document so you see the bottom of page 1 and the top of page 2 in Section 2.**
Two bulleted items appear at the bottom of page 1, and the remaining bulleted list continues on the next page.

(Continues)

To Keep Text from Separating Across Page Breaks (Continued)

3 **Click and drag to select the entire bulleted list, which spans both pages.**
You need to select the text that you want to keep from separating across pages (see Figure 6.14).

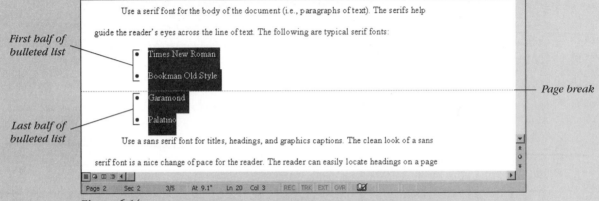

First half of bulleted list

Last half of bulleted list

Page break

Figure 6.14

4 **Choose F̲ormat, P̲aragraph.**
The Paragraph dialog box is displayed.

5 **Click the _Line and P̲age Breaks_ tab.**
The _Widow/Orphan control_ check box is selected. Although it keeps at least two lines of a paragraph together on each page, it does not keep lines together that end with a hard return. You need to select the _Keep with ne̲xt_ check box (see Figure 6.15).

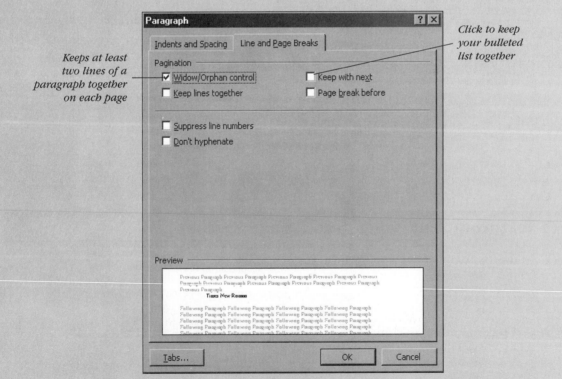

Keeps at least two lines of a paragraph together on each page

Click to keep your bulleted list together

Figure 6.15

To Keep Text from Separating Across Page Breaks

 If you have problems...

Don't select the *Keep lines together* option to attempt to keep bulleted lists from separating across page breaks. This option keeps an entire paragraph together—not individual lines created by hard returns.

6 **Click the *Keep with next* check box, and then click OK.**

Word now keeps the entire bulleted list together. Because the bulleted list can't fit at the bottom of page 1, the bulleted list appears at the top of page 2 (see Figure 6.16).

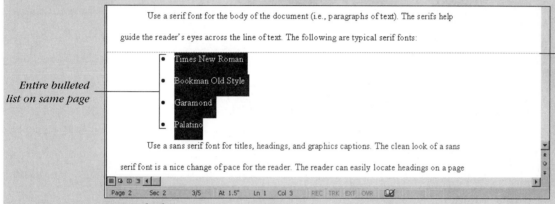

Entire bulleted list on same page

Automatic page break

Figure 6.16

 If You Have Problems...

If the entire bulleted list does not appear at the top of page 2, switch to Print Layout view and then back to Normal view.

7 **Deselect the bulleted list.**

8 **Save the document, and keep it onscreen to continue with the next lesson.**

Lesson 6: Creating Headers and Footers

A **header** contains standard data (text and graphics) in the top margin of most document pages. A **footer** contains standard data in the bottom margin of most document pages. You can insert text, page numbers, dates, filenames, and logos in headers and footers. Headers and footers are typically used in long documents, such as reports, legal briefs, medical transcripts, and proposals.

Each section in a document can have different information in a header. For example, the header in your textbook changes to reflect the project number and topic.

In this lesson, you create a header containing the title of the report.

To Create Headers

1 **In the *Desktop Publishing-WB6L* document, press** Ctrl+Home **to position the insertion point at the top of the document.**

(Continues)

To Create Headers (Continued)

2 **Choose <u>V</u>iew, <u>H</u>eader and Footer.**
Word switches to the Print Layout view. The header area is outlined at the top of the document window, and the Header and Footer toolbar appears (see Figure 6.17).

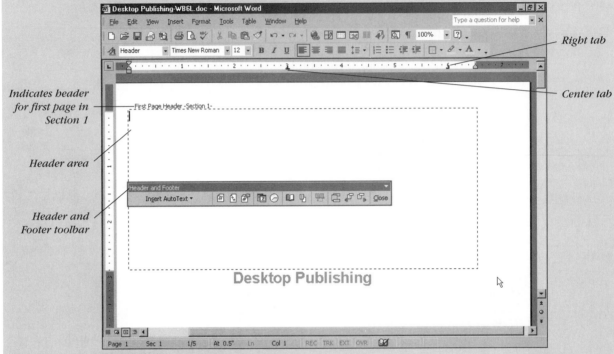

Indicates header for first page in Section 1

Header area

Header and Footer toolbar

Right tab

Center tab

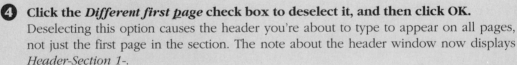

Figure 6.17

Word displays information that the header will appear on the first page in Section 1. You want to display the header on all pages.

3 **Click the Page Setup button on the Headers and Footers toolbar.**
The Page Setup dialog box appears with the layout options displayed. Notice that the *Different first <u>p</u>age* option is selected, which means that the header on the first page of each section is different from the rest of the pages.

4 **Click the *Different first <u>p</u>age* check box to deselect it, and then click OK.**
Deselecting this option causes the header you're about to type to appear on all pages, not just the first page in the section. The note about the header window now displays *Header-Section 1-*.

5 **Type** Desktop Publishing.
You want to insert the date at the right side of the header.

6 **Press** Tab **twice—once to get to the center point and again to align text at the right side of the header.**

7 **Click the Insert Date button on the Header and Footer toolbar.**
Word inserts a date field right-aligned at the 6″ mark.

8 **Click <u>C</u>lose on the Header and Footer toolbar.**
When you click <u>C</u>lose, the Header and Footer toolbar disappears, and the insertion point is inside regular document text. The header does not appear in Normal view.

To Create Headers

⑨ Click the Print Layout View button, click the Zoom drop-down arrow, and choose *Two Pages*.

The header appears on the title page. Notice that the page number now displays on the title page because you deselected the *Different first page* option for the header. However, the *Different first page* option is still in effect (see Figure 6.18).

Header on page 1 in Section 1

No header on page 1 in Section 2

Page number appears on title page

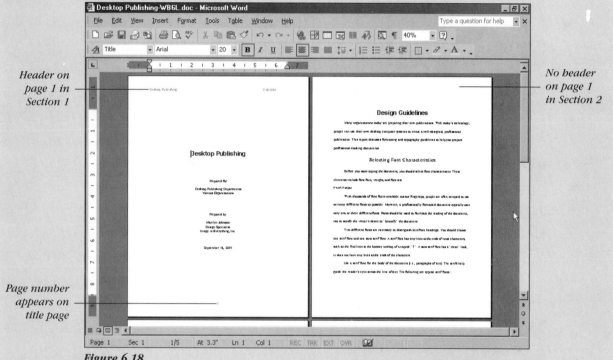

Figure 6.18

⑩ Press `Ctrl`+`PgDn` two times to see the header continue on the rest of the pages in Section 2.

⑪ Save the document, and keep it onscreen to continue with the next lesson.

Table 6.3 lists and describes the Header and Footer toolbar buttons.

Table 6.3	Header and Footer Toolbar Buttons	
Button	**Button Name**	**Description**
Insert AutoText ▾	Insert AutoText	Inserts items such as the filename, filename and path, and creation data.
[#]	Insert Page Number	Inserts a code to display the page number.
[⊡]	Insert Number of Pages	Inserts a code to display the total number of pages in a document.
[⊡]	Format Page Number	Lets you choose the page-number format, such as the number format and whether you want continuous page numbers or new page numbers for a section.
[⊡]	Insert Date	Inserts a code to display the current date.
[⊙]	Insert Time	Inserts a code to display the current time.
[⊡]	Page Setup	Displays the Page Setup dialog box, so you can set different headers and footers for odd- and even-numbered pages and different headers and footers for the first page in a section.
[⊡]	Show/Hide Document Text	Shows or hides the document text.
[⊡]	Same as Previous	Links the header or footer to the same header or footer in the previous section when clicked. Click to set different headers and footers for the current section.
[⊡]	Switch Between Header and footer window.	Switches between the header and Footer
[⊡]	Show Previous	Shows the previous header or footer.
[⊡]	Show Next	Shows the next header or footer.
Close	Close Header and Footer	Closes the header or footer window, and hides the Header and Footer toolbar.

To extend your knowledge...

Creating a Footer

You can create a footer by clicking the Switch Between Header and Footer button on the Headers and Footers toolbar.

Suppressing a Header or Footer on the First Page

If you don't want a header or footer to appear on the first page, make sure that the *Different first page* option is selected in the Page Setup dialog box; then click the Show Next button on the toolbar to go to the next page within the section. The header you create will appear on all pages except the first page in the section.

Creating Multiple or Odd/Even Headers and Footers

Use the Help feature to learn how to create multiple headers or different headers for odd and even pages.

Lesson 7: Navigating Through a Document

You learned how to scroll and how to use the Go To feature in Project 2,"Working with a Document."Although those navigation features are helpful, you are now ready to learn additional navigation features for longer documents.

The **Document Map** feature displays a window that lists the structure of headings in your document. You can quickly display a particular section by clicking the heading in the Document Map. Furthermore, you use the Select Browse Object button to browse by footnotes or sections.

To Navigate Through Documents

1 In the *Desktop Publishing-WB6L* document, press Ctrl+Home, and click the Normal View button.

2 Click the Document Map button on the Standard toolbar.
The Document Map appears on the left side of the document window (see Figure 6.19).

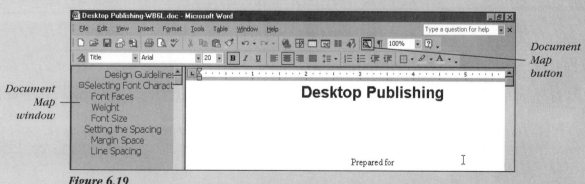

Figure 6.19

3 Click *Setting the Spacing* in the Document Map window.
Word takes you to that section immediately (see Figure 6.20).

(Continues)

To Navigate Through Documents (Continued)

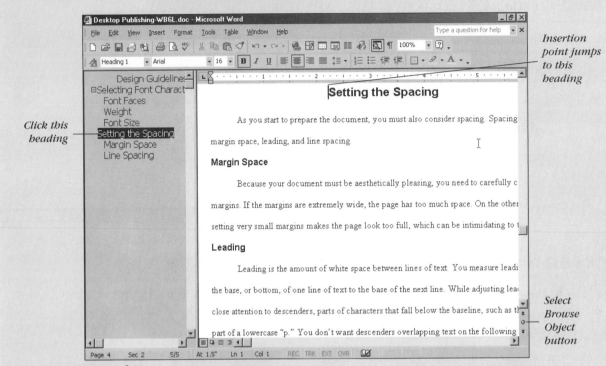

Figure 6.20

4 **Click the Document Map button to turn off this feature.**
Now, you want to scroll by jumping from heading to heading.

5 **Click the Select Browse Object button below the vertical scrollbar buttons.**
The Select Browse Object palette appears (see Figure 6.21).

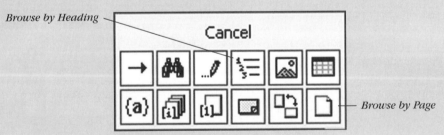

Figure 6.21

6 **Click the Browse by Heading button.**
Word moves the insertion point to the next heading: *Margin Space.* Notice that the Previous and Next buttons turn blue, indicating that you are browsing by any object *except* by page. When you position the mouse on top of these buttons, the ScreenTip displays *Previous Heading* and *Next Heading*, respectively.

7 **Click the Next Heading button.**
The insertion point jumps to the next heading, *Leading.*

8 **Click the Next Heading button again.**
The next heading is *Line Spacing.*

9 **Click the Select Browse Object button, and click the Browse by Page button.**

To Navigate Through Documents

This changes the browse back to the original default, which is browsing by page. The Previous and Next buttons are black again.

10 **Save the document, and close it.**

To extend your knowledge...

Select Browse Object Options

As you position the mouse pointer over a button on the Browse Object palette, the top of the palette displays the name of the button, such as *Browse by Edits*.

 Summary

You learned a lot of valuable document-formatting features. You can set margins, center text vertically, insert page numbers, create headers, and insert section and page breaks. In addition, you learned how to keep bulleted lists from separating across page breaks, and how to navigate quickly through your documents using the Document Map and the Select Browse Object options.

You can now expand your knowledge and skills of these and related features by using Help. For example, you might want to learn more about section breaks and the other buttons on the Header and Footer toolbar. In addition to using Help, complete the following exercises to reinforce and expand your skills.

Multiple Choice

Circle the letter of the correct answer for each of the following.

1. What is the keyboard shortcut for inserting a manual page break? [L2]

    a. `↵Enter`

    b. `Ctrl`+`↵Enter`

    c. `Ctrl`+`Break`

    d. `Pause`+`Break`

2. The *Vertical alignment* option is found in which tab of the Page Setup dialog box? [L3]

    a. Margins

    b. Line and Page Breaks

    c. Paper Source

    d. Layout

3. Which option should you use to keep a selected numbered list together? [L5]

   a. <u>W</u>idow/Orphan control

   b. <u>K</u>eep lines together

   c. Keep with ne<u>x</u>t

   d. Page <u>b</u>reak before

4. Which of the following is a default setting for page numbers? [L4]

   a. The number is positioned at the top of the page within a header.

   b. The page numbers continue from one section to another.

   c. The page numbers appear as lowercase Roman numerals.

   d. Page numbers appear left-aligned.

5. What types of items can you put into a header or footer? [L6]

   a. page numbers

   b. text

   c. date

   d. all of the above

Discussion

1. Describe a section page break and when you need section breaks in a document. [L2]

2. Look at the location of page numbers in this textbook. What position and alignment options would you choose to produce this effect? [L4]

3. What type of formatting is different in bulleted lists that the Widow/Orphan Control can't help keep the items from separating between page breaks? [L5]

Skill Drill exercises reinforce project skills. Each skill reinforced is the same, or nearly the same, as a skill presented in the project. Detailed instructions are provided in a step-by-step format.

1. Setting Margins

You created an information report for your business communication class. After reviewing the instructor's guidelines, you realize that you need to change the left and right margins.

   1. Open *ew1-0602*, and save it as `Interview Paper-WB6SD`.

   2. Choose <u>F</u>ile, Page Set<u>u</u>p.

   3. Click the *Margins* tab, if needed, to see the margin options.

   4. Press Tab two (or three) times, and type 1 in the <u>L</u>eft box.

   5. Press Tab, and type 1 in the <u>R</u>ight box.

   6. Click OK.

   7. Save the document, and keep it onscreen to continue with the next exercise.

2. Inserting a Section Break and Centering Text Vertically

You need to replace a manual page break with a section break, so you can vertically center the title page without centering the rest of the document.

1. In the *Interview Paper-WB6SD* document, click the Normal View button.
2. Scroll down on the first page, and click on the page break line between the title page and the next page.
3. Press ⌈Del⌉ to remove the hard page break.
4. Choose **I**nsert, **B**reak. Click the *Next page* option, and click OK to insert a section break.
5. Press ⌈Ctrl⌉+⌈Home⌉ to position the insertion point on the title page.
6. Choose **F**ile, Page Set**u**p, and click the *Layout* tab.
7. Click the *Vertical alignment* drop-down arrow, and choose *Center*.
8. Check to see that the *Apply to* option displays *This section*; then click OK.
9. Click the Print Layout View button.
10. Click the Zoom drop-down arrow, and choose *Whole Page*.
    You can see that the title page is centered vertically.
11. Press ⌈Ctrl⌉+⌈End⌉ to see the last page.
    This page is not vertically centered because the vertical alignment is Top.
12. Save the document and keep it onscreen to continue with the next exercise.

3. Using the Document Map and Inserting Manual Page Breaks

You need to use the Document Map to navigate quickly through the document. In addition, you want to insert manual page breaks to create page breaks within the same section.

1. In the *Interview Paper-WB6SD* document, change the zoom to 100%.
2. Click the Document Map button on the Standard toolbar.
3. Click *Pre-interview Impression Effects* in the Document Map window to move the insertion point there.
4. Press ⌈Ctrl⌉+⌈↵Enter⌉ to insert a manual page break.
5. Click *Perception in the Interview* in the Document Map window; then press ⌈Ctrl⌉+⌈↵Enter⌉ to insert a manual page break.
6. Click the Document Map button to remove the Document Map from the screen.
7. Save the document, and keep it onscreen to continue with the next exercise.

4. Inserting Page Numbers

You decide to insert page numbers in your document so your readers can easily locate specific sections of the paper. You want page numbers to begin with the main document, and not the title page. In addition, you need to keep a heading from being isolated at the bottom of a page.

1. In the *Interview Paper-WB6SD* document, position the insertion point at the top of the document (the title page).
2. Make sure that you are displaying the document in Print Layout view with the Two Pages zoom option. (If the Document Map appears, turn it off.)
3. Choose **I**nsert, Page N**u**mbers.
4. Click the *Alignment* drop-down arrow, and choose *Center*.
5. Click the *Show number on the first page* check box to deselect this option (if it is selected) and then click OK.
6. Click the Zoom drop-down arrow and choose 100%. Scroll to the bottom of page 3 to check the placement of the page number.
7. Position the insertion point at the top of page 2, the first page of the body of the document.
8. Choose **I**nsert, Page N**u**mbers, and deselect the *Show number on the first page* check box, if needed.
9. Click **F**ormat to display additional options.
10. Click the *Start at* option, and type 1.
11. Click OK and then click OK in the Page Numbers dialog box.
12. Notice that the page number indicator is *Page 1* on the status bar.

5. Keeping a Heading with the Following Paragraph

While reviewing the latest version of the document, you notice that a heading is the last line of a page with the following paragraph at the top of the next page. Although you want to keep the heading with the paragraph, you don't necessarily want to insert a manual page break because the heading does not always need to be at the top of a page; it just needs to be kept with its paragraph.

1. In the *Interview Paper-WB6SD* document, click the Normal View button.
2. Scroll through the document so you see the bottom of page 2 and the top of page 3 in Section 2.
3. Drag across the heading *The Bias of Information Processing* and the first two lines of the following paragraph.
4. Choose F<u>o</u>rmat, <u>P</u>aragraph to display the Paragraph dialog box.
5. Click the *Line and <u>P</u>age Breaks* tab.
6. Click the *Keep with <u>n</u>ext* check box, and click OK. If the heading does not appear at the top of page 3, click the Print Layout View button and then click the Normal View button again.
7. Repeat this process with any other headings that have separated incorrectly.
8. Save the document, and keep it onscreen to continue with the next exercise.

6. Creating a Header

You decide to create a header to appear in the second section of your document.

1. In the *Interview Paper-WB6SD* document, click the Normal View button.
2. Display the first page in Section 2.
3. Choose <u>V</u>iew, <u>H</u>eader and Footer.
4. Click the Page Setup button on the Header and Footer toolbar.
5. Deselect the *Different first page* option and then click OK to use the same header on the first and subsequent pages in the header.
6. Click the Same as Previous button on the Header and Footer toolbar to disconnect the header from the (non) header in Section 1.
7. Type `The Personal Interview`, press `Tab⇆` twice, and type your name.
8. Select the header text, and choose 11-point Arial.
9. Click the Close button on the Header and Footer toolbar.
10. Save the document, print it, and close it.

Challenge exercises expand on or are somewhat related to skills presented in the lessons. Each exercise provides a brief narrative introduction, followed by instructions in a numbered-step format that are not as detailed as those in the Skill Drill section.

1. Formatting a Status Report

You composed a status report for division managers concerning an upcoming Information Technology Training Conference. You open it, and make a few changes before sending it out.

1. Open *ew1-0603*, and save it as `Status Report-WB6CH1`.
2. On the blank line above the title, create the title page shown in Figure 6.22.

14-point Arial,
bold, Blue

Information Technology Training Conference

Status Report

Press ⏎Enter
8 times

Prepared for

Division Managers
Premium Distributors, Inc.

Press ⏎Enter
8 times

Prepared by

Press ⏎Enter
4 times

Renee Foster
IT Director

Use today's date —————————————April 21, 2004

Figure 6.22

3. Apply bold to the two-line title only; the rest of the title page should *not* be bold.

4. Change Renee's name to your name.

5. Apply Center alignment for the text you typed on the title page.

6. Insert a section break after the date. Then, vertically center text in the first section only (that is, the title page).

7. Select text, starting with the first full paragraph to the end of the document, and apply Justify alignment.

8. Select the bulleted list, and use the feature that prevents a page break within this text.

9. Insert page numbers in the bottom center of the pages. Do not display a page number on the title page. Make sure that the page number value starts at 1 on the first page of the body of the report.

10. Save the document, print it, and close it.

2. Formatting the Annual Report

The top corporate officials have reviewed the annual report you worked on. After making the revisions they requested, you want to reformat it to look more professional by controlling page breaks and creating a footer with identification information.

1. Open *ew1-0604*, and save it as **Annual Report-WB6CH2**.

2. Set 1″ left and right margins.

3. Use the appropriate feature to keep any tabulated list or bulleted list from separating across page breaks.

4. Create a *footer* that displays **Seatek-Parkway Enterprises** at the left side, the page number in the center, and **2003 Annual Report** on the right side of the footer.
   Hint: Use the Header and Footer toolbar to insert the page number *within* the footer.

5. Edit the footer by moving the center tab to 3.25″ and the right tab to 6.5″.

6. Display the Document Map, and use it to display each heading within the report; then, remove the Document Map.

7. Save, print, and close the document.

3. Formatting a Document for Lab Assistants

You work for the College of Business Lab Center. Your supervisor typed a memo and job description list for the lab assistants. You need to finish formatting the document for your supervisor.

1. Open *ew1-0605*, and save it as `Lab Assistant-WB6CH3`.
2. Insert a section break at the beginning of the title *College of Business*.
3. Vertically center text in the first section.
4. Create a footer with this information: `Lab Assistant Rules` at the left side, automatic page number in the center, and automatic date at the right side. Use the Header and Footer toolbar to insert automatic components.
5. Insert a manual page break before *Classroom Lab Assistant Expectations*.
6. Set 1″ left and right margins for Section 2.
7. Save, print, and close your document.

4. Formatting a Job Screening Guidelines Document

As the Human Resources Director at Woodward State College, you are responsible for informing and training screening committees on equal opportunity regulations. These rules are important to ensure fair and legal hiring practices at your college. You need to format a document to distribute to hiring committees.

1. Open *ew1-0606*, and save it as `Screening Guidelines-WB6CH4`.
2. Set 1″ left and right margins, and a 1.25″ bottom margin.
3. Insert section page breaks at the beginning of *Applicant Evaluation* and *Referral, Selection, and Protection* headings.
4. Select all items except the last item in the first bulleted list, and set `8 pt` spacing after paragraph.
5. Repeat the last step to format the other bulleted lists.
6. Select the entire document and turn on the Widow/Orphan Control.
7. Select the *Human Resources Director…* heading and the first bulleted item on the next page; use the feature to keep the heading and first bulleted item from separating across a page break. (Do *not* insert a section or manual page break.)
8. Insert page numbers in the bottom center of all pages.
9. Save, print, and close the document. (To save paper, consider changing the *Pages per sheet* option in the Print dialog box to `2 pages`.)

Discovery Zone exercises help you gain advanced knowledge of project topics and/or application of skills. These exercises focus on enhancing your problem-solving skills. Numbered steps are not provided, but you are given hints, reminders, screen shots, and/or references to help you reach your goal for each exercise.

1. Customizing the Contents of a Footer

You want to try some other formatting for the personal interview paper you created. You want to create a footer with filename and page number fields. Open *ew1-0602*, and save it as `Personal Interview-WB6DZ1`.

Delete the page break after the title page, and insert a section page break. In addition, insert section page breaks for the other two centered titles. Use appropriate vertical alignment for the title page.

Starting on the first page of Section 2, make sure that the *Headers and footers* options are deselected in the Page Setup dialog box. Then, create a footer starting in Section 2 that is not the same as the previous section. Insert a filename field (left side), your name (centered), and *Page X of Y* page-numbering format field (right side). Within the footer, change the page number to start the page number at 1 with the first page of Section 2.

If you need assistance, study the Header and Footer toolbar options to create this effect. Apply 11-point Arial Narrow font face to the footer.

Check for headings isolated at the bottom of pages and then use the appropriate feature to keep the headings with their following paragraphs.

Save, print, and close the document. (To save paper, consider changing the *Pages per sheet* option in the Print dialog box to `2 pages`.)

2. Creating and Printing a Booklet with Page Numbers

You want to create a double-sided booklet for the screening committee document. Use Help to learn about creating and printing booklets in Word Version 2002.

Open *ew1-0606*, and save it as `AAEO Booklet-WB6DZ2`. Set 0.75″ left and right margins; 1″ top and bottom margins; and landscape orientation. Set the option to lay out the document as a booklet with 0.75″ inside and outside space.

Insert page numbers at the bottom of all pages, except the first page of the first section. Select the alignment option that places odd page numbers on the right side, and places even page numbers on the left side.

Insert section page breaks for the three centered headings. Apply the Widow/Orphan Control to the entire document and then use the appropriate feature to prevent headings from being isolated at the bottom of a page, while the following paragraph appears on the next page. (**Hint:** You might want to choose the Two Pages zoom to see how text flows from page to page.) In addition, apply `8 pt` spacing after paragraph for all bulleted items except the last item in each bulleted list. Keep the *Administrators are responsible for* heading on the same page as its entire bulleted list using a page break.

The title should be the only text on the first page. Add appropriate, relevant information to make the first page. Use other formats as needed for the title page.

Save the document. If your printer has duplexing capabilities, print the document. If your printer does not have duplexing capabilities, choose the appropriate option in the Print dialog box to manually duplex the document. Your document should be printed on both sides of the paper. Collate the booklet and then close the document.

Creating and Formatting Tables

Objectives

In this project, you learn how to

- ✔ Create a Table
- ✔ Enter Text into a Table
- ✔ Insert Rows and Columns
- ✔ Delete Rows and Columns
- ✔ Adjust Column Widths and Row Height
- ✔ Format Cells
- ✔ Apply Shading and Borders
- ✔ Move and Position a Table

Key terms introduced in this project include

- ❏ cell
- ❏ column
- ❏ column headings
- ❏ column width
- ❏ gridlines
- ❏ row
- ❏ row height
- ❏ table
- ❏ table alignment

Why Would I Do This?

Sometimes, you might want an easy way to organize a series of data in a columnar list format. Although you can align text with tabs, you have more format control when you create a table. A ***table*** is a series of rows and columns that neatly organizes data. Each ***row*** presents data going horizontally (across the table from left to right), and each ***column*** presents data going vertically in the table. The intersection of a row and column is called a ***cell***.

You can create tables to store customer names and addresses, phone lists, personal inventories, calendars, project forms, and so on. After you complete this project, you'll probably think of additional ways you can use tables in your own documents.

Visual Summary

Figure 7.1 shows the structure of a table in Word.

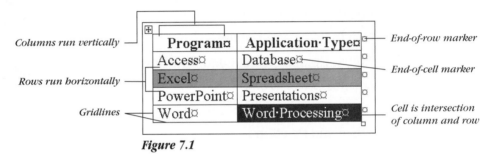

Figure 7.1

Figure 7.2 shows a table that you create within a business letter in this project.

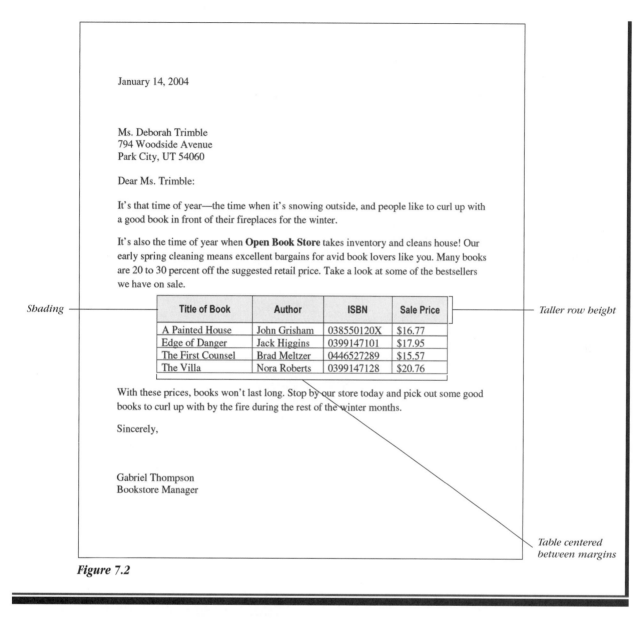

January 14, 2004

Ms. Deborah Trimble
794 Woodside Avenue
Park City, UT 54060

Dear Ms. Trimble:

It's that time of year—the time when it's snowing outside, and people like to curl up with a good book in front of their fireplaces for the winter.

It's also the time of year when **Open Book Store** takes inventory and cleans house! Our early spring cleaning means excellent bargains for avid book lovers like you. Many books are 20 to 30 percent off the suggested retail price. Take a look at some of the bestsellers we have on sale.

Shading

Taller row height

Title of Book	Author	ISBN	Sale Price
A Painted House	John Grisham	038550120X	$16.77
Edge of Danger	Jack Higgins	0399147101	$17.95
The First Counsel	Brad Meltzer	0446527289	$15.57
The Villa	Nora Roberts	0399147128	$20.76

With these prices, books won't last long. Stop by our store today and pick out some good books to curl up with by the fire during the rest of the winter months.

Sincerely,

Gabriel Thompson
Bookstore Manager

Table centered between margins

Figure 7.2

Lesson 1: Creating a Table

You can create a table between paragraphs in a letter, memo, or report; or you can create a table as a separate document. Before you create a table, plan what data you want to include and how you want to organize it. Doing so helps you create an appropriate table structure from the beginning, but you can always change the table later.

In this lesson, suppose that you work for a local bookstore named Open Book Store. Your manager, Gabriel Thompson, asked you to insert a table that lists some books that are on sale. You need to create a table that lists book titles, authors, ISBN numbers, and sale prices.

To Create a Table

1 Open *ew1-0701*, and save it as Book Letter-WB7L.

2 Scroll down through the document, and position the insertion point on the blank line above *Sincerely*.

(Continues)

To Create a Table (Continued)

You need to position the insertion point where you want to create the table.

③ Click the Insert Table button on the Standard toolbar.
Word displays a table grid. You click and drag through the grid to specify how many columns and rows you want in your table.

④ Position the mouse pointer on the fourth cell down in the fourth column.
The grid shows that you are creating a table with four rows and four columns (see Figure 7.3).

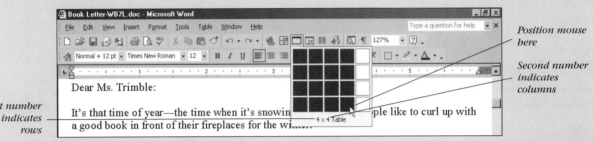

First number indicates rows

Position mouse here

Second number indicates columns

Figure 7.3

⑤ Click the mouse button in the cell on the grid.
You now have a new table in your document. By default, Word creates evenly spaced columns between the left and right margins. Your table contains *gridlines*, which are lines that separate cells within the table (see Figure 7.4).

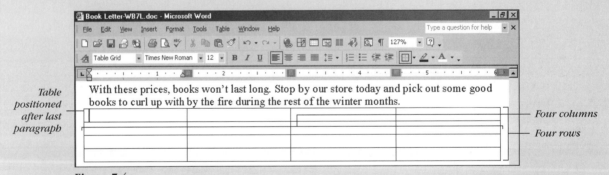

Table positioned after last paragraph

Four columns

Four rows

Figure 7.4

 ## If you have problems...

If you accidentally choose the wrong number of columns and rows for the table, click the Undo button to remove the table. Then, click the Insert Table button again to create the table.

⑥ Save the document, and keep it onscreen to continue with the next lesson.

 ## To extend your knowledge...

Creating a Table

You can also create a table by choosing Table, Insert, Table and then specifying the number of columns and rows you want in the Insert Table dialog box (see Figure 7.5).

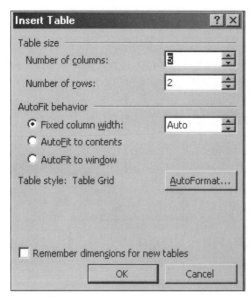

Figure 7.5

Lesson 2: Entering Text in a Table

After creating a table, you are ready to enter text into the cells. Type directly in the cell, letting the text word-wrap within the cell. When you are ready to type in the next cell, press Tab⁺.

You are now ready to type book titles, author names, ISBN numbers, and sale prices in your table. The insertion point is in the first cell, so you can start typing the first item now.

To Enter Text in a Table

❶ **In the *Book Letter-WB7L* document, type the following book title in the first cell of the table:** From the Corner of His Eye
The book title wraps within the same cell, making the first row taller.

 ## If you have problems...

Do not press ↵Enter within the cell. Let Word word-wrap the text within the cell. Inserting a hard return can cause problems when you adjust the column widths later. If you think you pressed ↵Enter within a table, display the nonprinting symbols to identify the paragraph marks and then delete them.

❷ **Press Tab⁺ to move the insertion point to the next cell to the right on the same row.**

❸ **Type** Dean R. Koontz **in the cell.**

❹ **Press Tab⁺, and type** 0553801341.

❺ **Press Tab⁺, and type** $16.17.
You are ready to type text on the next row. When you press Tab⁺ in the last cell on a row, Word moves the insertion point to the first cell on the next row.

(Continues)

To Enter Text in a Table (Continued)

6 Press Tab↹ and then type the data in the last three rows of the table, as shown in Figure 7.6. Do not press Tab↹ after typing $15.57 in the last cell.

From the Corner of His Eye	Dean R. Koontz	0553801341	$16.17
A Painted House	John Grisham	038550120X	$16.77
Edge of Danger	Jack Higgins	0399147101	$17.95
The First Counsel	Brad Meltzer	0446527289	$15.57

Figure 7.6

If you have problems...

If you accidentally press Tab↹ in the last cell and create a new row at the end of the table, click the Undo button to remove the extra row.

7 Save the document, and keep it onscreen to continue with the next lesson.

Table 7.1 lists different methods for moving around in a table.

Table 7.1 Moving the Insertion Point in a Table

To Move to the	Press
Next cell to the right	Tab↹
Cell to the left	⬆Shift + Tab↹
First cell in column	Alt + PgUp
Last cell in column	Alt + PgDn
First cell in current row	Alt + Home
Last cell in current row	Alt + End

To extend your knowledge...

Sorting Table Data

You can rearrange the rows within a table by using the Sort command. To do this, select the rows you want to arrange (minus the headings on the first row), choose Table, Sort. Specify how you want to sort the table, and click OK. Refer to Help for more information on sorting table data.

Lesson 3: Inserting Rows and Columns

After creating the table, you might decide to add another row or column. For example, you might realize that you left out information in the middle of the table, or you might want to create a row for **column headings**—text that appears at the top of each column describing that column.

In this lesson, you insert a row at the top of the table to type in column headings and a row at the end of the table for an additional book.

To Insert a Row

① **In the *Book Letter-WB7L* document, position the insertion point within any cell on the first row of the table.**

Remember that rows go across, not down. If the insertion point is not on the first row, the new row might not be inserted in the correct location.

② **Choose T_a_ble, _I_nsert to display the Table Insert menu options for inserting columns and rows (see Figure 7.7).**

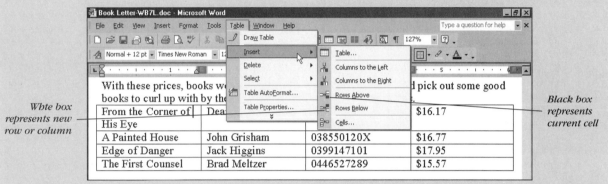

White box represents new row or column

Black box represents current cell

Figure 7.7

③ **Choose Rows _A_bove.**

Word inserts a new row above the current one. The new row is currently selected.

④ **Click in the first cell, and type the following data in cells on the first row:**

```
Title of Book     Author    ISBN     Sale Price
```

Your table now contains all the data you want to include (see Figure 7.8).

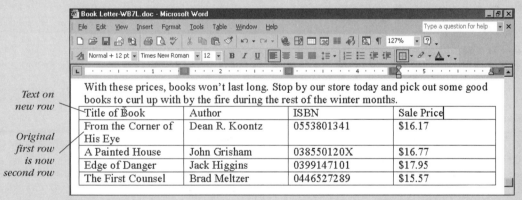

Text on new row

Original first row is now second row

Figure 7.8

⑤ **Click in the last cell on the last row—the cell containing *$15.57*.**

You want to add a row below the last row for another book that's on sale.

⑥ **Press Tab.**

Pressing Tab in the last cell on the last row creates a new row below the original last row.

⑦ **Type the following information on the last row:**

```
The Villa     Nora Roberts     0399147128     $20.76
```

(Continues)

To Insert a Row (Continued)

Your table contains data on the new row at the bottom of the table (see Figure 7.9).

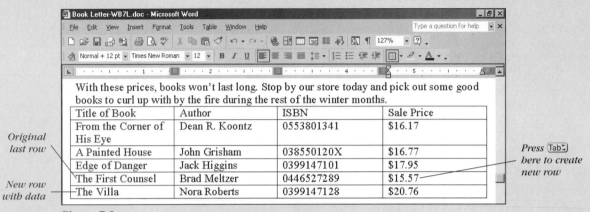

Original last row

New row with data

Press Tab⇄ *here to create new row*

Figure 7.9

8 **Save the document, and keep it onscreen to continue with the next lesson.**

To extend your knowledge...

Inserting Columns

Use the Table, Insert menu to insert a new column to the left or right of the column containing the insertion point. For example, if the insertion point is in the second column and you insert a column to the left, the new column becomes the second column, and the original second column becomes the third column. When you insert a column, the existing columns decrease in width to make room for the new column.

Lesson 4: Deleting Rows and Columns

After creating a table, you might decide that you no longer need a particular row or column. You can delete a row or column just as easily as you insert rows and columns. In this lesson, you realize that your bookstore only has one copy of *From the Corner of His Eye*, and will not receive more for another month. Therefore, you decide to remove this book from your list of sale items.

To Delete a Row

1 **In the *Book Letter-WB7L* document, position the insertion point in the second row of the table—the row that contains *From the Corner of His Eye*.**
You must first position the insertion point in any cell on the row that you want to delete.

2 **Choose Table, Delete.**
The Delete options include Table, Columns, Rows, Cells.

3 **Choose Rows.**
Word deletes the row containing the insertion point (see Figure 7.10).

To Delete a Row

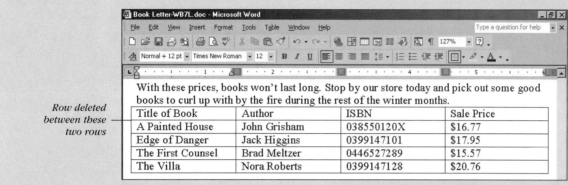

Row deleted between these two rows

Figure 7.10

❹ Save the document, and keep it onscreen to continue with the next lesson.

To extend your knowledge...

Deleting Cell Contents

Instead of deleting a row or column, you might want to keep the table structure but delete the text in the cells. To delete just the text, select the cells containing the text you want to delete and then press [Del]. This process leaves empty cells in which you can type new text.

Lesson 5: Adjusting Column Width and Row Height

When you create a table, Word creates evenly spaced columns. *Column width* is the horizontal space or width of a column. You may, however, need to adjust the column widths based on the type of data you type in the column. For example, the columns in your table should be narrower.

Furthermore, you might want to adjust the row height. *Row height* is the vertical distance from the top of the row to the bottom of the row. By default, Word expands the row height when text word-wraps within a cell on that row. To make the column headings on the first row stand out, you want to make this row taller.

To Adjust Row Height and Column Widths

❶ In the *Book Letter-WB7L* document, click the Print Layout View button, and change the zoom to 100%.

❷ Position the mouse pointer on the gridline that separates the first and second rows of the table.
As Figure 7.11 shows, the mouse pointer turns into a two-headed arrow, indicating that you can adjust the height by clicking and dragging the gridline.

(Continues)

To Adjust Row Height and Column Widths (Continued)

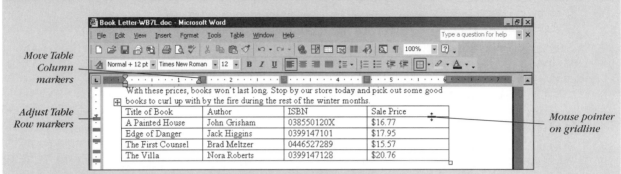

Move Table Column markers

Adjust Table Row markers

Mouse pointer on gridline

Figure 7.11

If you have problems...

You won't see the two-headed mouse arrow in Normal view. You must be in Print Layout view to see the two-headed arrow on the table gridlines.

❸ Click and drag the gridline down to make the row about twice its original height, as shown in Figure 7.12.

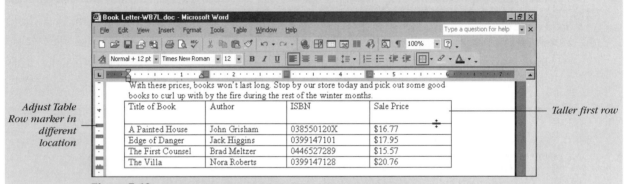

Adjust Table Row marker in different location

Taller first row

Figure 7.12

You now need to decrease the column widths.

❹ Position the mouse pointer on the vertical gridline on the right side of the Sale Price column.

The mouse pointer is a two-headed arrow, indicating that you can change the column width (see Figure 7.13).

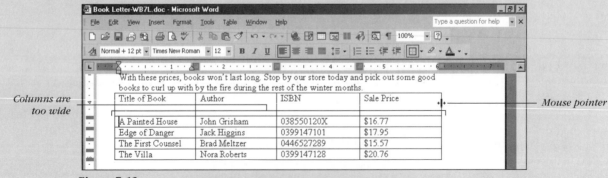

Columns are too wide

Mouse pointer

Figure 7.13

To Adjust Row Height and Column Widths

5 **Double-click the gridline.**
Double-clicking a vertical gridline adjusts the column width based on the text in that column. The fourth column is now narrower.

6 **Double-click the vertical gridline between the third and fourth columns to decrease the width of the third column.**

7 **Double-click the vertical gridline between the second and third columns.**
The columns look better than they did when they were wider (see Figure 7.14).

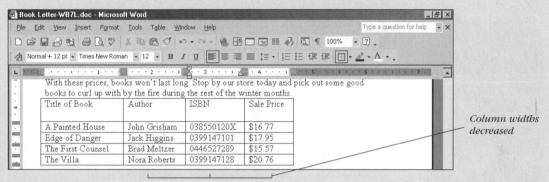

Column widths decreased

Figure 7.14

8 **Save the document, and keep it onscreen to continue with the next lesson.**

To extend your knowledge...

Decreasing Widths Before Increasing Other Widths

Before making a column *wider*, adjust other columns that need to be *narrower*. If you make one wider and then decrease other column widths, you might have to increase the first column width again.

Using the Markers to Adjust Width and Height

You can click and drag the Adjust Table Row marker to change the row height and the Move Table Column marker to change a column width (refer to Figure 7.11 in the previous exercise).

Adjusting Exact Column Widths

If instructed, you can specify an *exact* measurement for column widths. To do this, click inside a cell within the column for which you want to adjust its width. Choose Table, Table Properties. Then, click the Column tab, click the *Preferred width* check box, and set a specific setting (see Figure 7.15).

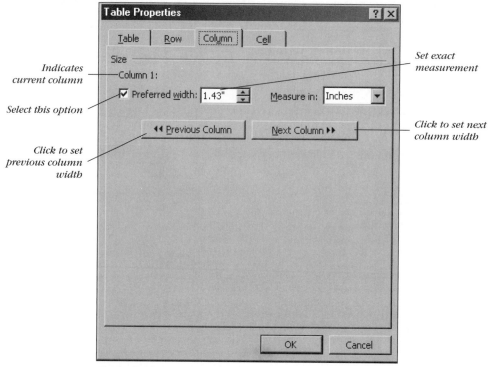

Indicates current column — Column 1:

Select this option

Click to set previous column width

Set exact measurement

Click to set next column width

Figure 7.15

If you want to set the same width for all columns, click the Table tab in the Table Properties dialog box and set the Preferred width there.

Setting a Specific Row Height

Instead of clicking and dragging a horizontal gridline to change row height, you can display the Table Properties dialog box and set an exact row height under the *Row* tab. Click the *Specify height* check box and then type the exact height in the text box.

Lesson 6: Formatting Cells

After creating a table, entering data, and adjusting the structure, you need to format data within the cells. You can use many common formatting techniques you already know, such as bold, font color, font, font size, bullets, and more.

In this lesson, you make the first-row text stand out by choosing center alignment, boldface, and center vertical alignment. In addition, you set cell margins for the cells in the first column.

To Apply Cell Formats

❶ In the *Book Letter-WB7L* document, click and drag across the text in the first row of the table.
You must select the text in the first-row cells to format them simultaneously.

❷ Click the Font button and choose Arial Narrow, click the Bold button, and then click the Center button on the Formatting toolbar.
The text on the first row is now bold and centered horizontally in Arial Narrow font.

❸ Choose Table, Table Properties, and click the *Cell* tab, if needed.
Figure 7.16 shows the Cell options in the Tables Properties dialog box.

To Apply Cell Formats

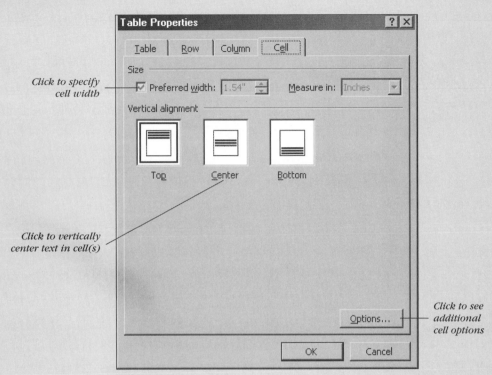

Click to specify cell width

Click to vertically center text in cell(s)

Click to see additional cell options

Figure 7.16

❹ **Click *Center*, click OK, and deselect the text.**
Figure 7.17 shows the first-row text centered vertically within the respective cells.

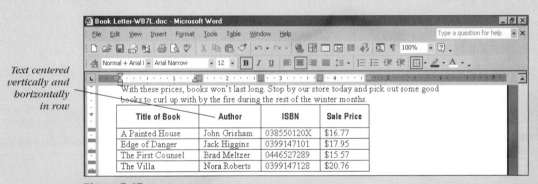

Text centered vertically and horizontally in row

Figure 7.17

Now, you want to adjust cell margins for the first column.

❺ **Select the entire first column—the column containing the book titles.**

❻ **Choose T̲able, Table P̲roperties.**

❼ **Click the O̲ptions button.**

(Continues)

To Apply Cell Formats (Continued)

The Cell Options dialog box appears (see Figure 7.18) so that you can adjust cell margins and wrap options.

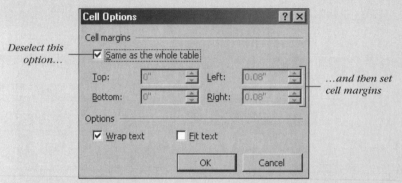

Figure 7.18

8 **Click the *Same as the whole table* check box to deselect it.**
After deselecting the check box, the four margin setting options are available.

9 **Click both the *Left* and *Right* spin buttons to display *0.16".***
Increasing the left and right cell margins helps balance the text within the cells.

10 **Click OK to close each open dialog box; then deselect the column.**
The first-column text looks balanced after increasing the cell margins (see Figure 7.19).

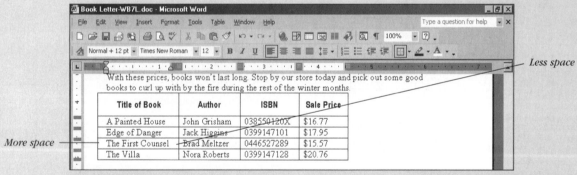

Figure 7.19

11 **Save the document, and keep it onscreen to continue with the next lesson.**

To extend your knowledge...

Selecting a Row

Instead of clicking and dragging across a row, you can position the mouse pointer to the left side of a row (in the selection bar area). When the mouse pointer is an arrow pointing to the top right, click to select the row.

Lesson 7: Applying Shading and Borders

You can also enhance the appearance of a table by selecting shading and border options. Shading refers to the background color within a cell or group of cells. Table shading is similar to the High-light feature that places a color behind text. Border refers to the line style around each cell in the table. The default line style is a single line.

In this lesson, you enhance the table by shading the first row, so it stands out.

To Select Table Shading

① **In the *Book Letter-WB7L* document, choose <u>V</u>iew, <u>T</u>oolbars, Tables and Borders.**
The Tables and Borders toolbar appears onscreen (see Figure 7.20).

Figure 7.20

② **Select the text on the first row of the table.**

③ **Click the drop-down arrow to the right of the Shading Color button on the Tables and Borders toolbar.**
You see the Shading Color palette, as shown in Figure 7.21.

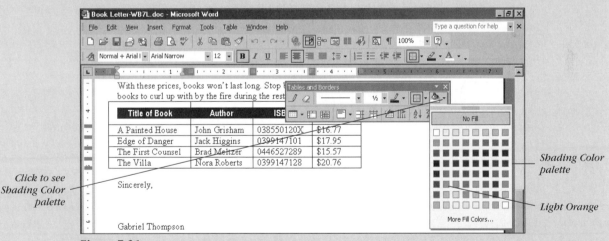

Click to see
Shading Color
palette

Shading Color
palette

Light Orange

Figure 7.21

When you position the mouse pointer on a color, Word displays a ScreenTip that tells you the exact name of the color, such as Sky Blue.

④ **Click the Light Orange color.**

⑤ **Deselect the row to see the color and then close the Tables and Borders toolbar.**
The first row contains a Light Orange shading color, as shown in Figure 7.22.

(Continues)

To Select Table Shading (Continued)

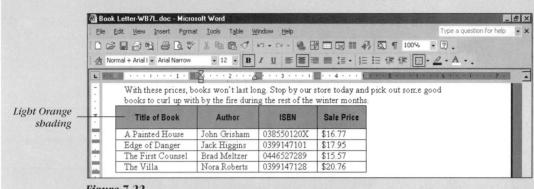

Light Orange shading

Figure 7.22

6 Save the document, and keep it onscreen to continue with the next lesson.

To extend your knowledge…

Table Borders

In Project 5, "Formatting Documents," you learned how to insert a border around a paragraph. Although you see borders for your table, you can customize the borders. To do this, click inside the table, and choose Table, Table Properties. Click the Table tab and then click the Borders and Shading button. You'll see options similar to those you used for paragraph borders. When choosing shading colors, be sure to specify whether you want to apply the shading to the entire table or the selected cells.

Remember that some colors do not print well or might cause text to be difficult to read on a black-and-white printout.

Lesson 8: Moving and Positioning a Table

After creating a table, you might decide to move it to a different location. You might also want to change the **table alignment**, the location of a table between the margins. In this lesson, you move the table above the last paragraph, make sure there is a blank line before and after the table, and choose center table alignment.

To Move the Table

1 In the *Book Letter-WB7L* document, adjust the view to see the table and the first two paragraphs.

2 Make sure the insertion point is inside the table; then position the mouse pointer on the table marker.
You should see a four-headed arrow, indicating that you can move the entire table.

3 Click and drag the table marker to the blank line above the last paragraph.
As you drag the table marker, you see a dotted line, indicating where you're moving the table. When you release the mouse, Word moves the table to that location (see Figure 7.23).

To Move the Table

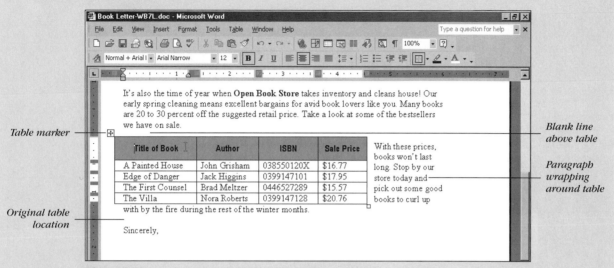

Figure 7.23

The last paragraph might word-wrap around the table. You need to take off the word-wrapping, and also center the table between the left and right margins.

4 **Right-click in the table, and choose Table Properties.**
When you right-click in a table, a shortcut menu appears. You can choose options from this menu or from the Table menu on the menu bar.

5 **Click the Table tab.**
Figure 7.24 shows the table options.

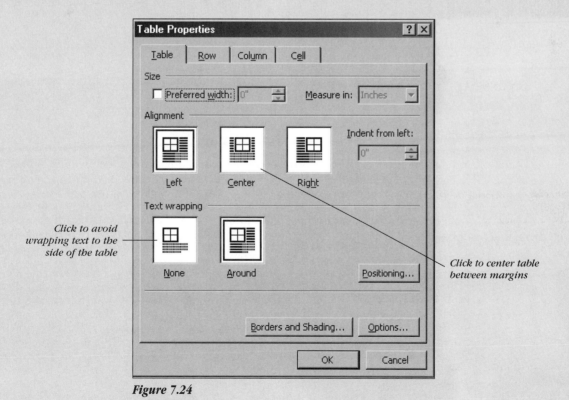

Figure 7.24

(Continues)

To Move the Table (Continued)

6 **Click the _Center_ alignment option.**
This option centers the table between the left and right margins.

7 **Click _None_ in the text-wrapping options and then click OK.**
This option prevents text from wrapping on the left or right side of the table.

8 **If necessary, press ⏎Enter at the end of the paragraph above the table.**
Figure 7.25 shows the centered table with text that does not wrap around the table.

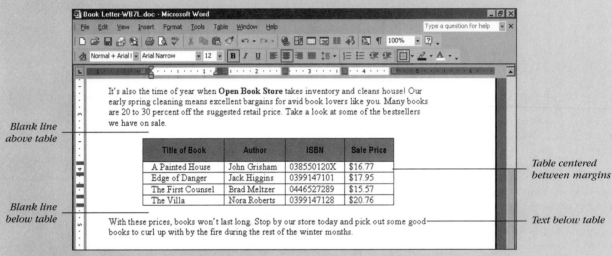

Blank line above table

Blank line below table

Table centered between margins

Text below table

Figure 7.25

9 **Save, print, and close the document.**

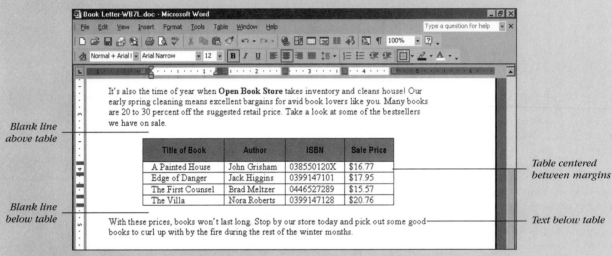
Summary

After completing these lessons, you know how to create a table, adjust the structure, and format the data. You can create exciting tables that look professional by centering text, shading cells, and positioning the table. In addition, you know how to move a table to a new location.

You probably noticed a lot of different buttons on the Tables and Borders toolbar. To learn more about these buttons, point to the button to see the ScreenTip displaying the button's name. Then, access onscreen Help to learn about these additional table buttons.

Checking Concepts and Terms

Multiple Choice

Circle the letter of the correct answer for each of the following.

1. If the insertion point is in the last cell on the first row, what key(s) should you press to go to the first cell on the next row? [L2]

   a. Ctrl+G

   b. ⬆Shift+Tab

   c. Alt+Home

   d. Tab

2. Assume that you created a table with the names of the months in the first column. Each row lists data for that particular month. The insertion point is in the first cell on the third row. This row list goals for April. You realize that you left out the goals for March. What should you do? [L3]

   a. Choose Table, Insert, Columns to the Left.

   b. Choose Table, Insert, Columns to the Right.

   c. Choose Table, Insert, Rows Above.

   d. Choose Table, Insert, Rows Below.

3. What happens when you press Tab when the insertion point is in the last cell in the last row? [L3]

   a. Word inserts a new row above the current row.

   b. Word inserts a new row below the current row.

   c. The insertion point appears in the paragraph below the table.

   d. The insertion point stays in the cell because it's already in the last cell of the table.

4. Refer to Figure 7.25 in Lesson 8. If the insertion point is in the cell that contains *$15.57*, and you choose Table, Delete, Rows, what happens? [L4]

   a. You delete just the *$15.57* text.

   b. You delete the Sale Price column.

   c. You delete the entire fourth row.

   d. You delete the entire third row.

5. All of the following help make the first row stand out, except _____. [L6,7]

   a. shading

   b. boldface

   c. taller height

   d. smaller font size

Discussion

1. Look through magazines, brochures, reports, and other documents that contain tables. Discuss the types of data conveyed in the tables. Evaluate the effectiveness of the table designs and formats. Provide suggestions for improving the tables. [L1–8]

2. Why should you adjust column widths instead of using the default column widths? [L5]

3. Describe the difference between table alignment and text alignment. [L8]

Skill Drill exercises reinforce project skills. Each skill reinforced is the same, or nearly the same, as a skill presented in the project. Detailed instructions are provided in a step-by-step format.

1. Creating a Table of Seminars

As the assistant to David Zaugg, you need to create a table that lists upcoming seminars for employees in the Dallas area.

1. Open *ew1-0702*, and save it as `Dallas Seminars-WB7SD`.
2. Position the insertion point between the first and second paragraphs.
3. Choose Table, Insert, Table.
4. Type **4** in the *Number of columns* box, press Tab, and type **5** in the *Number of rows* box. Then, click OK.
5. Type the data shown in Figure 7.26.

October 17	8:00-10:00 a.m.	Working with Difficult Customers	Baker Room
October 17	1:30-3:30 p.m.	Communicating with Subordinates	Texas Ballroom
October 18	8:00-10:00 a.m.	Resolving Customer Complaints	Suite 495
October 18	9:30-11:30 a.m.	Climbing the Corporate Ladder	Texas Ballroom
October 18	3:30-5:30 p.m.	Analyzing Data	Suite 495

Figure 7.26

6. Save the document, and keep it onscreen to continue with the next exercise.

2. Adjusting the Table Structure

You need to add a row at the top of the table to enter column headings to identify the data. You also need to add a row at the bottom of the table. Your supervisor, David Zaugg, just informed you that one seminar was canceled; therefore, you need to delete that row.

1. With the *Dallas Seminars-WB7SD* document onscreen, position the insertion point in any cell on the first row.
2. Choose Table, Insert.
3. Choose Rows Above.
4. Click in the first cell.
5. Type the following data in cells on the first row:
   Date   Time   Topic   Room
6. Click in the last cell on the last row—the cell containing *Suite 495*—and press Tab.
7. Type the following data in the cells on the new row:
   October 19   9:30-11:30 a.m.   Working with Managers   Suite 495
8. Click in the cell containing *Climbing the Corporate Ladder*.
9. Choose Table, Delete, Rows to delete the row.
10. Save the document, and keep it onscreen to continue with the next exercise.

3. Adjusting Column Width and Row Height

You need to adjust the column widths in the table. Most columns are too wide. In addition, you want to increase the height of the first row.

1. In the *Dallas Seminar-WB7SD* document, position the mouse pointer on the vertical gridline on the right side of the last column, and double-click to decrease its width.

2. Double-click the vertical gridline between the Date and Time columns.

3. Double-click the vertical gridline between the Time and Topic columns.

4. Double-click the vertical gridline between the Topic and Room columns.

5. Click the Print Layout View button.

6. Click and drag the horizontal gridline between the first and second rows down to double the height of the first row.

7. Save the document, and keep it onscreen to continue to the next exercise.

4. Formatting Table Cells

You want the column headings to stand out, so you plan to add bold, centering, and shading to the first row. In addition, you want to right-align text in the second column.

1. In the *Dallas Seminars-WB7SD* document, select the first row by positioning the mouse pointer between the left gridline and the text in the first cell, and double-click.

2. Choose T̲able, Table P̲roperties.

3. Click the *C̲ell* tab.

4. Click the *C̲enter* vertical alignment option and then click OK.

5. Click the *T̲able* tab and then click the B̲orders and Shading button.

6. Click the *S̲hading* tab in the Borders and Shading dialog box.

7. Click Light Green (fourth from the left on the last row) on the palette.

8. Make sure the *Apply to* option is *Cell*.

9. Click OK to close each open dialog box.

10. Click the Bold and Center buttons on the Formatting toolbar.

11. Deselect the first row.

12. Click and drag to select the times (but not the column heading) in the second column.

13. Click the Align Right button on the Formatting toolbar.

14. Deselect the text.

15. Save the document and keep it onscreen to continue with the next exercise.

5. Moving the Table

You want to move the table to a different location within the memo. In addition, you need to make sure you have one blank line above and below the table.

1. In the *Dallas Seminar-WB7SD* document, scroll down to see the table and the last two paragraphs.

2. Click in the table, and position the mouse pointer on the table marker.

3. When you see the four-headed arrow, click and drag the table marker straight down, and position the table between the second and third paragraphs.

4. Click at the end of the second paragraph, and press ⏎Enter.

5. Make sure you have one blank line above and below the table.

6. Save, print, and close the document.

C hallenge

Challenge exercises expand on or are somewhat related to skills presented in the lessons. Each exercise provides a brief narrative introduction, followed by instructions in a numbered-step format that are not as detailed as those in the Skill Drill section.

1. Creating an Alternative Book Sales Letter

Gabriel Thompson, manager of Open Book Store, has asked you to create another sales letter with different book choices. As you create the table, Gabriel provides continual input for changes.

1. Open *ew1-0701*, and save it as `Book Letter2-WB7CH1`.
2. Between the second and third paragraphs, create a table with the data shown in Figure 7.27.

Shreve, Anita	Where or When	April 1999	240
Connelly, Michael	Blood Work	September 1998	528
McFarland, Dennis	Singing Boy	February 2001	320
Shreve, Anita	Last Time They Met, The	April 2001	320
Diamant, Anita	Red Tent, The	September 1997	321
Connelly, Michael	Darkness More than Night, A	January 2001	432

Figure 7.27

3. Insert a row at the top of the table and enter the following information:
   `Author    Book Title    Publication Date    Pages`
4. Format the first row with bold, center horizontal alignment, 0.4″ row height, center vertical alignment, and Pale Blue shading.
5. Decrease all column widths to fit the data.
6. Center-align the text in the third and fourth columns.
7. Make sure you have one blank line above and below the table.
8. Center the table itself between the left and right margins.
9. Save and print the document.
10. Delete the publication date column, and insert a new column on the far right side of the table.
11. Enter the following data in the last column:
    ```
    Sale Price
    $11.70
    $6.75
    $20.00
    $19.96
    $19.96
    $15.57
    ```
12. Save the revised letter as `Book Letter 3-WB7CH1`, print it, and close the document.

2. Creating a Table in a Flier

The Life and Learning Center at a college is sponsoring two series of workshops: one series to improve student success and one series on effective writing. You were asked to create and format a table in the flier that will be distributed on campus.

1. Open *ew1-0703*, and save it as `Workshops-WB7CH2`.
2. Create a table with two columns and six rows. Place the table between the *Free Workshops* and *Sponsored By* text lines. Use the following information to create the table:

   ```
   Student Success Series        Effective Writing Series
   Taking Notes                  Using Proper Punctuation
   Using Textbooks Effectively   Writing Creatively
   Improving Concentration       Correcting Common Mistakes
   Managing Time                 Streamlining Prose
   Taking Tests                  Proofreading Carefully
   ```

3. Select the table, and apply 16-point Times New Roman.
4. Emphasize the *first row* by applying these formats: Arial Narrow, bold, 0.5″ row height, and centered vertically and horizontally.
5. Apply Yellow font color and Blue shading for the first row.
6. Double-click the vertical gridlines to adjust the column widths.
7. Center the table between the left and right margins.
8. Add some blank lines between *Workshops* and the table, and between the table and *Sponsored By*.
9. Center the document vertically.
10. Insert a row after the fourth row. Type the following information in the new row:

    ```
    Overcoming Test Anxiety       Revising Globally
    ```

11. Apply the Pencil art page border to the document. You might need to custom-install Office XP if the art page borders are not available.
12. Save, print, and close the document.

3. Creating a Table of People Involved in a Book Project

You are an assistant for a book publisher. Your supervisor wants you to create a table that lists the key people involved with an Office XP book.

1. In a new document window, type the title `Office XP Book Project`, and triple-space after the title.
2. Apply these formats to the title: center-align, bold, 16-point Antique Olive or Arial Rounded MT Bold, and Dark Blue font color. Choose Arial Black if you don't have Antique Olive or Arial Rounded MT Bold fonts.
3. Create a table after the hard returns. Use the information shown in Figure 7.28.

Name	Job Title	Phone Number
Monica Stewart	Author	801.555.8237
Susan Layne	Developmental Editor	580.555.7033
Justin Fields	Project Editor	201.555.4387
Melody Devereaux	Proofreader	419.555.2031
Louisa Jayaraman	Indexer	734.555.2499
Andy Ottley	Layout Technician	201.555.8108
Geoff Scovel	Usability Tester	801.555.1634

Figure 7.28

4. Insert a row above the developmental editor, and enter the following data:

`Nick Lopez`   `Acquisitions Editor`   `201.555.8642`

5. Insert a row below the project editor, and enter the following data:

`Josie Rynbrandt`   `Copy Editor`   `201.555.8265`

6. Apply Pale Blue shading to the entire table.

7. Set a 0.25″ row height for the entire table.

8. Apply a vertical center alignment to the cells within the table.

9. Horizontally center the text in the third column.

10. Center-align and bold the text on the first row.

11. Adjust the column widths, as needed.

12. Center the table between the left and right margins. (Make sure you center the *table*, not the text.)

13. Select the first column, set a **1.75″** cell width, and **0.21″** left and right cell margins.

14. Save the document as `Book Project-WB7CH3`, print it, and close it.

4. Creating Tables for Candle Scents and Prices

You work for Heavenly Scents Candles, a company that makes and distributes a variety of candle fragrances. You just wrote a letter to a customer who is interested in your candles. Now, you need to create two tables: one to list candle fragrances, and one for sizes and pricing.

1. Open *ew1-0704*, and save it as `Candle Letter-WB7CH4`.

2. Create the first table below the first paragraph. Use the information shown in Figure 7.29.

Standard Scents	Exotic Scents
Cinnamon	Pina Colada
Peach	Raspberry Delight
Mulberry	Mango
Vanilla	Passion Fruit

Figure 7.29

3. Add a row at the bottom of the table for `Apple Spice` and `Tropical Mist`, two popular standard and exotic scents.

4. Delete the row containing *Peach* and *Raspberry Delight* because you ran out of those scents and won't have any more for another month.

5. Apply these formats to the first row: centered vertically and horizontally, bold, 11-point Arial, Violet font color, Yellow shading color, and 0.35″ row height.

6. Apply a Light Yellow shading color to the rest of the table.

7. Adjust the column widths.

8. Create another table after the second paragraph, using the information shown in Figure 7.30.

Size	Price
8 ounce	$9.95
16 ounce	$17.95
26 ounce	$19.95
28 ounce	$22.95

Figure 7.30

9. Insert a column between the two existing columns in the second table. Enter this data:

```
Description
Round Jar
Round Jar
Octagon Jar; 2 Wicks
Square Jar; 2 Wicks
```

10. Apply these formats to the first row of the second table: centered vertically and horizontally, bold, 11-point Arial, Yellow font color, Violet shading color, and 0.35″ row height.

11. Apply Lavender shading color to the rest of the second table.

12. Adjust column widths as needed for the second table.

13. Center-align the data in the first and third columns of the second table.

14. Right-align the dollar values in the last column.

15. Center both tables between the left and right margins.

16. Make sure you have one blank line above and below each table.

17. Select the second table, and apply a 1.5-point Box border with Violet border to the outside of the table. (This process applies a thicker outside border and removes the cell borders inside the table.)

18. Replace the regular hyphens with nonbreaking hyphens in the phone number.

19. Save, print, and close the document.

Discovery Zone

Discovery Zone exercises help you gain advanced knowledge of project topics and/or application of skills. These exercises focus on enhancing your problem-solving skills. Numbered steps are not provided, but you are given hints, reminders, screen shots, and/or references to help you reach your goal for each exercise.

1. Sorting and Aligning Decimals in a Table

Gabriel Thompson wants you to make a few more changes to your latest book letter that you completed in Challenge 1. Open *Book Letter 3-WB7CH1*, and save it as `Book Letter 4-WB7DZ1`.

Set a `0.75"` cell width for the entire last column. Also, select left alignment and a decimal tab for the prices within the last column. (Make sure the cells are selected first.)

Sort the table by author in ascending order and then further sort by title. Study the options in the Sort dialog box, and select the appropriate options based on the table data.

Save, print, and close the document.

2. Enhancing the Candle Letter Tables

You want to further enhance the tables you created in Challenge 3. Open *Candle Letter-WB7CH4*, and save it as `Candle Letter-WB7DZ2`.

Use Help to learn how to create captions for tables. Create a caption for each table that reflects the table content. Keep the caption brief. Use the option to place the caption above the tables. After creating the captions, center them above their respective tables.

Select the first table, and apply these border options: Grid setting, ninth line style, Pink line color, and applied to the table. Also, choose a Rose shading color for the table. Italicize the fragrance names, but not the column headings. Apply the same border style to the bottom of the first row. *Hint:* Look at the buttons in the Preview section of the dialog box to apply a border to a certain part of the cell.

Select the second table, and apply these border options: Box setting, Yellow line color, 3 pt width, and applied to table. Also, add a Yellow bottom border to the first row only.

Save, print, and close the document.

3. Creating a Table of Potential Computer Systems

Your supervisor asked you to research six different computer systems and provide the following details in a table: brand name and model number, hard-drive capacity, RAM, megahertz, other features (such as CD-ROM or DVD; Jazz or Zip drive), and price. Choose one major computer retailer to complete your research. You might want to conduct Internet research by looking at the retailer's Web site. Choose models with similar features so the comparison will be appropriate.

Write a memo to your supervisor that explains where you got the research, and create a table that compares the computer systems. Apply appropriate formatting that you learned in this project. For example, select shading and borders; set column widths and row height; and choose fonts, font sizes, and font color to make the table look good. Use Help to learn how to select landscape page orientation. Explore the Tables and Borders toolbar.

Save your document as `Computer Memo-WB7DZ3`, print it, and close it.

Inserting and Formatting Graphics

Objectives

In this project, you learn how to

- ✔ Insert an Image
- ✔ Move and Delete an Image
- ✔ Size an Image
- ✔ Wrap Text Around an Image
- ✔ Apply Borders and Fills
- ✔ Copy Images with the Clip Organizer
- ✔ Download and Insert an Online Clip
- ✔ Create a Watermark
- ✔ Create WordArt

Key terms introduced in this project include

- ❑ clip art
- ❑ Clip Organizer
- ❑ fill
- ❑ Insert Clip Art task pane
- ❑ keyword

- ❑ sizing handles
- ❑ tight wrap
- ❑ watermark
- ❑ WordArt
- ❑ wrapping style

Why Would I Do This?

Some of the most exciting features of Word are its graphic capabilities. You can insert *clip art*, graphic images, or drawings in any document. Clip art and images provide visual appeal for a variety of documents. People use clip art, images, drawings, and scanned photographs to enhance brochures, newsletters, and announcements.

Visual Summary

Figure 8.1 shows various visual elements in a document that you complete in this project.

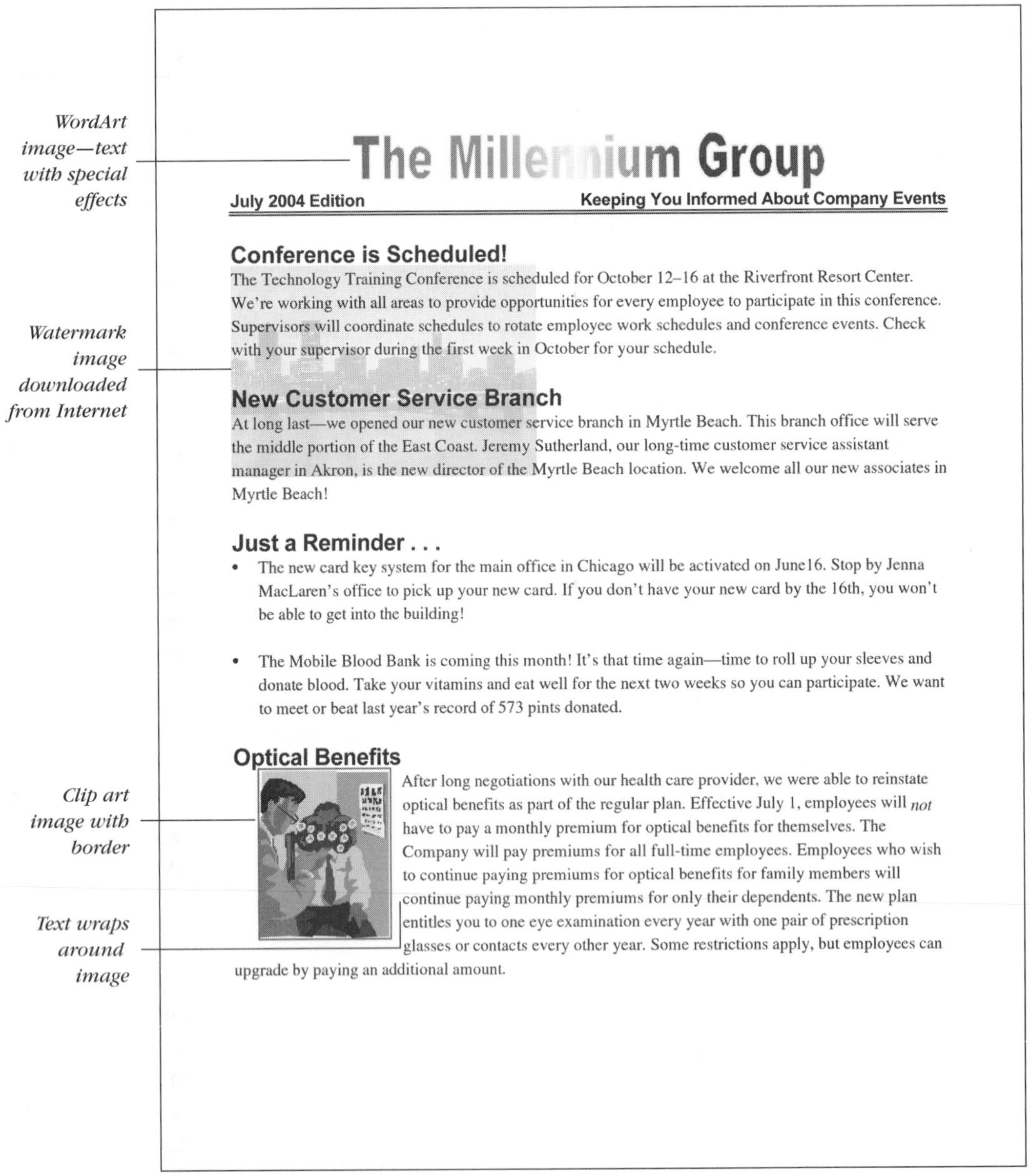

WordArt image—text with special effects

The Millennium Group

July 2004 Edition   **Keeping You Informed About Company Events**

Conference is Scheduled!

The Technology Training Conference is scheduled for October 12–16 at the Riverfront Resort Center. We're working with all areas to provide opportunities for every employee to participate in this conference. Supervisors will coordinate schedules to rotate employee work schedules and conference events. Check with your supervisor during the first week in October for your schedule.

Watermark image downloaded from Internet

New Customer Service Branch

At long last—we opened our new customer service branch in Myrtle Beach. This branch office will serve the middle portion of the East Coast. Jeremy Sutherland, our long-time customer service assistant manager in Akron, is the new director of the Myrtle Beach location. We welcome all our new associates in Myrtle Beach!

Just a Reminder . . .

- The new card key system for the main office in Chicago will be activated on June16. Stop by Jenna MacLaren's office to pick up your new card. If you don't have your new card by the 16th, you won't be able to get into the building!

- The Mobile Blood Bank is coming this month! It's that time again—time to roll up your sleeves and donate blood. Take your vitamins and eat well for the next two weeks so you can participate. We want to meet or beat last year's record of 573 pints donated.

Optical Benefits

Clip art image with border

After long negotiations with our health care provider, we were able to reinstate optical benefits as part of the regular plan. Effective July 1, employees will *not* have to pay a monthly premium for optical benefits for themselves. The Company will pay premiums for all full-time employees. Employees who wish to continue paying premiums for optical benefits for family members will continue paying monthly premiums for only their dependents. The new plan entitles you to one eye examination every year with one pair of prescription glasses or contacts every other year. Some restrictions apply, but employees can

Text wraps around image

upgrade by paying an additional amount.

Figure 8.1

Lesson 1: Inserting an Image

Office XP comes with an enormous number of clip art images. You can find images representing people, animals, special occasions, and more! Depending on how Office XP was installed on your computer, you may have just a few or all of these images. You can also obtain clip art from the Microsoft Design Gallery Live, Microsoft's online clip gallery, or you can purchase clip art packages at a computer supply store.

Be sure to read about the legal uses of clip art images, whether you're using Microsoft's clip art or other clip art you purchased. Although clip art is often acceptable for education or non-profit use, it may not be legal to use in some advertising situations.

In this lesson, you insert clip art in a company newsletter by using the ***Insert Clip Art task pane***, a window pane in which you search for and select clip art, photographs, movies, and sounds.

To Insert an Image

❶ Open *ew1-0801*, and save it as `July Newsletter-WB8L`.

❷ Press Ctrl+End **to position the insertion point at the end of the document.**
You want to insert an image after the last paragraph.

❸ Choose Insert, Picture, Clip Art.

If you have problems...
If you see the Add Clips to Organizer dialog box, click the Later button to see the Insert Clip Art task pane.

The Insert Clip Art task pane appears so that you can search for clip art and other media (see Figure 8.2).

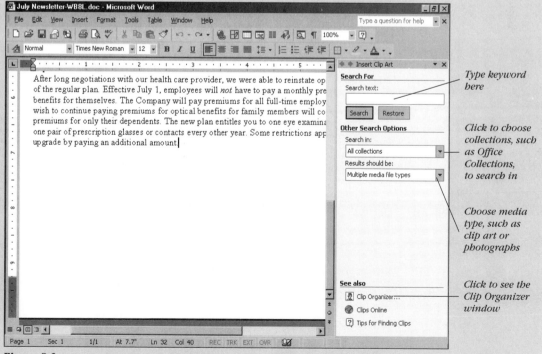

Figure 8.2

(Continues)

To Insert an Image (Continued)

You want to select an image that depicts an optometrist. To display clips, you type a **keyword**, a word or phrase that describes the type of clip you're looking for. You can type very specific keywords, such as `optometrist`, or general keywords, such as `medicines`.

4 Type `medicine` in the *Search text* box.
The keyword *medicine* provides more results than *optometrist*.

5 Click the *Search in* drop-down arrow, select *Office Collections*, deselect the other options, and then click the drop-down arrow to close the menu.
The Office Collection refers to the clips that are stored on your computer when you installed the software. Although you could leave all options selected, doing so would slow down the search process.

6 Click the *Results should be* drop-down arrow, and deselect all check boxes except *Clip Art*, which should be selected, and then click the drop-down arrow to close the *Results should be* list.
You should check the media types you want to find to expedite the search process.

7 Click the Search button in the task pane.
Word searches through the clips to find ones that contain the keyword you typed for the media you selected (see Figure 8.3).

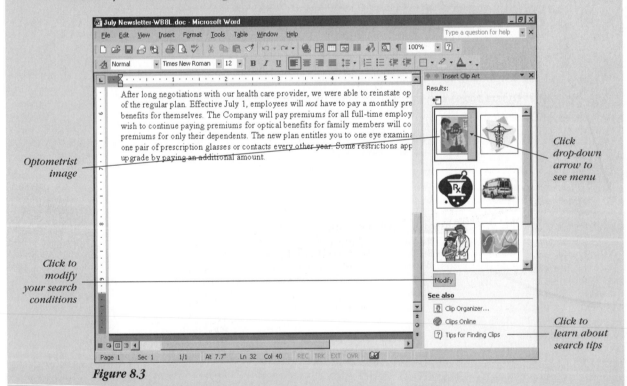

Figure 8.3

8 Position the mouse pointer on the optometrist image and then click the down-pointing arrow to the right of the image.
A menu of options appears (see Figure 8.4).

To Insert an Image

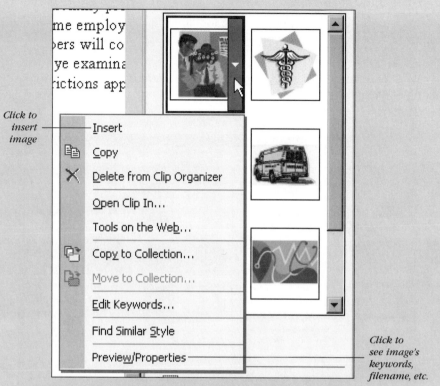

Click to insert image

Click to see image's keywords, filename, etc.

Figure 8.4

9 Click Insert from the menu and then click the task pane's Close button.
Word inserts the image at the insertion point location, causing the last line of the paragraph to align with the bottom of the image (see Figure 8.5).

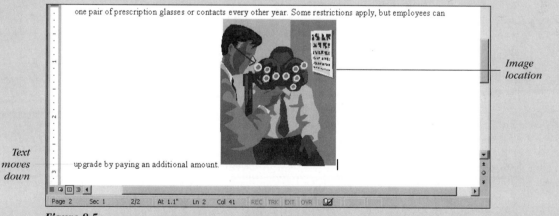

Image location

Text moves down

Figure 8.5

10 Save the document, and keep it onscreen to continue with the next lesson.

To extend your knowledge...

Using the Clip Organizer

Instead of entering keywords and searching for clips, you can display the **Clip Organizer**, which is a gallery of clips organized on your hard drive with access to download and organize clips from Microsoft's Web site.

To use the Clip Organizer, click *Clip Organizer* at the bottom of the Insert Clip Art task pane. Within the Clip Organizer window, click *Office Collections*, and click a category such as *Business*. Figure 8.6 shows a sample palette of clip art you can choose from.

Figure 8.6

Using Other Images

You can insert almost any type of image by choosing Insert, Picture, From File. Some image file types you can use include Joint Photographic Experts Group (.jpg), Windows Bitmap (.bmp), Graphics Interchange Format (.gif), and Windows Metafile (.wmf). Word can insert these types of files without any special conversion.

If you want to insert other types of graphics files, such as a WordPerfect (.wpg) graphics image, you must install the graphics filters from the installation CD first.

Scanning a Picture

If you have a scanner attached to your computer, you can scan a picture to use as an image within Word. Choose Insert, Picture, From Scanner or Camera. Type `insert picture` in the Answer Wizard section of the Help window and then click *Insert a picture directly from a scanner or digital camera* for more information about inserting an image into your document by using a scanner.

Lesson 2: Moving and Deleting an Image

After inserting an image, you might want to move it around on the page until you are satisfied with its location. If you want to move an image to another area that you currently see onscreen, you can click and drag the image there.

In this lesson, you move the image below the *Optical Benefits* heading, and position it at the left margin.

To Move an Image

❶ In the *July Newsletter-WB8L* document, click the Normal View button.
Because you want to drag the image from the second to the first page, you need to display the document in Normal view.

❷ Click the image to select it.
When you click an image, the Picture toolbar appears. Word displays *sizing handles*—little black boxes that appear around the image so you can adjust the image's size and move it elsewhere (see Figure 8.7).

Picture toolbar

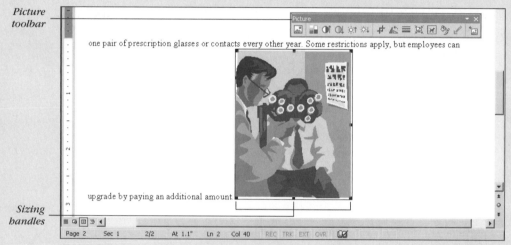

Sizing handles

Figure 8.7

? If you have problems...
If you don't see the Picture toolbar, choose <u>V</u>iew, <u>T</u>oolbars, Picture to display the Picture toolbar.

❸ Click the scroll up button about six times to see the last heading and paragraph on page 1.
You can see the beginning of the paragraph without the bottom and top margin space in Normal view. Without the margin space, it is easier for you to click and drag the image to the correct place.

❹ Click and drag the image to the beginning of the paragraph immediately below *Optical Benefits.*
A shadow cursor follows your mouse pointer, letting you know where the image will appear when you release the mouse button.

? If you have problems...
If you can't see the part of the document to which you want to move the image, do *not* click and drag. Doing so might cause your screen to scroll so quickly through the document that you won't be able to stop at the place you want to drop the image.

Instead, click the image and then click the Cut button. Position the insertion point where you want the image to appear and click the Paste button. The cutting and pasting process is easier than clicking and dragging the image from page to page.

(Continues)

To Move an Image (Continued)

The image appears at the beginning of the paragraph, as shown in Figure 8.8.

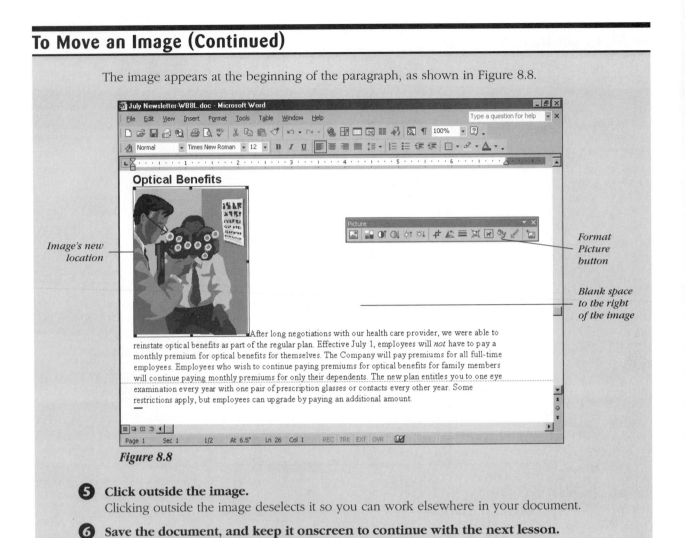

Figure 8.8

⑤ **Click outside the image.**
Clicking outside the image deselects it so you can work elsewhere in your document.

⑥ **Save the document, and keep it onscreen to continue with the next lesson.**

To extend your knowledge...

Deleting an Image

If you want to delete an image, click it to select it. Then, press Del.

Lesson 3: Sizing an Image

When you insert an image in a document, it comes in at a predetermined size. Most of the time, you need to adjust the image's size so it fits better within the document.

In this lesson, you decide on a specific size for the image. You want it to be 1.6″ tall and 1.29″ wide. To set a specific size, you need to access the Format Picture dialog box.

To Change the Image's Size

❶ In the *July Newsletter-WB8L* document, click the image to select it.
The Picture toolbar should appear. If it doesn't, right-click the Standard toolbar, and choose Picture.

❷ Click the Format Picture button on the Picture toolbar.
The Format Picture dialog box appears. You use this dialog box to select the format settings for your images.

❸ Click the Size tab.
You see the options for setting the size of your image, as shown in Figure 8.9.

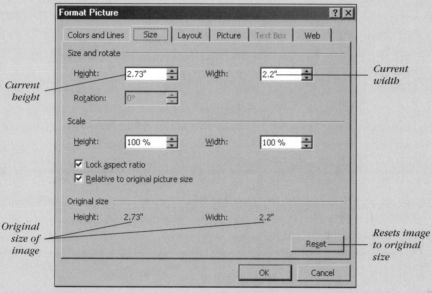

Figure 8.9

❹ Highlight 2.73″ in the *Height* box.

❺ Type 1.6 and click OK.
You don't need to set the width because it automatically adjusts when you click OK to maintain a proportionate size. Figure 8.10 shows the smaller image.

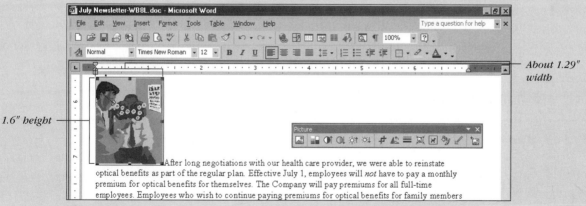

Figure 8.10

❻ Click outside the image, save the document, and keep it onscreen to continue with the next lesson.

To extend your knowledge...

Using the Sizing Handles

If you don't need an exact size, you can click and drag the sizing handles to adjust the image's size. Table 8.1 describes how to use the sizing handles.

Table 8.1 Adjusting the Image's Size with the Sizing Handles	
Desired Result	**Do This:**
Increase the width	Click and drag either the middle-left or middle-right sizing handle away from the image.
Decrease the width	Click and drag either the middle-left or middle-right sizing handle toward the image.
Increase the height	Click and drag the upper-middle or bottom-middle sizing handle away from the image.
Decrease the height	Click and drag the upper-middle or bottom-middle sizing handle toward the image.
Adjust the height and width at the same time	Click and drag a corner sizing handle at an angle to adjust the height and width. Hold down (⬆Shift) to maintain the image's proportions.

Displaying the Format Picture Dialog Box

You can also double-click an image or right-click an image and choose Format Picture to display the Format Picture dialog box.

Lesson 4: Wrapping Text Around an Image

When you first insert an image, Word treats it as a character on the line of text; therefore, the text line allows a lot of empty space on the left or right side of the image. You probably want to allow text to wrap differently. **Wrapping style** refers to the way text wraps around an image. You can have text appear on top of or behind an image, wrap tightly around the outer edges of the image itself, or wrap above or below the image.

In this lesson, you choose a square wrap style to let the paragraph wrap on the right side of the image.

To Wrap Text Around an Image

❶ In the *July Newsletter-WB8L* document, click the image to select it.

❷ Click the Text Wrapping button on the Picture toolbar.
A list of text-wrapping options appears (see Figure 8.11).

To Wrap Text Around an Image

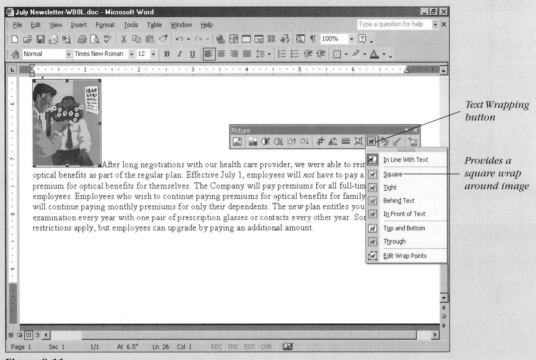

Figure 8.11

❸ **Choose Square from the menu.**
Text now wraps square around the right side of the image (see Figure 8.12).

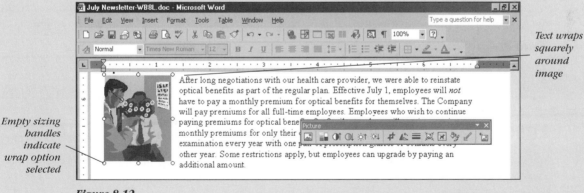

Figure 8.12

❹ **Deselect the image, save the document, and keep it onscreen to continue with the next lesson.**

To extend your knowledge...

Selecting Wrap Style and Alignment

You can display the Format Picture dialog box and then click the Layout tab to select a wrapping style, the image's horizontal alignment, or advanced options (see Figure 8.13).

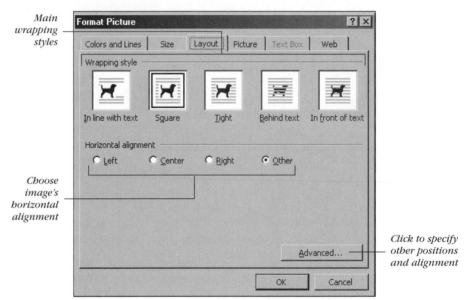

Main wrapping styles

Choose image's horizontal alignment

Click to specify other positions and alignment

Figure 8.13

The Horizontal alignment options are available for any wrapping style except *In line with text*.

Top and Bottom Wrap

If you want to place an image between paragraphs without text wrapping on either the left or right sides, you need to choose *Top and Bottom* as the wrap option. You can choose this option by clicking the Text Wrapping button on the Picture toolbar or by clicking the Advanced button within the Layout tab of the Format Picture dialog box.

Tight Wrap

The **tight wrap** option wraps text around the edge of the image itself—contouring around the image—instead of the square boundary of the image.

Lesson 5: Applying Borders and Fills

You can apply a *border* or *fill* to an image. A border is a line style that creates a frame around an object. **Fill** refers to a shading color that appears in the background of a text box or around the image within its square boundaries.

In this lesson, you apply a border around the optometrist image in your newsletter.

To Apply a Border

❶ In the *July Newsletter-WB8L* document, click the optometrist image.

❷ Click the Format Picture button on the Picture toolbar.
The Format Picture dialog box appears.

❸ Click the Colors and Lines tab in the dialog box.
You see options for selecting border lines and fill colors (see Figure 8.14).

To Apply a Border

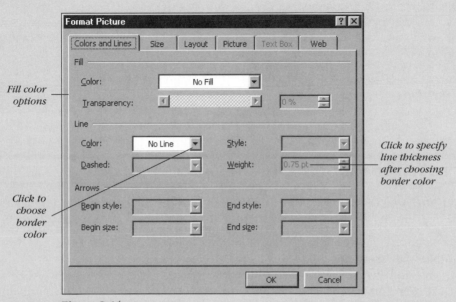

Fill color options — Fill

Click to choose border color — Line

Click to specify line thickness after choosing border color

Figure 8.14

4 **Click the Teal color, the fifth color on the second row.**
You see a ScreenTip that displays the color, such as *Teal*, when you position the mouse pointer over a color.

5 **Click the Weight spin button to display *1.25 pt*.**
Choosing 1.25 pt provides a thicker border line.

6 **Click OK and then deselect the image.**
The image is enclosed in a 1.25 pt Teal-colored border (see Figure 8.15).

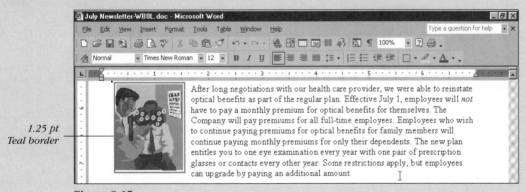

1.25 pt Teal border

Figure 8.15

7 **Save the document, and keep it onscreen to continue with the next lesson.**

To extend your knowledge...

Using the Line Style Button

You can apply a border line by clicking the Line Style button on the Picture toolbar. When you click this button, you see a list of point sizes that indicates the thickness of the line. Word applies a black line around the image.

Lesson 6: Copying Images with the Clip Organizer

Microsoft provides additional clips on its Web site—Microsoft Design Gallery Live. The Web site contains several thousand clips to choose from. From within the Clip Organizer, you can view online clips or link to the Web site, download images to the Clip Organizer, and then insert the images in your documents.

In this lesson, you look at the Web Collections clips—clips found on Microsoft's Web site—and then copy a clip art image to your computer.

To Copy an Image with the Clip Organizer

1 **In the *July Newsletter-WB8L* document, position the insertion point at the beginning of the first paragraph after the *Conference is Scheduled!* heading.**
This is the location where you eventually insert a downloaded clip.

2 **Make sure you have a live connection to the Internet.**
If you are using a computer with a direct Internet connection, you can continue with the next step. If you are using a home computer, you need to connect to your Internet Service Provider (ISP), such as America Online, before continuing to the next step.

3 **Choose Insert, Picture, Clip Art to display the Insert Clip Art task pane.**

If you have problems...
Although the task pane contains the *Clips Online* option, do not use it. You must have the Clip Organizer window open in order to download to it.

4 **Click *Clip Organizer* at the bottom of the task pane and then click its Maximize button.**
The Clip Organizer dialog box appears. You can organize clips, choose from the Office Collections clips that are stored on your computer, or choose Web Collections to see online clips.

5 **Double-click *Web Collections* in the Collection List, and then double-click *Design Gallery Live.***
You see a list of categories, similar to the categories shown in Figure 8.6 at the end of Lesson 1.

6 **Scroll through the list and click *Office.***
You see office clips that are in the Microsoft Design Gallery Live Web site (see Figure 8.16).

To Copy an Image with the Clip Organizer

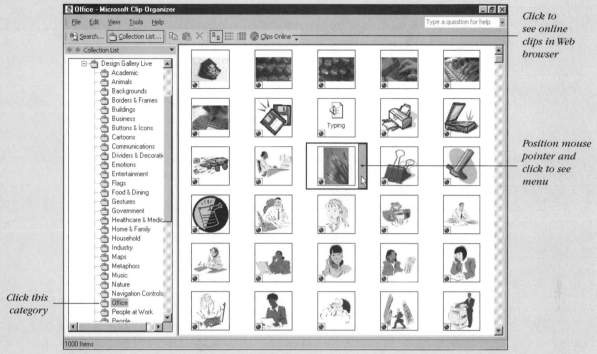

Click to see online clips in Web browser

Position mouse pointer and click to see menu

Click this category

Figure 8.16

If you have problems...

Depending on your Internet connection, you might see icons instead of the actual images. If this happens, read the rest of this exercise without completing the steps. You can study the steps and figures to see what happens when you have a higher-speed Internet connection.

7 **Position the mouse pointer on the photograph clip of pencils, and click the drop-down arrow.**

A menu appears so that you can choose what to do. For example, you can copy the image to the Clipboard and then click the Paste button in the document window to paste the clip there.

8 **Click *Copy to Collection*, choose Favorites, and then click OK.**

Choosing *Copy to Collection* displays a dialog box so that you can copy the image from the online Web site to your hard drive. This gives you access to the clip without being connected to the Internet.

9 **Scroll up through the Collection List, and click *Favorites*.**

You see the image stored in this location within the Clip Organizer. Next time you need this image, you don't have to have a live Internet connection; you can simply select it from your Favorites list.

10 **Keep the document and Clip Organizer window open to continue with the next lesson.**

Lesson 7: Downloading and Inserting an Online Clip

If your computer can't load the images in the Web Collections category of the Clip Organizer, you need to click the *Clips Online* button to actually go to the Design Gallery Live Web site, search for images, and download them.

In the next exercise, you go to the Microsoft Design Gallery Live and download a photo of a city to the Clip Organizer.

To Download an Image from the Web Site

1 **Click the Clips Online button at the top of the Clip Organizer window.**
Your Internet browser window opens. If you see the End-User License Agreement, read it to learn about acceptable uses of the clips, and then click the Accept button.

 If you have problems...
If you use another browser instead of Internet Explorer, the images might not download correctly. Make sure that Internet Explorer is the default browser.

The Microsoft Design Gallery Live Web page appears (see Figure 8.17).

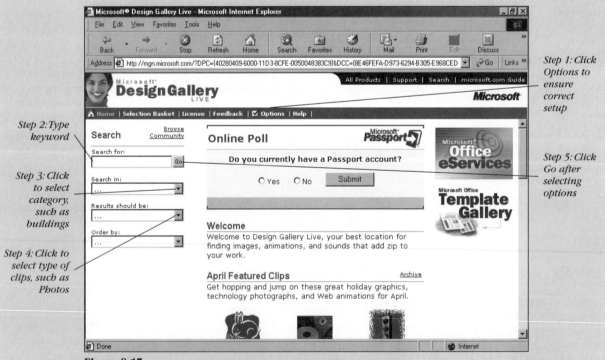

Figure 8.17

Web pages constantly change; therefore, the gallery might look different from the figures shown in this book.

To Download an Image from the Web Site

Before searching for a photograph of a city, you need to ensure that the correction option is selected in order to download correctly.

2   **Click the *Options* link in the top middle section of the Web page.**
You need to specify the appropriate file type to download.

3   **Scroll down to see *Specify preferred file type to download* options, click the *MPF (Media Package File)* option, and then click the *Update* button.**
The MPF option is required to download to Office XP applications, such as Word 2002.

4   **Type `cities` in the *Search for* text box.**
You want to find images of cities.

5   **Click the *Search in* drop-down arrow, and choose *Buildings*.**

6   **Click the *Results should be* drop-down arrow, and choose *Photos*.**

7   **Click the Go button to the right of the *Search for* box.**
You should see photos of cities.

8   **Click the photo of the city with the waterfront and orange skyline background.**
The image appears in a separate preview window, along with keywords formatted as hypertext links that display another Web page of images when clicked (see Figure 8.18).

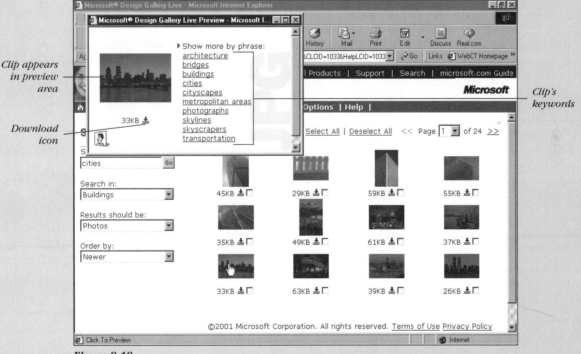

Clip appears in preview area

Download icon

Clip's keywords

Figure 8.18

9   **Click the download icon to download the image.**
The picture is downloaded into the Clip Organizer (see Figure 8.19).

(Continues)

To Download an Image from the Web Site (Continued)

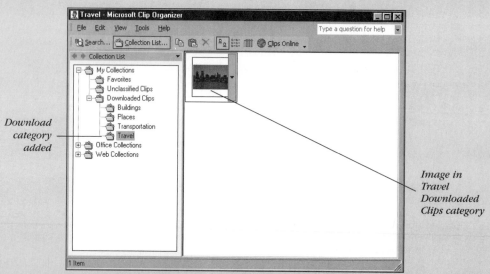

Download category added

Image in Travel Downloaded Clips category

Figure 8.19

 ### If you have problems...

If the image does not download to your Clip Organizer, save it as an image. Right-click the preview image in your Web browser; choose Save Picture As; choose a storage location, filename, and file type—such as gif or bmp; and then click the Save button. You can then choose Insert, Picture, From File to insert the image file.

🔟 **Keep the Clip Organizer onscreen to continue with the next exercise.**

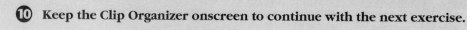

 ### To extend your knowledge...

Searching for Online Clips from the Insert Clip Art Task Pane

Instead of clicking the Clips Online button and searching for clips, you can use the Insert Clip Art task pane to search for online clips from the Microsoft Design Gallery Live. To do this, type your keyword in the *Search text* box; click the *Search in* drop-down arrow, and choose only *Web Collections*; click the *Results should be* drop-down arrow, and choose the type of clip you want; and click the Search button.

You are ready to insert the downloaded photograph into your document.

To Insert the Downloaded Image

❶ **Make sure you can see the image in the *Travel Downloaded Clips* category in the Collection List.**

 ### If you have problems...

If you saved the image instead of downloading it in the last exercise, close the Clip Organizer. Choose Insert, Picture, From File; locate the gif or bmp

To Insert the Downloaded Image

image you saved; and click Insert. The image is inserted in your document. Save the document and skip the rest of the steps in this exercise.

2 **Click the drop-down arrow for the city photograph you downloaded and then choose Copy.**
The drop-down arrow in the Clip Organizer does not have an Insert option, so you must copy the image and then paste it into the document.

3 **Click the Minimize button to minimize the Clip Organizer and then close the Insert Clip Art task pane.**

4 **Click the Paste button on the Formatting toolbar.**
The image is pasted at the insertion point's location (see Figure 8.20).

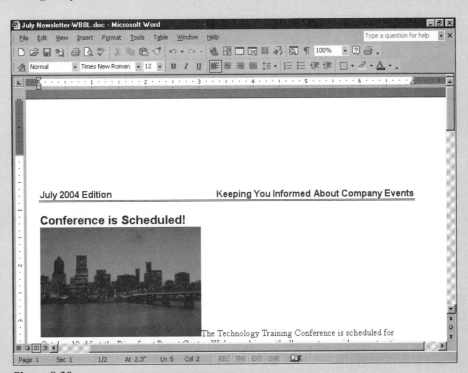

Figure 8.20

5 **Save the document, and keep it onscreen to continue with the next lesson.**

Lesson 8: Creating a Watermark

A *watermark* is a "washed-out" graphic object or text that typically appears behind text. People use watermarks as an imprint for a logo that helps people to remember and identify a company's image. You can also use watermarks as visual effects for creative documents, such as fliers, brochures, and newsletters.

In this lesson, you format the photograph as a watermark.

To Create a Watermark from an Image

1 In the *July Newsletter-WB8L* document, click the photograph to select it.

2 Click the Color button on the Picture toolbar.
A list of color options appears.

3 Choose <u>W</u>ashout.
The image appears washed-out, which is how watermarks appear.

4 Click the Text Wrapping button and choose Behin<u>d</u> Text.
Figure 8.21 shows the watermark image behind the text.

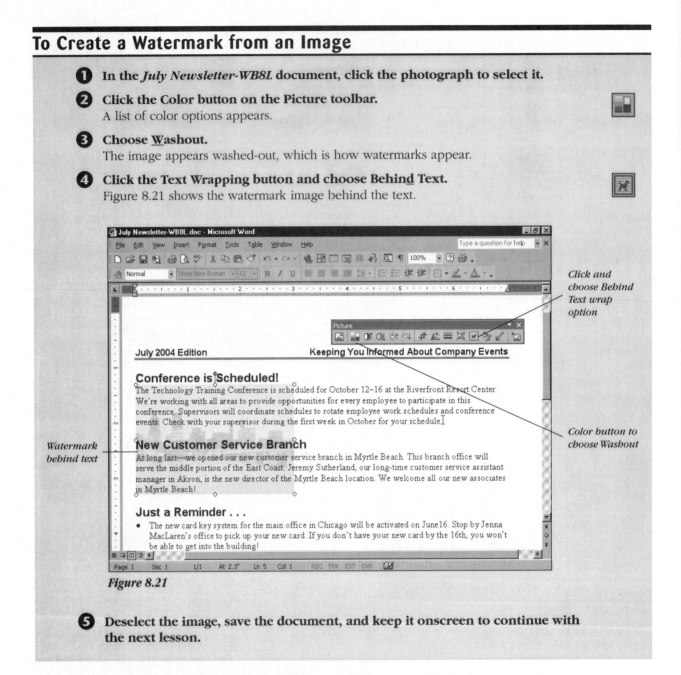

Figure 8.21

5 Deselect the image, save the document, and keep it onscreen to continue with the next lesson.

To extend your knowledge…

Creating a Watermark in a Header

You can create a watermark within a header. After displaying the header window, insert the image and set a larger width—typically one that spans the image from the left to the right margins. Click the Color button, and choose <u>W</u>ashout. Click the Text Wrapping button, and choose Behin<u>d</u> Text. Adjust the contrast using the buttons on the Picture toolbar.

Lesson 9: Creating WordArt

Another exciting graphic feature is WordArt. *WordArt* shapes text into designs for you. You can use WordArt to create unique banners and titles for fliers, brochures, and other advertising documents. Because WordArt is a graphic object, you can use similar options to those you used to customize your clip art.

In this lesson, you create a WordArt object for the title of your newsletter.

To Create WordArt

1 In the *July Newsletter-WB8L* document, position the insertion point at the top of the document.

2 Choose **I**nsert, **P**icture, **W**ordArt.
The WordArt Gallery dialog box appears so that you can select a WordArt style (see Figure 8.22).

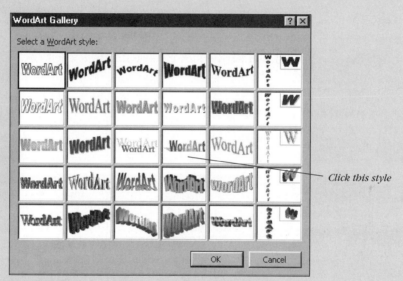

Figure 8.22

3 Click the fourth style on the third row and then click OK.
The Edit WordArt Text dialog box appears, so that you can enter text and select the font and font size (see Figure 8.23).

(Continues)

To Create WordArt (Continued)

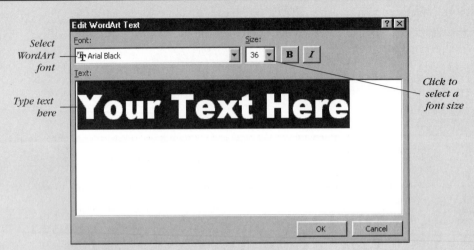

Select WordArt font

Type text here

Click to select a font size

Figure 8.23

④ **Type** The Millennium Group **in the text area.**
You need to choose a smaller font size for your title.

⑤ **Click the Size drop-down arrow and choose 28; then click OK.**
The WordArt appears where you positioned the insertion point prior to creating the WordArt.

⑥ **Click the WordArt.**
The WordArt is selected, and the WordArt toolbar appears so that you can customize it (see Figure 8.24).

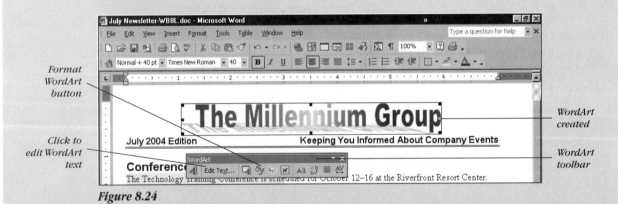

Format WordArt button

Click to edit WordArt text

WordArt created

WordArt toolbar

Figure 8.24

⑦ **Deselect the WordArt object, save the document, print it, and then close the document.**

To extend your knowledge...

Customizing WordArt

If you need to edit your WordArt object later, double-click the WordArt object to change the text, font, or font size.

Use the WordArt toolbar to customize the WordArt's appearance. For example, you can rotate the object, select a different style from the gallery, or choose a different shape. Table 8.2 lists the functions of different WordArt toolbar buttons.

Table 8.2 WordArt Buttons

Button	Button Name	Description
	Insert WordArt	Displays the WordArt Gallery dialog box, so you can choose a style and then type WordArt text.
Edit Text...	Edit Text	Displays dialog box to edit text, font, and font size.
	WordArt Gallery	Displays Gallery to choose a different style.
	Format WordArt	Displays the Format WordArt dialog box to change size, layout, and so on.
	WordArt Shape	Displays palette of various shapes for WordArt.
	Text Wrapping	Displays list of text-wrapping options, such as Top and Bottom.
	WordArt Same Letter Heights	Adjusts WordArt letters so they are the same height.
	WordArt Vertical Text	Changes WordArt to a vertical object.
	WordArt Alignment	Displays palette of alignment options, such as Stretch Justify.
	WordArt Character Spacing	Lets you adjust spacing between characters.

Summary

You should be able to create exciting graphics in your documents now. You can insert clip art and images from the Insert Clip Art task pane, Clip Organizer, or Microsoft Design Gallery Live. After inserting an image, you can change the image's size and location, apply a border, and adjust the way text wraps around the image. Finally, you learned how to create watermarks and design exciting WordArt objects to make headings and banners.

Although much information about graphics is included here, Word provides many more choices for customizing pictures, watermarks, and WordArt. You can learn a lot by exploring the different options on the toolbars and by using onscreen Help.

Checking Concepts and Terms

Multiple Choice

Circle the letter of the correct answer for each of the following.

1. All of the following are graphic image types except _____. [L1]

   a. .jpg
   b. .gif
   c. .doc
   d. .bmp

2. You can use the sizing handles to do all of the following except _____. [L2–4]

   a. adjust the image's width
   b. move the image to a different location
   c. increase the height of the image
   d. adjust the text-wrapping around the image

3. Which wrap option contours text around an image in your document? [L4]

   a. Square
   b. Tight
   c. Top to Bottom
   d. Through

4. What two options should you select to format an image as a watermark? [L8]

   a. Tight wrap and WordArt Gallery
   b. Through wrap and fill color
   c. Washout and Behind Text wrap
   d. More Brightness and Square wrap

5. What term refers to interesting, colorful shapes for text? [L9]

   a. WordArt
   b. Microsoft Design Gallery Live
   c. watermark
   d. clip art

Discussion

1. Look through several magazines, newsletters, and brochures. Evaluate the use of clip art. Notice which types of clip art or images are used, how are they placed, and so on. [L1–9]

2. Review the license agreements for different clip art programs. What are some commonalities? [L1]

3. Create a variety of WordArt images, and print them on a color printer and a black-and-white printer. What warnings or suggestions do you have about using various WordArt images? [L9]

Skill Drill exercises reinforce project skills. Each skill reinforced is the same, or nearly the same, as a skill presented in the project. Detailed instructions are provided in a step-by-step format.

1. Inserting and Sizing a Bitmap Image

The local Parent Educator Association (PEA) has asked you to create this month's newsletter about school activities for parents. You have been given the basic text, but you decide that graphic elements will enhance the newsletter's appearance and encourage parents to read it.

1. Open *ew1-0802*, and save it as **PEA Newsletter-WB8SD**.
2. With the insertion point aligned at the right at the beginning of the document, choose Insert, Picture, From File.
3. Choose the drive and folder that contains files for this project, click *PEA.bmp*, and click the Insert button.
4. Click the image to display the sizing handles.
5. Click the Format Picture button on the Picture toolbar.
6. Click the Size tab.
7. Select the current *Height* setting, type **1.5**, and click OK.
8. Deselect the image.
9. Save the document, and keep it onscreen to continue with the next exercise.

2. Inserting an Image from the Clip Organizer

You want to insert clip art by the *New School Buses* section of the newsletter. The Clip Organizer contains an image of a school bus in the Transportation section of the Office Collections category.

1. In the open *PEA Newsletter-WB8SD* document, position the insertion point at the beginning of the *New School Buses* heading.
2. Choose Insert, Picture, Clip Art.
3. Click the *Clip Organizer* link at the bottom of the Insert Clip Art task pane.
4. Double-click *Office Collections* in the Collection List, double-click the *Transportation* category, and double-click the *Land* category.
5. Click the drop-down arrow for the school bus image, and choose Copy.
6. Minimize the Clip Organizer.
7. Click the Paste button on the Formatting toolbar to paste the image.
   If text is pasted instead of the image, click the Undo button, display the Office Clipboard, and click the clip art object in the Office Clipboard task pane to paste it in the document.
8. Deselect the image and close the Clip Organizer.
9. Save the document, and keep it onscreen to continue with the next exercise.

3. Adjusting the Size, Wrap, and Border Options

After inserting the image, you need to reduce its size and select a text-wrapping option for it. You want the text to wrap on the right side of the image.

1. In the *PEA Newsletter-WB8SD* document, click the school bus image to select it.
2. Click the Format Picture button on the Picture toolbar.
3. Click the Size tab.
4. Select the width, type **1″**, and click OK.

5. Click the Text Wrapping button on the Picture toolbar, and choose <u>S</u>quare.

6. Click the Format Picture button.

7. Click the Colors and Lines tab.

8. Click the *Line C<u>o</u>lor* drop-down arrow, and choose Gold.

9. Click the *Weight* spin button to display *1.5 pt*, and then click OK.

10. Deselect the image, save the document, and keep it onscreen to continue with the next exercise.

4. Creating a WordArt Banner

The newsletter needs a title or banner. Instead of typing the banner in a larger font size, you decide to create a WordArt banner for a better visual effect.

1. In the open *PEA Newsletter-WB8L* document, position the insertion point at the top of the document.

2. Choose <u>I</u>nsert, <u>P</u>icture, <u>W</u>ordArt.

3. Click the third style on the third row, and click OK.

4. Type `Maple Elementary` in the <u>T</u>ext area.

5. Make sure that the font is Times New Roman.

6. Click the <u>S</u>ize drop-down arrow, choose 40, and click OK.

7. Click the WordArt to select it.

8. Click the Text Wrapping button on the WordArt toolbar, and choose <u>S</u>quare.

9. Drag the WordArt to the left of the triangle image you inserted in the first exercise. The top of the uppercase letters in the WordArt should align with the top of the triangle.

10. Deselect the WordArt.

11. Save, print, and close the document.

Challenge exercises expand on or are somewhat related to skills presented in the lessons. Each exercise provides a brief narrative introduction, followed by instructions in a numbered-step format that are not as detailed as those in the Skill Drill section.

1. Creating an Announcement for Pictures with Santa

The management at the local mall will have a picture day with Santa. You have been asked to create a flier with two pages per sheet with the announcement.

1. Open *ew1-0803*, and save it as `Santa Photo-WB8CH1`.

2. Delete the asterisk, and keep the insertion point there.

3. Display the Insert Clip Art task pane, and search for holiday clip art in the Office Collections.

4. Insert the Santa clip art.

5. Apply the I<u>n</u> Front of Text wrap style, and center-align the image.

6. With the image selected, press ⬆ about six times to bring the image higher on the page.

7. Apply the art page border that looks like poinsettias.

8. Choose *2 pages per sheet* as the <u>M</u>ultiple pages option in the Page Setup dialog box.

9. Copy the document, press ⏎Enter below the last line, and paste to get a duplicate announcement on the same sheet of paper.

10. Save, print, and close the document.

2. Creating an Independence Day Announcement with a Watermark

You are in charge of promoting your local town's Independence Day celebration. You decide to create an eye-catching flier you can print and post around town. You want it to have a watermark and appropriate page border.

1. Open *ew1-0804*, and save it as `July 4 Celebration-WB8CH2`.
2. Apply the Fireworks Art border to the page. It is the 28th border option in the A<u>r</u>t border drop-down list.
3. Position your insertion point at the top of the document, and search for clips with these specifications:
   - `Fireworks` keyword
   - Web Collections only
   - Photograph clips
4. Insert a fireworks clip with a black background and a couple of explosions. (The clip is taller than it is wide.)
5. Convert the clip to a watermark with the necessary wrapping option, centered. Set a 9.9″ height and 7.7″ width; deselect the *Lock <u>a</u>spect ratio* option in order to change both the height and width.
6. Save, print, and close the document.

3. Enhancing a Halloween Invitation

You created a Halloween invitation. You want to search the Microsoft Clip Gallery Live to find an appropriate image. In addition, you want to create a title using WordArt.

1. Open *ew1-0805*, and save it as `Halloween Party-WB8CH3`.
2. At the top of the document, create a WordArt image using the third style on the fourth row in the Gallery. Enter `Halloween Party!` as the text in 44-point Comic Sans MS. Select the text-wrapping option that does not allow text on the left and right sides of the image, and then center-align the WordArt.
3. Apply 24-point Comic Sans MS, bold, Orange font color to the last line in the document. With the text still selected, create a 3-point Orange paragraph border with Tan shading.
4. In the blank space below *Let the Good Times Roll*, insert a clip art image from Microsoft's Web site. Access Microsoft's Web site from within the Clip Organizer. Search for clips by using the keyword `jack-o-lantern`. Search through the images to find an image with contains a jack-o-lantern, a ghost, and a tombstone. Download it to your Clip Organizer and then insert it into your invitation. Adjust the size, wrap style, and alignment of the image as needed. Make sure you have a little space above and below the image.
5. Apply a page border using the pumpkin art border. Change the color of the art border to orange.
6. Choose the option to vertically center the page.
7. Save, print, and close the document.

4. Creating an Airline Information Sheet

You work for a small airline service that provides transportation from Oklahoma City to special-attraction vacation spots, such as Las Vegas, Denver, and Salt Lake City. You want to design an attractive information sheet about safety instructions for the passengers.

1. Open *ew1-0806*, and save it as `Airline Information-WB8CH4`.
2. If the current font is unreadable, change the text to Comic Sans MS or Bookman Old Style font.
3. Select the list of rules at the bottom of the document. Use the Bullets and Numbering dialog box to create a customized bulleted list using the Wingdings symbol of an airplane. *Note:* The airplane symbol is on the fourth row of symbols. Change the symbol font color to Blue, but make sure the text remains in Black.

4. Apply a Blue paragraph border around the selected bulleted list. Select Light Yellow shading.

5. Position the insertion point at the beginning of the document, and access the Microsoft Design Gallery Live from within the Clip Organizer.

6. Search for **airplane** photographs in the Transportation category.

7. Preview the clip of the plane with the sun in the background; then download it.

8. Insert the clip at the beginning of the first paragraph. Move it to the right side of the paragraph. Set a 2″ height, Behind Text wrapping style in the Layout section, and a 58% picture Brightness.

9. Create a WordArt banner using the third style in the first column of the Gallery. Type **Sunset Airlines** for the text. Move the WordArt above the first paragraph, apply a Top and Bottom wrap, and center it between the left and right margins.

10. Select Center vertical alignment in the Page Setup dialog box.

11. Save, print, and close the document.

Discovery Zone exercises help you gain advanced knowledge of project topics and/or application of skills. These exercises focus on enhancing your problem-solving skills. Numbered steps are not provided, but you are given hints, reminders, screen shots, and/or references to help you reach your goal for each exercise.

1. Creating a Watermark in a Header

The top administrators at Seatek-Parkway Enterprises paragraph are pleased with your work on the annual report. They have one more request before finalizing the report: They want you to insert a watermark that appears on all pages. Use Help to learn how to use a watermark within a header.

Open *ew1-0807*, and save it as **Annual Report-WB8DZ1**. From the Insert Clip Art task pane, search the Web Collections to find clip art images of **profits**. After you find a bar chart that depicts increasing profits, select it, and insert it. Convert the image to a watermark, and apply all necessary image formats to make the watermark look correct, including an approximate 1.15″ absolute vertical position and 90% contrast. Make sure that the watermark appears on all document pages.

Create a footer that displays the page number in the center.

Save, print, and close the document.

2. Inserting Scanned Images in a Flier

You were assigned to create a flier for a Hawaiian Touring Agency. The company has sent you three scanned photographs from the island of Kauai for you to include in the flier. Open *ew1—0808*, and save it as **Hawaiian Paradise-WB8DZ2**.

Insert a WordArt image that displays the text **Escape to Paradise: Island of Kauai**, using the fifth row in the fifth column of the gallery. Display the Drawing toolbar, and use Help to learn how to remove the 3-D style. Center the WordArt above the first paragraph, and set a 0.44″ WordArt height.

Insert Hawaii1.jpg, Hawaii2.jpg, and Hawaii3.jpg from the location of your data files for this project. Apply a Square wrap for the three images. Use Help to learn how to overlap the images with the Order option. Use the Click and Type method to insert the descriptions of the photos.

Apply paragraph formatting and WordArt formatting—use WordArt help if needed for the last two— as indicated in Figure 8.25.

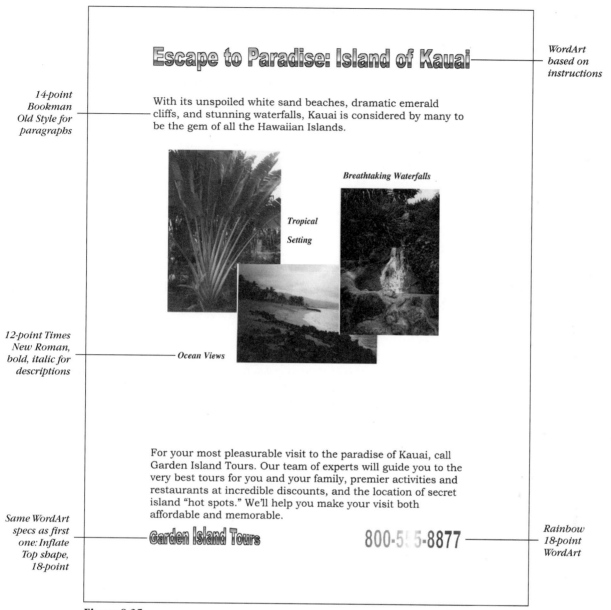

14-point Bookman Old Style for paragraphs

WordArt based on instructions

12-point Times New Roman, bold, italic for descriptions

Same WordArt specs as first one: Inflate Top shape, 18-point

Rainbow 18-point WordArt

Figure 8.25

The phone number in the WordArt is **800-555-8877**, and the other WordArt is `Garden Island Tours`. Save, print, and close the document.

Overview of Windows

APPENDIX

Objectives

In this appendix, you learn how to

- ✔ Start Windows and Use the Mouse
- ✔ Use the Start Button and the Taskbar
- ✔ Work with a Window
- ✔ Manage Folders Using Windows Explorer
- ✔ Manage Files Using Windows Explorer
- ✔ Use the Windows Help System
- ✔ Shut Down Your Computer

Key terms in this appendix include

- ❑ desktop
- ❑ dialog box
- ❑ file
- ❑ filename
- ❑ file extension
- ❑ folder
- ❑ format (a disk)
- ❑ graphical user interface (GUI)
- ❑ horizontal scrollbar
- ❑ icon
- ❑ maximize
- ❑ menu bar
- ❑ message box
- ❑ minimize
- ❑ mouse pointer
- ❑ operating system

- ❑ restore
- ❑ scrollbox
- ❑ shortcut menu
- ❑ Start button
- ❑ status bar
- ❑ subfolder
- ❑ submenu
- ❑ taskbar (Windows)
- ❑ title bar
- ❑ toolbar
- ❑ vertical scrollbar
- ❑ window
- ❑ Windows
- ❑ Windows Explorer
- ❑ windows, cascading
- ❑ windows, tiled
- ❑ WordPad

Why Would I Do This?

An *operating system* is a computer program that manages all the computer's resources and sets priorities for programs running at the same time. A computer cannot run without an operating system. The basic tasks performed by the operating system include recognizing input, sending output to the screen or a printer, keeping track of stored documents, and providing security. When you turn on your computer, it automatically loads the operating system into its memory and turns control of the computer over to the operating system.

The term *Windows* refers to a group of operating systems developed for personal computers by Microsoft. Microsoft Office XP works with Windows 95, Windows 98, Windows NT, Windows 2000, Windows 2000 Professional, and Windows ME. Windows is an example of a *graphical user interface (GUI)*, a program interface that incorporates graphics to make the program easier to use.

The version of Windows you are using does not make a difference in the way an Office XP application (such as the Excel spreadsheet program) works. The version does influence the look of your screen for some of the topics that are covered in this appendix. For example, the Help topics vary in the newer Windows versions, as does the layout of the Help window. A *window* is an enclosed, rectangular area onscreen that enables you to see the output from a program. In this appendix, the instructions and figures are based on Windows 2000 Professional.

To use Microsoft Office XP applications effectively, you should have a basic familiarity with the Microsoft Windows operating system. Suggested skills include opening a program and switching among open programs; opening, closing, moving, and resizing windows; creating folders; moving, copying, and deleting files and folders; and using the Windows onscreen Help system. A *file* is a collection of data stored on disk that has a name, called the *filename*. A *folder* is an object that can contain multiple files. Folders are used to organize files.

Visual Summary

In this appendix, you first become familiar with the Windows desktop. The *desktop* consists of icons, a taskbar, and a Start button (see Figure A.1 for an example of a Windows desktop). It provides a quick means to open and close programs, and to control the components of your computer system.

An *icon* is a small picture that represents an object or program. Double-clicking a program icon starts the program. Right-clicking an icon displays a menu of options related to the icon. The *taskbar (Windows)* displays, in button form, the names of the files and programs currently in use. The taskbar can also include icons, such as the picture of a printer in the lower-right corner of Figure A.1, which provide a shortcut to printer control. The *Start button* provides a menu approach to opening and closing programs, managing files and folders, getting onscreen Help about Windows, and controlling system components. The *mouse pointer* is a small arrow on the display screen that moves as you move the mouse.

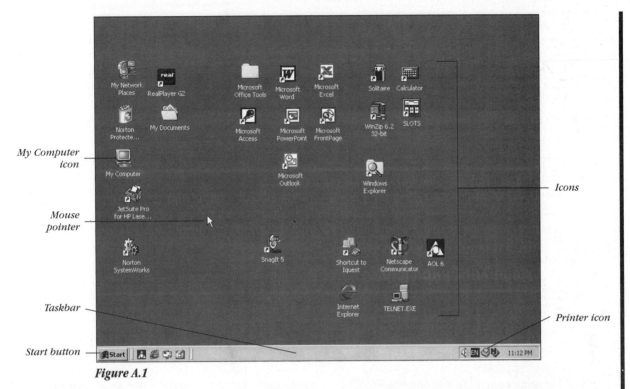

My Computer icon

Mouse pointer

Taskbar

Start button

Icons

Printer icon

Figure A.1

The remainder of the appendix focuses on those features of Windows that support using Office XP applications: opening and viewing multiple windows, performing tasks related to file storage, using the Windows Help system, and shutting down your computer.

Lesson 1: Starting Windows and Using the Mouse

In most cases, starting Windows is an automatic procedure. You turn on the computer and Windows (whichever version you are using) appears. The items you see onscreen are likely to vary from the Windows screens displayed in this lesson because your computer has different software installed, different shortcuts on the desktop, and/or a different version of Windows.

In this lesson, you start Windows and use the mouse to open and close the My Computer window. Every window includes a title bar at the top of a window and a status bar at the bottom. A ***title bar*** includes the name of the open object or program at its left end, and a series of buttons at its right end. The buttons enable you to minimize, maximize or restore, and close the window, respectively. A ***status bar*** provides information about the current operation or workspace. Windows can also include a menu bar and one or more toolbars. A ***menu bar*** contains common menu names that, when activated, display a list of related commands. A ***toolbar*** is a set of buttons; each button on the toolbar performs a predefined task.

If an instruction tells you to *click* an item, click the left mouse button. An instruction to click the right mouse button includes the phrase *right-click*.

To Start Windows and Use the Mouse

1 **Turn on your computer.**
After several screens of text and the Windows opening screen, the Windows desktop displays (refer to the sample Windows desktop shown in Figure A.1). The look of the screen varies, depending on which version of Windows you are using and the programs installed on your system.

If you have problems...
If the taskbar does not appear at the bottom of the desktop, one of two actions is likely to restore its display. First, move the pointer to the bottom of the screen. If the taskbar property *Auto hide* is set, this is the only action needed to temporarily display the hidden taskbar. If the cursor changes to a two-headed arrow when you move the pointer to the bottom of the screen, click and drag the taskbar up onto the screen. If the taskbar still does not appear, it may have been moved to the top or one of the sides of the desktop.

2 **Move the mouse pointer until it points to the center of the My Computer icon on the desktop.**
My Computer represents one of two ways to access the programs and documents stored on your computer; the other is the Windows Explorer. The My Computer icon looks like a miniature computer.

3 **Click the My Computer icon.**
The icon turns dark, indicating that it has been selected. However, a single click does not start the program represented by the icon.

If you have problems...
If single-clicking the My Computer icon opens the My Computer window, the Active Desktop feature is enabled. The feature makes your desktop look and work like a Web page, and its use is beyond the scope of this Windows Overview. Skip the next hands-on step, but read the explanation below it.

4 **Double-click the My Computer icon.**
The My Computer window displays (see the sample My Computer display shown in Figure A.2). Do not be concerned if the display in your My Computer window appears to be quite different from the one shown in Figure A.2. The display can be customized in many ways using the <u>V</u>iew menu option. For now, focus on simply opening and closing windows, and learning about the standard components of a window.

To Start Windows and Use the Mouse

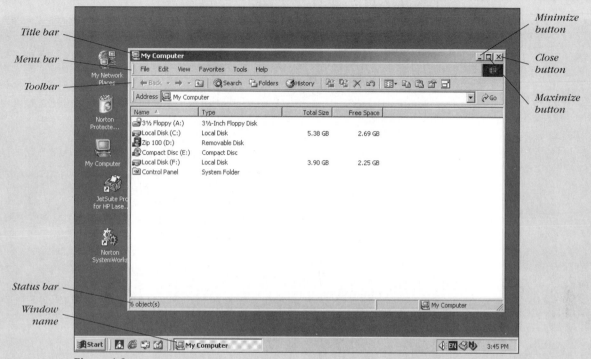

Title bar

Menu bar

Toolbar

Minimize button

Close button

Maximize button

Status bar

Window name

Figure A.2

If you have problems...

If the My Computer window does not open, you might have moved the mouse while you were double-clicking the mouse button. Or, you may not have clicked twice in rapid succession. In either case, try again. If you are unfamiliar with a mouse, it may take awhile to become proficient.

Another possible reason why the My Computer window does not open is that your computer is in a lab that has security installed. Some levels of security do not allow you to open the My Computer window. If the problem is a security level that cannot be changed, read the steps in this lesson and view the figures to get an understanding of the process.

5 **Click the Close button in the upper-right corner of the My Computer window title bar.**
The My Computer window closes.

6 **Right-click the My Computer icon.**
A shortcut menu displays. A ***shortcut menu*** enables you to perform an operation quickly without using a menu bar or toolbar. The options that appear may differ, depending on the version of Windows that is installed.

7 **Move the mouse pointer over the word** *Open* **in the My Computer shortcut menu.**

(Continues)

To Start Windows and Use the Mouse (Continued)

Dark highlighting indicates that the *Open* option is selected (see Figure A.3).

Dark highlighting indicates that the option is selected

Shortcut menu

Figure A.3

8 **Click within the dark highlighting to select the Open option.**
The My Computer window is displayed. Right-clicking the My Computer icon and selecting *Open* from the shortcut menu produces the same result as double-clicking the icon. In Microsoft Windows and Microsoft Office, many tasks can be performed in more than one way.

9 **Click the Close button in the title bar of the My Computer window (refer to Figure A.2).**
The My Computer window closes. Leave your computer on if you are continuing to the next lesson. Instructions about how to shut down your computer properly are provided in Lesson 7, "Shutting Down Your Computer."

To extend your knowledge...

Dialog and Message Boxes

A window can be a dialog box or message box within a program. A ***dialog box*** enables a user to input data or specify settings related to the current task. For example, if you are using a computer that is part of a network of computers, you are likely to see a dialog box requesting that you enter a user name and password.

A ***message box*** displays information—for example, a procedure has been completed or an error has occurred—but does not provide an opportunity for the user to respond, except to close the box.

Lesson 2: Using the Start Button and the Taskbar

One of the powerful features of the Windows operating system is that the user can have more than one window open at a time. This is particularly important when using Microsoft Office because you can have more than one application open, and easily move data between applications. For example, you can open the spreadsheet application Microsoft Excel and word-processing application Microsoft Word, and copy data from the spreadsheet to a word-processing document.

You can use buttons to determine the amount of the screen occupied by a window. For example, you can maximize or minimize a window (refer to the Maximize and Minimize buttons in Figure A.2). If you *maximize* a window, it fills the entire screen. If you *minimize* a window, it remains open, but it no longer appears on the screen.

In this lesson, you open and close three programs—a calculator program, Microsoft Word, and Microsoft Excel—and use the taskbar to switch between the programs. The way you open a Microsoft Office application depends on how your computer is set up. You may have a shortcut so that you can start the programs from the top of the Start menu. If there is an icon for Microsoft Word on the desktop, you can double-click it instead of using the Start menu. You may also have a toolbar at the top of your screen with icons that open Office applications. In the following steps, you open programs by using the Start button and selecting options from the Programs menu.

To Use the Start Button and the Taskbar

1 **Click the Start button at the left end of the Windows taskbar.**
The Start menu is displayed. Some of the options have arrows on the right. An arrow indicates that there is a submenu containing programs or folders containing more options. A *submenu* is a second-level set of options activated by selecting a menu item.

2 **Move the pointer up to the Programs menu option, but do not click the mouse button.**
The Programs menu is displayed (see the sample Programs menu in Figure A.4). The options reflect the programs installed on your computer system. If the list extends beyond the bottom of the screen, you can click on the double arrow at the bottom of the menu to scroll down (in earlier versions of Windows, a single arrow displays).

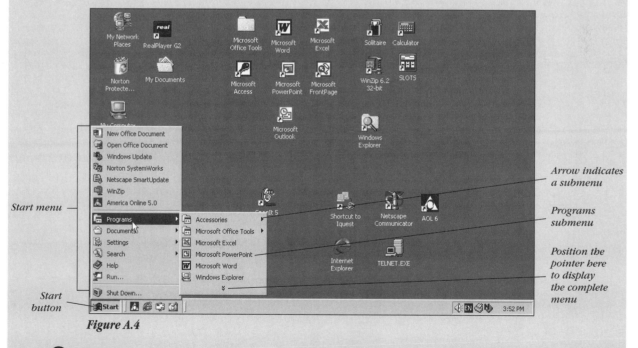

Figure A.4

3 **Move the pointer to the Accessories menu option, but do not click the mouse button.**

(Continues)

To Use the Start Button and the Taskbar (Continued)

The Accessories submenu is displayed. The expanded Accessories menu appears after a few seconds delay.

If you have problems...

If the Accessories option is not visible, move the pointer to the top of the menu, and hold it above the double-arrow. The menu scrolls to include options at the top.

④ Move the pointer into the Accessories submenu, and point to the Calculator option.
The Calculator option is highlighted.

⑤ Click the Calculator option.
The Calculator window is displayed (see Figure A.5). To use the calculator, click the calculator keys.

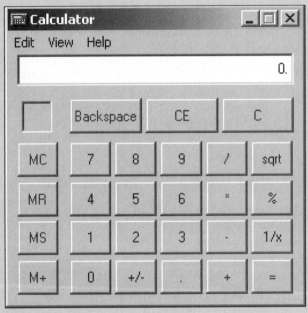

Figure A.5

⑥ Click the Start button and move the pointer to the Programs menu choice.
The Programs submenu is displayed.

⑦ Point to Microsoft Word, and click it.
Microsoft Word opens. A Microsoft Word button displays in the taskbar, indicating that the application is open. The Word window may or may not be maximized. If it is not, click the Maximize button at the right end of the Word title bar (refer to Figure A.2, if necessary).

⑧ Click the Start button, point to the Programs option, and select Microsoft Excel.
Microsoft Excel opens. Buttons for the Calculator, Word, and Excel appear in the taskbar (see Figure A.6). The buttons are displayed from left to right in the order the programs

To Use the Start Button and the Taskbar

were opened. The Excel window may or may not be maximized. If it is not, click the Maximize button at the right end of the Excel title bar.

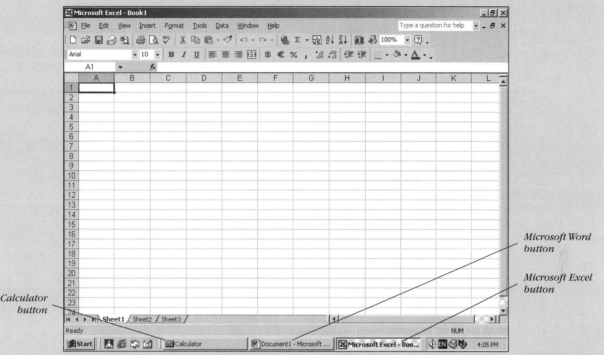

Calculator button

Microsoft Word button

Microsoft Excel button

Figure A.6

9 **Click the Microsoft Word button in the taskbar.**
The Microsoft Word window appears. The program was open, but hidden, so it did not have to be reloaded.

10 **Click the Calculator button in the taskbar.**
The Calculator window displays on top of the Word window.

11 **Click anywhere on the Word window.**
The Word window again becomes the active window (it appears in front).

12 **Click the Close button to close Word (click No if a message box asks whether you want to save your changes).**
Make sure that you click the Close button (the one with the *X* in it) at the right end of the Microsoft Word title bar. The Microsoft Word window closes, and the Microsoft Excel window is displayed behind the Calculator window.

13 **Click the Close button to close the Calculator, and click the Close button to close Excel. (Click *No* if a message box asks if you want to save your changes.)**
You closed the application programs that you opened during this lesson. Leave your computer on if you are continuing to the next lesson. Instructions about how to shut down your computer properly are provided in Lesson 7, "Shutting Down Your Computer."

To extend your knowledge...

Displaying All Open Windows

You can display all open windows in a cascading or tiled arrangement. In a ***windows, cascading*** view, open windows appear in a stack—each open window displays slightly to the right of, and lower than, the previous window. In a ***windows, tiled*** view, open windows display horizontally— each window to the right of the previous one—or vertically—each window below the previous one. To arrange all open windows, right-click a blank area on the taskbar; and choose Cascade Windows, Tile Windows <u>H</u>orizontally, or Tile Windows V<u>e</u>rtically. To restore windows to their original state, right-click a blank area on the taskbar, and click <u>U</u>ndo Cascade or <u>U</u>ndo Tile.

Lesson 3: Working with a Window

You know that you can minimize, maximize, and close windows using buttons in the title bar of the window. You can also change the size of a window by restoring or resizing it. When you ***restore*** a window, it automatically returns to the size it was before being maximized. You can also manually resize a window to the dimensions of your choice.

Scrollbars are automatically included in a window if the information in the window extends beyond the right or bottom edges of the window. A ***horizontal scrollbar*** enables you to shift window contents left and right to view information that expands beyond the width of a window. A ***vertical scrollbar*** enables you to shift window contents up and down to view information that extends beyond the height of a window.

Each scrollbar includes a ***scrollbox*** that you can drag to shift quickly the display within a window. The size of the scrollbox compared to the size of the scrollbar indicates the relative proportion of a window's contents that you can see. For example, if the scrollbox is nearly as large as the scrollbar, only a relatively small amount of information is not in view. The location of the scrollbox indicates the current position within the window's total contents, such as near the beginning or somewhat beyond the middle.

In this lesson, you open the Windows Explorer window, resize it, and move it. ***Windows Explorer*** is a utility program that you can use to access programs and documents; as well as copy, move, delete, and rename files (see the sample Windows Explorer screen in Figure A.7).

You also use scrollbars to view the contents of the window. You complete the lesson by maximizing, restoring, minimizing, and closing the Windows Explorer window. The methods you learn can be applied to any window.

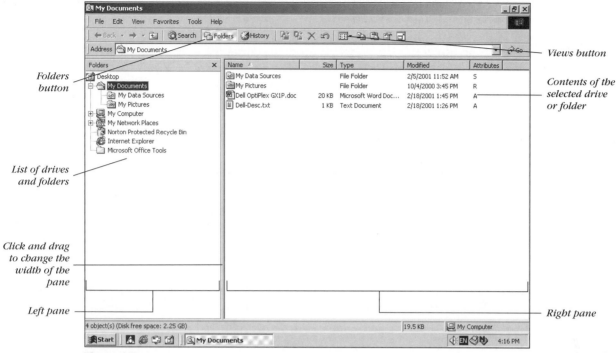

Views button

Contents of the selected drive or folder

Folders button

List of drives and folders

Click and drag to change the width of the pane

Left pane

Right pane

Figure A.7

To Work with a Window

① **Click the Start button, point to Programs, and click Windows Explorer in the list of programs (or right-click the Start button and select Explore from the shortcut menu).**

The Windows Explorer window is displayed. Your screen may look considerably different than the sample shown in Figure A.7. Now, alter your screen display in the next two steps, as necessary, so that it resembles the general display format shown in Figure A.7.

 If you have problems...

Make sure that you select Windows Explorer, not Internet Explorer. You may have to scroll down to find the Windows Explorer option in the list of programs. If it does not appear on your Programs menu, click the Accessories option and look for it there.

② **If the Windows Explorer window occupies the entire screen, click the Restore button—the middle button in the set of three buttons at the right end of the Windows Explorer title bar.**

③ **If icons appear instead of folders and files in the right side of the window, click the Views button on the toolbar, and select Details.**

④ **Move the pointer to the lower-right corner of the Windows Explorer window.**

The pointer changes to a diagonal two-headed arrow.

(Continues)

To Work with a Window (Continued)

5 **Click and hold down the left mouse button, and drag the corner of the window up and to the left about an inch in each direction.**
The window resizes as you move the pointer. If you are using an older version of Windows, the window is resized when you release the mouse button.

6 **Move the pointer to the Windows Explorer title bar; click and drag the title bar down and to the right, and release the mouse button.**
Releasing the mouse button completes the move. The Windows Explorer window is positioned in a different location.

7 **If a plus sign displays to the left of the My Computer icon in the left pane of the Windows Explorer window, click it and then click the drive labeled C:.**
Clicking a plus sign expands the view of the folder structure, and clicking a minus sign collapses the display to show less detail. The disk drives and Control Panel in My Computer display, as do the contents of drive C: (see Figure A.8).

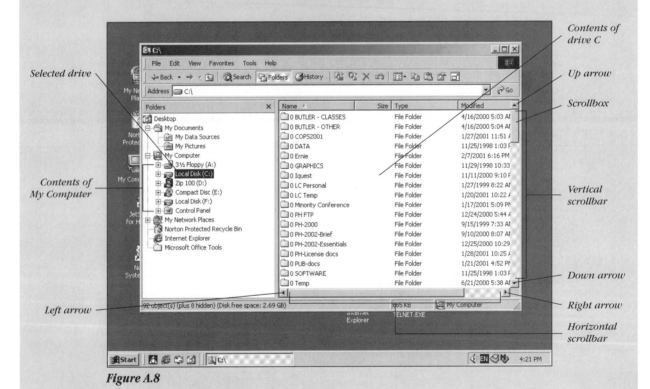

Figure A.8

8 **Click and hold the down arrow at the bottom of a vertical scrollbar.**
The items at the bottom of the pane scroll up so that you can see the folders and files that were not visible before.

9 **Click and hold the up arrow on the same scrollbar.**
The display within the pane shifts up slowly until the first items are displayed.

10 **Click and hold the right arrow on a horizontal scrollbar; click and hold the left arrow on the same scrollbar.**
The display within the pane shifts relatively slowly—first to the right, and then to the left.

To Work with a Window

⑪ Position the pointer on a scrollbox in a vertical scrollbar, and drag the scrollbox to the middle of the scrollbar.

The display shifts down relatively quickly. Approximately half of the window's contents are located above the current position.

⑫ Click the gray area below the scrollbox on the same vertical scrollbar.

Clicking the gray area above or below a scrollbox shifts the display one section at a time.

⑬ Click the Maximize button at the right end of the Windows Explorer title bar.

The Windows Explorer window now occupies the entire screen. The Restore button replaces the Maximize button (see Figure A.9).

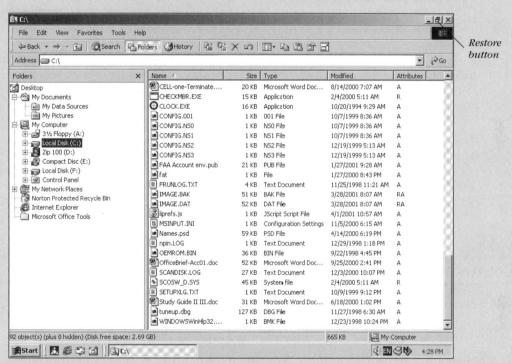

Restore button

Figure A.9

⑭ Click the Restore button.

The window returns to the size it was before you clicked the Maximize button.

⑮ Click the Minimize button.

The Windows Explorer window is still open, but it is stored on the taskbar at the bottom of the screen. The window has not been closed, just temporarily hidden.

⑯ Click the Windows Explorer button in the taskbar.

The window displays in the same location it was in when you clicked the Minimize button.

⑰ Click the Close button at the right end of the Windows Explorer title bar.

This concludes your brief experience working with windows. Leave your computer on if you are continuing to the next lesson. Instructions about how to shut down your computer properly are provided in Lesson 7, "Shutting Down Your Computer."

To extend your knowledge...

Other Scrollbar Buttons

Other buttons may display within a scrollbar, depending on the contents of the window. For example, the vertical scrollbar in an open Word document includes Previous Page and Next Page buttons. Recent versions of Word also include a Select Browse Object button, which you can use to switch from one subheading to the next, from one footnote to the next, and so forth.

Lesson 4: Managing Folders Using Windows Explorer

In Windows, folders are storage locations on disk that enable you to store multiple files by type or subject. You can create a multiple-level storage system by creating a folder within a folder—sometimes referred to as a **subfolder**. As a general guideline, folders are created on zip disks, hard disks, and other storage devices that also have large capacities. You can, however, create folders on smaller-capacity disks, such as a 3-1/2 inch high-density disk. The procedure is the same no matter what disk capacity is involved.

In this lesson, you create two folders on a blank 3 1/2-inch disk formatted to work on a Windows-based computer system. When you **format (a disk)**, the operating system prepares it to store files. Formatting also identifies and automatically isolates any bad spots on the surface of the disk, and sets up an area for a disk directory. You also rename one of the folders, and create several practice files that you use in the next lesson.

To Create and Rename Folders

1 **Insert a blank formatted 3 1/2-inch disk in drive A.**
All 3 1/2-inch disks sold in recent years are already formatted. Make sure that the disk you select is formatted for a Windows-based system.

2 **Open the Windows Explorer window, click the plus sign next to the My Computer icon, and click the icon representing drive A.**

3 **Move the pointer to a blank area in the right side of the window, and right-click.**
A shortcut menu is displayed. The contents of the shortcut menu depend on the version of Windows that you are using.

4 **Move the pointer to the New option.**
A submenu is displayed (see Figure A.10). An option to create a new folder or shortcut displays at the top of the menu; the remaining choices are determined by the programs installed on your computer.

To Create and Rename Folders

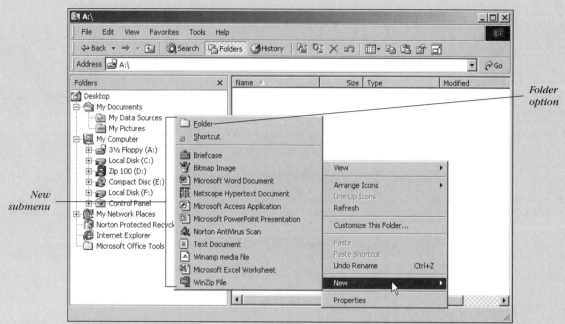

Figure A.10

5 **Click the Folder option.**

A new folder is created. The dark highlighting behind the words *New Folder* indicates that edit mode is active.

6 **Type** `Personal` **as the new folder name, and press** ⏎Enter.

The new folder has a meaningful name (see Figure A.11). Now, create another folder using the menu bar.

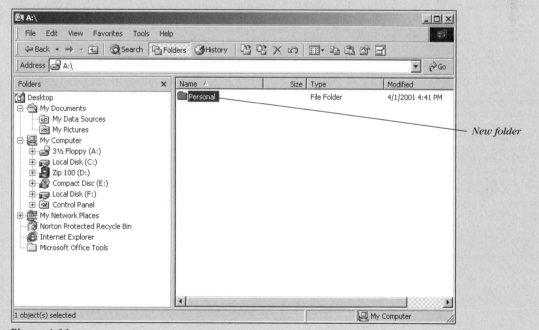

Figure A.11

(Continues)

To Create and Rename Folders (Continued)

If you have problems...

If you press ⏎Enter before you have a chance to name the folder, you can rename it. Right-click the folder, choose Rename from the shortcut menu, type the new folder name, and press ⏎Enter.

7 Choose File in the menu bar, point to New, and select <u>F</u>older.

8 Enter School as the name of the second new folder.

You now have two folders and no files on your disk in drive A (see Figure A.12).

Name column selector

Folders in alphabetical order

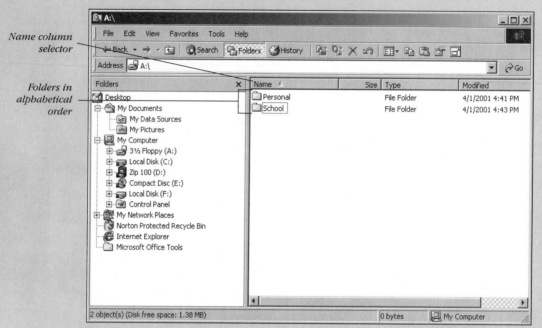

Figure A.12

9 Click the Start button, point to Programs, point to Accessories, and position the pointer on the double-down arrow at the bottom of the Accessories submenu.

10 Select WordPad.

The WordPad window opens. **WordPad** is a Windows utility program for creating small word-processing files in several formats.

11 Type This is a practice file. in the blank WordPad work area (see Figure A.13).

To Create and Rename Folders

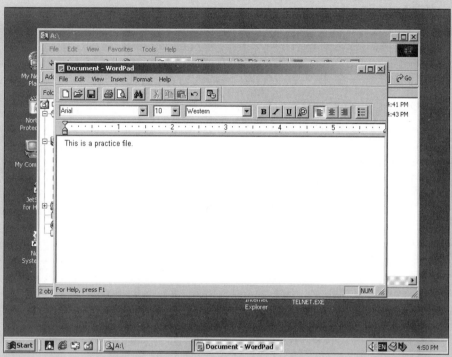

Figure A.13

12 Choose <u>F</u>ile, Save <u>A</u>s to open the Save As dialog box; click the drop-down arrow at the right of the Save in text box, and click *3 ½ Floppy [A:]*.

13 Type `Rename` in the *File <u>n</u>ame* text box (see Figure A.14).

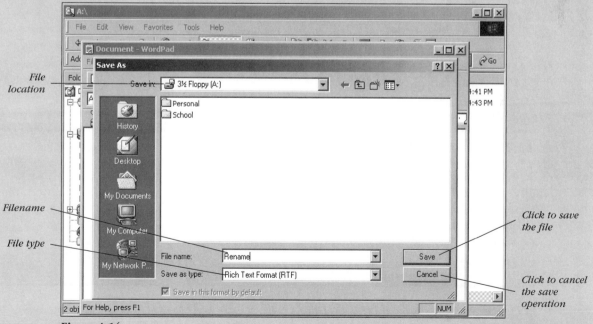

Figure A.14

(Continues)

To Create and Rename Folders (Continued)

If you do not change the default file type, WordPad creates a file with an RTF (rich text format) extension. A **_file extension_**, the last part of a filename, consists of three characters that represent the type of file.

⑭ **Click the Save button in the Save As dialog box.**

⑮ **Repeat the file save process described in the last three steps to create three more practice files; name the files** Copy, Move, **and** Delete.

⑯ **Click the Close button at the right end of the WordPad title bar.**
Two folders and four files display in the Windows Explorer window (see Figure A.15). Continue with the next lesson on managing files.

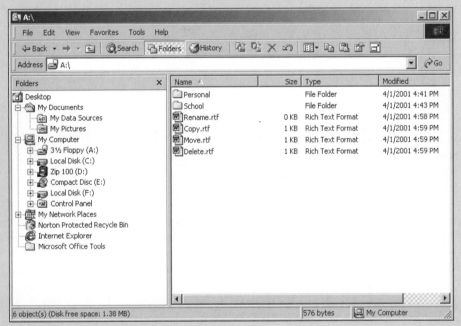

Figure A.15

To extend your knowledge...

Sorting by Name, File Size, Type, or Date Last Modified

You can click any of the column selectors in the contents area of a Windows Explorer screen to sort the files and folders in the current drive. Clicking once on the Name column selector (refer to Figure A.12) sorts in descending order (Z-to-A), and clicking again sorts in ascending order (A-to-Z). Clicking once on the Size column selector sorts the files by size, smallest to largest. Clicking it again sorts the files from largest to smallest. Because folders have no size, they are either all shown first or all shown last. You can use the same procedure to sort by date modified or by file type.

Lesson 5: Managing Files Using Windows Explorer

Common file-management tasks include copying, moving, renaming, and deleting files and folders. You should always make backup copies of important files, and store the backup copies in a separate physical location. If you want to copy a file to a 3 1/2-inch disk, the My Documents folder, the desktop, a Zip disk, or as an attachment to an e-mail message, you can right-click the name of the file in Windows Explorer and use the Send To option on the shortcut menu. If you want to copy a file to a hard drive or to a folder on any drive, you can select and copy the file, display the desired target location, and paste it. At times, you may want to move a file from one location to another. Perhaps you want to reorganize files, and place one in a new folder.

The process to copy or move a file or folder using Windows Explorer consists of four steps: Click the file or folder you want to work with; choose Edit, Copy to make a copy or choose Edit, Cut to move; open the folder or disk where you want to copy or move the item; and choose Edit, Paste. As an alternative to copying or cutting and then pasting files, you can drag and drop them in their new locations.

You can change the name of a file at any time by right-clicking it, choosing Rename, and typing a new name. When you are certain that you no longer need a file, it is a good idea to delete it, which makes its storage location available for another file(s).

In this lesson, you copy, move, delete, and rename files using Windows Explorer. You work with the practice files you created in the previous lesson.

To Manage Files Using Windows Explorer

1 **If necessary, insert the 3 1/2-inch disk used in the previous lesson in drive A, and open Windows Explorer.**

2 **Select the *3 ½ Floppy [A:]* disk drive in the left pane.**
The folders and files created in the previous lesson are displayed (refer to Figure A.15). Now, copy a file to a folder.

3 **Click the *Copy.rtf* filename; and choose <u>E</u>dit, <u>C</u>opy.**

4 **Open the Personal folder in the Folders pane by clicking the folder icon next to it.**

5 **Choose <u>E</u>dit, <u>P</u>aste.**
The original *Copy.rtf* file remains in the root directory of drive A. A copy of that file is stored within the Personal folder. Now, move a file to a folder.

6 **Select the *3 ½ Floppy [A:]* disk drive; click the *Move.rtf* filename; and choose <u>E</u>dit, Cu<u>t</u>.**

7 **Open the School folder in the left pane; and choose <u>E</u>dit, <u>P</u>aste.**
The original *Move.rtf* file is stored in one place only—the School folder. Now, delete a file.

8 **Select the *3 ½ Floppy [A:]* disk drive, right-click the *Delete.rtf* filename, and select <u>D</u>elete from the shortcut menu.**

9 **Choose Yes in the Confirm File Delete dialog box.**
The *Delete.rtf* file no longer exists. Now, rename a file.

10 **Right-click the *Rename.rtf* filename, and select Rena<u>m</u>e from the shortcut menu.**

(Continues)

To Manage Files Using Windows Explorer (Continued)

⑪ Type New Name.rtf, and press ⏎Enter.
You executed four basic file management tasks: copy, move, delete, and rename. The root directory of drive A includes two files: *Copy.rtf* and *New Name.rtf*. The Personal folder contains one file named *Copy.rtf*. The School folder contains one file named *Move.rtf*.

⑫ Close the Windows Explorer window.

To extend your knowledge...

Shortcut Keys to Copy, Cut, and Paste

You may prefer to use keyboard shortcuts as an alternative to choosing Copy, Cut, and Paste commands from menus. Use Ctrl+C in place of Edit, Copy; use Ctrl+X in place of Edit, Cut; and use Ctrl+V in place of Edit, Paste.

Copying and Moving Folders

When a folder name is selected, two new options appear on the Edit menu: Copy To Folder and Move To Folder. These options enable you to browse your system and choose the destination for the selected files. This is a useful feature when moving or copying files to a different disk drive. The feature is not available on Windows 98 or earlier operating systems.

Selecting Multiple Files or Folders

You can select multiple files before executing a copy, move, or delete operation. To select consecutive files or folders, click the first item, press and hold down ⇧Shift, click the last item, and release ⇧Shift. To select files or folders that are not consecutive, press and hold down Ctrl, click each item, and release Ctrl.

Lesson 6: Using the Windows Help System

If you want to perform an action in Windows, but don't know how, Windows has an onscreen Help feature that can guide you. Figure A.16 is a sample Help Viewer screen (earlier versions of Windows refer to this as a Help window).

Use the Contents tab to select among general Help topics. Use the Index tab to request help on a specified word or phrase. The Search tab enables you to look for individual words in the Help text. This is particularly important if you don't know the correct words and phrases to use with the Index feature. The Favorites tab (not included in earlier versions) enables you to bookmark the Help topics that you often refer to.

Favorites tab ———
Search tab ———
Index tab ———
Contents tab ———

Books (help
topics) ———

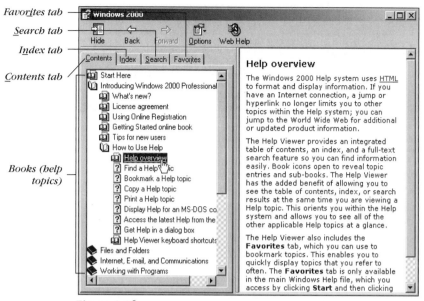

Figure A.16

In this lesson, you glimpse the power of the onscreen Windows Help by using the Contents and Index tabs in the Windows Help Viewer.

To Use the Windows Help Viewer

❶ Click the Start button, and select the Help option.
The Help Viewer window is displayed. There are four help tabs: Contents, Index, Search (called Find in the older versions of Windows), and Favorites.

❷ Click the Contents tab, if necessary, and select the *Introducing Windows 2000 Professional* book icon (or its equivalent).
The Contents window contains help in a book-like format. The *Introducing Windows 2000 Professional* book is opened to display topics and other books.

 ### If you have problems...

The look of the Help Viewer window varies widely, depending on which version of Windows you are using. For example, the Contents tab contains five books in Windows 95, ten books plus an introduction in Windows 98, and fifteen books plus a *Start Here* introduction in Windows 2000 Professional. The way these books are activated is also different. In Windows 95 and Windows NT 4.0, you need to double-click on the book, or select the book and click the Open button. If you are using Windows 98 or 2000, you simply need to click once on the book. This demonstrates the movement of the Windows operating system toward a Web structure.

❸ Open *How to Use Help*.

(Continues)

To Use the Windows Help Viewer (Continued)

Chapters consisting of a page with a question mark are displayed. The chapters vary with the version of Windows. (*Note:* To get to this book using Windows NT 4.0, click the *How To* book first.)

4 **Open any topic of your choice in the Contents tab; when you finish, click the Close button to close the Help Viewer window.**

5 **Click the Start button, select the Help option, and click the Index tab.**

6 **Type** Start **in the keyword text box near the top of the window.**
Related topics are shown in the box below (see Figure A.17).

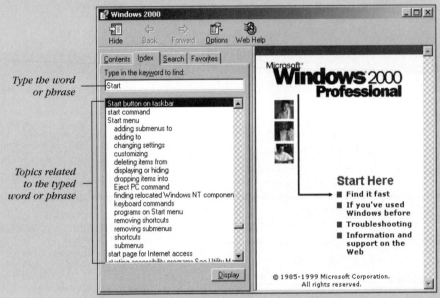

Figure A.17

7 **Select the topic of your choice, and click the Display button near the lower-right corner of the left pane.**
Information about the selected topic is displayed in the right pane.

8 **Enter other words or phrases of your choice, and read the related topics; close the Help Viewer window when you finish.**

Lesson 7: Shutting Down Your Computer

It is important that you shut down your computer properly. To do this, you need to use the Shut Down option from the Start menu. The Shut Down option gives the computer a chance to close many of the programs that are going on in the background—programs that you probably don't even know are running. Simply turning off the computer can cause problems.

To Shut Down Your Computer

1 **Click the Start button.**
The Start menu is displayed.

To Shut Down Your Computer

② Select Shut Down from the Start menu.
The Shut Down Windows dialog box is displayed (see Figure A.18). The contents of the dialog box depend on the version of Windows you are using. Windows 2000 Professional and Windows ME provide a drop-down menu of choices. Earlier versions display the list of options immediately. If you are working in a lab, you might get a completely different message, asking if you want to log out or log in as a new user.

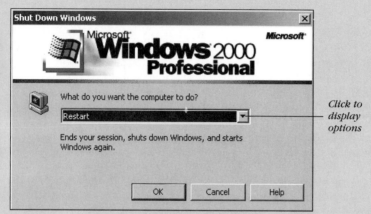

Figure A.18

③ Make sure the *Shut down the computer?* (or *Shut down*) option is selected, and click OK (or Yes in Windows 95).
If you have a file that you forgot to close, Windows prompts you to save your work and then shuts the computer down. Depending on the computer you are using, you may get a message telling you that *It's now safe to turn off your computer.* Some computers automatically shut down.

ummary

In this appendix, you had a brief introduction to Windows on topics that support your work with Microsoft Office applications. There are many more topics that might be of interest to you. You can start adding to your arsenal of Windows knowledge by going through the Help menu and exploring topics of interest. You might also want to pick up a Windows tutorial or reference manual—you can find several at www.prenhall.com.

Task Guide

A book in the *essentials* series is designed to be kept as a handy reference beside your computer, even after you have completed all the projects and exercises. Any time you have difficulty recalling the sequence of steps or a shortcut needed to achieve a result, look up the general category in the following alphabetized listing and then quickly find your task. For your convenience, some tasks have been duplicated under more than one category. If you have difficulty performing a task, turn to the page number listed in the third column to locate the step-by-step exercise or other detailed description. For the greatest efficiency in using this Task Guide, take a few minutes to familiarize yourself with the main categories and keywords before you begin your search.

Continues ▶

To Do This	Use This Command	Page Number
Next page	Press Ctrl+PgDn, or click the Next Page button.	33
Normal view	Choose View, Normal.	42
Office Assistant: display	Choose Help, Show the Office Assistant.	21
Office Assistant: turn off	Click Office Assistant. Click Options and click the Options tab. Deselect the *Use the Office Assistant* check box, and click OK.	21
Previous page	Press Ctrl+PgUp, or click the Previous Page button.	33
Print Layout view	Choose View, Print Layout.	42
Print Preview	Click Print Preview button.	17
ScreenTip about button's purpose	Position the mouse pointer over the button or icon.	8
Task Pane: display/hide	Choose View, Task Pane.	8
Task Pane: Insert Clip Art	Choose Insert, Picture, Clip Art.	209
Task Pane: Office Clipboard	Choose Edit, Office Clipboard.	95
Task Pane: Reveal Formatting	Choose Format, Reveal Formatting.	139
Toolbar: Standard and Formatting on separate rows	Choose Tools, Customize. Click the *Show Standard and Formatting toolbars on two rows* check box, and click Close.	9
Toolbar: Tables and Borders	Choose View, Toolbars, Tables and Borders.	195
Zoom dialog box	Choose View, Zoom.	43

Edit Text

Clear formatting	Select text. Choose Edit, Clear, Formats.	139
Copy text	Select text; click the Copy button or press Ctrl+C.	94
Cut text	Select text; click the Cut button or press Ctrl+X.	93
Delete character: left of insertion point	Press ◆Backspace.	40
Delete character: right of insertion point	Press Del.	40
Delete word: left of insertion point	Press Ctrl+◆Backspace.	40
Delete word: right of insertion point	Press Ctrl+Del.	40
Grammar-check	Right-click on text with wavy green underlining, and choose correct grammar.	16
Overtype mode: activate	Double-click OVR on the status bar.	41
Paste	Click the Paste button, or press Ctrl+V.	94
Redo an Undo action	Click the Redo button.	100
Select a block of text	Click and drag the mouse.	38
Select entire document	Press Ctrl+A.	38
Select multiple items	Select one area. Press and hold Ctrl. Select another area.	40

To Do This	Use This Command	Page Number
Select paragraph	Triple-click the paragraph.	38
Select sentence	Hold down Ctrl while clicking the sentence.	38
Select word	Double-click the word.	38
Spelling-check	Right-click on the word with wavy red underlining, and choose correct spelling.	16
Synonym: choose	Right-click in the word, choose Synonyms, and choose appropriate synonym from list.	103
Undo single action	Click the Undo button, or press Ctrl+Z.	99
Undo multiple actions	Click the drop-down arrow to the right of the Undo button. Select the sequence of actions you want to undo.	99

Format Characters

To Do This	Use This Command	Page Number
Bold existing text	Select text. Click the Bold button, or press Ctrl+B.	60
Bold text as you type	Click the Bold button, type text, and click the Bold button again.	60
Case of text: change	Select text. Choose Format, Change Case. Choose option, and click OK. Alternatively, select text, and press ♠Shift+F3 until you see the casing you want.	91
Cells in a table	Select cells, and choose formats, such as font, font size, bold, and so on.	192
Character effects	Choose Format, Font. Click the check boxes for the effects you want, and click OK.	64
Character spacing	Choose Format, Font. Click the Character Spacing tab. Choose spacing options, and click OK.	64
Font: select	Click the Font drop-down arrow. Choose the desired font.	62
Font color: select	Click the Font Color drop-down arrow. Choose the desired color.	63
Font size: set	Click the Font Size drop-down arrow. Choose the desired font size.	62
Format Painter	Click inside the formatted text, and double-click the Format Painter button. Click and drag across other instances of text to copy the character formats. Then, click the Format Painter button, or simply press Esc to turn off the feature.	67
Highlight text	Select the text. Click the Highlight button.	70
Italicize existing text	Select text. Click the Italic button, or press Ctrl+I.	59

Continues ▶

To Do This	Use This Command	Page Number
Italicize text as you type	Click the Italic button, type text, and click the Italic button.	59
Underline existing text	Select text. Click the Underline button, or press Ctrl+U.	59
Underline text as you type	Click the Underline button, type text, and click the Underline button.	59

Format Paragraphs

To Do This	Use This Command	Page Number
Align: center	Click the Center button.	121
Align: justify	Click the Justify button.	121
Align: left	Click the Align Left button.	121
Align: right	Click the Align Right button.	121
Border and shading: select	Choose Format, Borders and Shading. Click a border setting, choose a color, select other options, and click OK.	131
Bulleted list: create	Click the Bullets button. Type text, and press ↵Enter to continue list. Press ←Backspace to delete the extra bullet and end list when done.	124
Cells in a Table	Select cells, and choose formats, such as font, font size, bold, and so on.	192
First line indent	Choose Format, Paragraph. Click the *Special* drop-down arrow. Choose *First Line*. Click OK.	124
Format Painter	Select an entire paragraph, and double-click the Format Painter button. Select other paragraphs to which you want to reapply the formatting of the original paragraph. Click the Format Painter button, or press Esc to turn off the feature when you finish.	67
Hanging indent: create	Click in the paragraph, and choose Format, Paragraph. Click the Indents and Spacing tab. Click the *Special* drop-down arrow, and choose Hanging. Click OK.	124
Indent from both margins	Choose Format, Paragraph. Type a value in the *Left* and *Right* Indentation boxes. Click OK.	123
Indent from left margin	Choose Format, Paragraph. Type a value in the *Left* Indentation box, and click OK.	123
Line spacing: change	Click the Line Spacing button. Choose desired line spacing.	116
Numbered list: create	Click the Numbering button. Type text, and press ↵Enter to continue list. Press ←Backspace to delete extra number and end list when done.	126

To Do This	Use This Command	Page Number
Outline numbered list	Choose F_ormat, Bullets and N_umbering. Click the O_utline Numbered tab. Choose a style, and click OK.	128
Paragraph spacing	Choose F_ormat, P_aragraph. Set the _Before_ and _After_ spacing. Click OK.	118
Same page as next paragraph: keeping on	Select text. Choose F_ormat, P_aragraph. Click the Line and P_age Breaks tab. Click the _Keep with next_ option, and click OK.	167
Sort paragraphs	Select paragraphs. Choose T_able, S_ort. Click OK.	124
Tabs: display dialog box	Choose F_ormat, T_abs.	138
Tabs: set	Click tab alignment button until you see desired alignment type. Click on ruler to set tab.	134

Format Document

To Do This	Use This Command	Page Number
Booklet: creating	Choose F_ile, Page Set_up. Click the _Multiple pages_ option, and choose _Book fold._ Click OK.	179
Center text vertically	Choose F_ile, Page Set_up. Click the L_ayout tab. Click the _Vertical alignment_ drop-down arrow, and choose _Center_. Select the _Apply to_ option, and click OK.	160
Margins: set	Choose F_ile, Page Set_up. Type margin settings in the boxes, and click OK.	153
Page border: select	Choose F_ormat, B_orders and Shading. Click the P_age Border tab. Choose options, and click OK.	131
Page break: insert	Press Ctrl+⏎Enter.	158
Page numbers: insert	Choose I_nsert, Page N_umbers. Choose the _Position._ Choose the _Alignment._ Select or deselect _Show number on first page,_ and click OK.	162
Page numbering: restart for section	Choose I_nsert, Page N_umbers. Click Format. Click the _Start at_ option, and type 1. Click OK; then click OK again.	164
Paragraphs: keeping together on same page	Select text. Choose F_ormat, P_aragraph. Click the Line and P_age Breaks tab. Click the _Keep with next_ option, and click OK.	165

Continues ▸

To Do This	Use This Command	Page Number
Section break: insert	Choose Insert, Break. Click the *Next page* option, and click OK.	156

Graphics: Clip Art and Objects

To Do This	Use This Command	Page Number
Clip art image: insert	Choose Insert, Picture, Clip Art. Type a keyword, choose search conditions, and click Search. Click down arrow by image, and click Insert.	209
Download image from Microsoft Web site	Choose Insert, Picture, Clip Art. Click the Clip Organizer link. Click the Clips Online link. Type a keyword, choose search options, click Go. Click the image's download button.	222
Fill and Border: select	Click the image. Click the Format Picture button on the Picture toolbar. Click the Colors and Lines tab. Select fill and lines options, and click OK.	218
Image: move to nonvisible area	Click the image. Click the Cut button. Move the insertion point to the new location. Click the Paste button.	213
Image: move to visible area	Click the image to see sizing handles. Click and drag to a new location within view onscreen.	213
Picture: insert from file	Choose Insert, Picture, From File. Select the path and filename, and click Insert.	212
Save images from Internet as graphics	Right-click an image. Choose Save Picture As.	224
Size image: "eyeball approach"	Click and drag a sizing handle to adjust the width and height.	216
Size image: specific setting	Click an image. Click the Format Picture button. Click the Size tab. Set the height and width, and click OK.	215
Watermark: convert image	Click an image. Click the Color button, and choose Washout. Click the Text Wrapping button, and choose Behind Text.	226
WordArt object: create	Choose Insert, Picture, WordArt. Select a shape from the gallery, and click OK. Type text, select the font and font size, and click OK.	227
Wrap and align text around image	Click an image. Click the Format Picture button. Click the Layout tab. Select the text-wrapping option and alignment, and click OK.	216

To Do This	**Use This Command**	**Page Number**
	Help	
Ask a Question	Click in the *Ask a Question* text box. Type the topic or question. Press ⏎Enter.	19
Get Help	Choose <u>H</u>elp, Microsoft Word <u>H</u>elp.	19
Help Index	With the Office Assistant turned off, choose <u>H</u>elp, Microsoft Word <u>H</u>elp. Click the <u>I</u>ndex tab. Type what you are looking for in the *Type keywords* text box and click <u>S</u>earch, or choose keywords in *Or choose keywords*. Then, click a topic in the *Choose a topic* list.	19
Office Assistant: change	Click the Office Assistant. Click <u>O</u>ptions. Click the <u>G</u>allery tab; click <u>B</u>ack or <u>N</u>ext to display other assistants. When you find the one you want, click OK.	21
Office Assistant: display	Choose <u>H</u>elp, Show the <u>O</u>ffice Assistant.	21
Office Assistant: turn off	Click the Office Assistant. Click <u>O</u>ptions, click the <u>O</u>ptions tab, deselect the <u>U</u>se the Office Assistant check box, and click OK.	21
	Insert	
Clip art image	Choose <u>I</u>nsert, <u>P</u>icture, <u>C</u>lip Art. Type a keyword, choose search conditions, and click Search. Click the down arrow by an image, and choose Insert.	209
Column in table: insert to left	Choose T<u>a</u>ble, <u>I</u>nsert, Columns to the <u>L</u>eft.	188
Column in table: insert to right	Choose T<u>a</u>ble, <u>I</u>nsert, Columns to the <u>R</u>ight.	188
Date and time	Choose <u>I</u>nsert, Date and <u>T</u>ime. Choose format, and click OK.	88
Headers and footers	Choose <u>V</u>iew, <u>H</u>eader and Footer. Type the header text for the first section, or leave blank. Click the Show Next button on the Header and Footer toolbar, and deselect the Same as Previous button. Type the header text for the second section.	167
Line break	Press ⬆Shift+⏎Enter.	135
Nonbreaking space	Type the first word. Press Ctrl+⬆Shift+Spacebar. Type the second word to keep together.	75
Nonbreaking hyphen	Type the first word. Press Ctrl+⬆Shift+-. Type the second word to keep together.	75
Page break	Press Ctrl+⏎Enter.	159

Continues ▸

To Do This	Use This Command	Page Number
Page numbers	Choose Insert, Page Numbers. Choose the Position, and choose the Alignment. Select or deselect *Show number on first page*, and click OK.	162
Picture	Choose Insert, Picture, From File. Select path and filename, and click Insert.	212
Row in table: insert above	Choose Table, Insert, Rows Above.	187
Row in table: insert below	Choose Table, Insert, Rows Below.	187
Section break	Choose Insert, Break. Click Next page, and click OK.	156
Symbol	Choose Insert, Symbol. Choose the symbol, and click the Insert button.	71
WordArt object	Choose Insert, Picture, and WordArt. Select a shape from the gallery, and click OK. Type the text, select the font and font size, and click OK.	227

Tables

To Do This	Use This Command	Page Number
Cells: shade	Click the drop-down arrow to the right of the Shading Color button on the Tables and Borders toolbar; then click a color.	195
Column width: adjust automatically	Double-click the Move Table Column marker to adjust the width of the column based on text in the column.	189
Column width: adjust manually	Click and drag the Move Table Column marker.	189
Create	Click the Insert Table button. Choose the number of rows and columns.	183
Delete current column	Choose Table, Delete, Columns.	188
Delete current row	Choose Table, Delete, Rows.	188
Delete text in table	Select cell(s), and press Del.	189
Format cells in table	Select cells, and choose formats, such as font, font size, bold, and so on.	192
Insert column to the left	Choose Table, Insert, Columns to the Left.	188
Insert column to the right	Choose Table, Insert, Columns to the Right.	188
Insert row above the current row	Choose Table, Insert, Rows Above.	187
Insert row below the current row	Choose Table, Insert, Rows Below.	187
Move	Click and drag the table marker to a new location.	196
Position horizontally	Choose Table, Table Properties. Choose an option in the Alignment section.	197
Row height: adjust	Click the Adjust Table Row marker, and click and drag to change the row height.	189
Tables and Borders toolbar: display	Choose View, Toolbars, Tables and Borders.	195

To Do This	Use This Command	Page Number
	Tools	
AutoCorrect entry: create	Choose Tools, AutoCorrect. Type in the *Replace* box. Type in the *With* box. Click Add.	100
AutoText entry	Choose Tools, AutoCorrect. Click the AutoText tab.	100
Envelope: create	Choose Tools, Letters and Mailings, Envelopes.	45
Grammar-check	Right-click on text with wavy green underlining, and choose correct grammar.	15
Labels: create	Choose Tools, Letters and Mailings, Labels.	48
Spell-check	Right-click on word with wavy red underlining, and choose correct spelling.	15
Synonym: replace word with	Right-click in the word. Choose Synonyms. Choose the appropriate synonym from the list.	103
Thesaurus	Choose Tools, Language, Thesaurus.	102

Glossary

action Any task or change you make in a document. [pg. 99]

active document window The window that contains a document with the insertion point; the title bar is blue or another color. [pg. 96]

alignment The placement of text between the left and right margins. The default alignment is left, which perfectly aligns text at the left margin. [pg. 121]

AutoComplete A feature that helps you complete text that's saved in the AutoText feature. For example, if you start typing today's date, you'll see a ScreenTip that displays the entire date. Press ⏎Enter to complete the date automatically. [pg. 35]

AutoCorrect A feature that automatically corrects typos and some capitalization errors "on the fly." [pg. 100]

automatic page break Page break inserted by Word when you fill an entire page. These breaks adjust automatically when you add and delete text. [pg. 158]

bar tab A tab marker that produces a vertical bar or line between columns when you press Tab↹. [pg. 134]

border A line style that surrounds text, table cells, or an object. [pg. 131]

bullet A special symbol to attract attention to text on a page. [pg. 124]

bulleted list An itemized list or enumeration that contains bullet symbols at the left side of each item. [pg. 124]

case Capitalization style of text. [pg. 91]

cell The intersection of a column and row in a table or Excel worksheet. [pg. 182]

character effects Special font formats, such as strikethrough and emboss, that you apply to characters. [pg. 64]

character formats Text formats, such as bold and font color, that emphasize ideas and help improve readability and clarity. [pg. 59]

character spacing The amount of space between printed characters. [pg. 66]

Click and Type feature In Print Layout view, this feature lets you double-click in any area of the document and then type new text. Depending on where you double-click, Word inserts left tabs, centers the text, or aligns text at the right margin. [pg. 12]

clip art Graphic images, pictures, or drawings. [pg. 208]

Clip Organizer Gallery of clips—clip art, photos, sounds, and movies—stored on your hard drive. It has the capability to help the user organize clips, including from other sources. [pg. 212]

close The process of removing an open file or a dialog box from the screen. [pg. 21]

column A group of table cells arranged vertically. [pg. 182]

column headings Text that appears at the top of table columns to identify the contents of each column. [pg. 186]

column width The setting or horizontal measurement of a column. [pg. 189]

copy To make a copy of the selected text or object and place it temporarily in the Office Clipboard. [pg. 93]

cut To remove text or an object from its location and place it temporarily in the Office Clipboard. [pg. 92]

date or time field A placeholder for a date or time that needs to change to reflect the current date or time when opened or printed. [pg. 87]

default Refers to a standard setting determined by Microsoft that is used unless you change it. For example, the default top margin is one inch. [pg. 10]

designer font A special font used in creative documents, such as wedding announcements, fliers, brochures, and other special-occasion documents. Examples of designer fonts include Broadway BT, Comic Sans MS, and Keystroke. [pg. 61]

desktop   A screen that provides a quick means to open and close programs, and control the components of your computer system; consists of icons, a taskbar, and a Start button. [pg. 238]

dialog box   A window that enables a user to input data or specify settings related to the current task. [pg. 242]

Document Map   Displays a window that lists the structure of headings in your document. [pg. 171]

document window   Area of Word window in which you type and format your documents. [pg. 5]

double indent   Indenting text from both the left and the right margins. [pg. 122]

double-space   Text that leaves one blank line between text lines. [pg. 116]

em dash   A dash the width of a lowercase m (—) that indicates a pause or change in thought. [pg. 71]

en dash   A dash the width of a lowercase n that indicates a series; for example, pages 9–15. [pg. 71]

end-of-document marker   Small horizontal line that indicates the end of the document in Normal view. [pg. 4]

exit   The process of closing an application, such as Word. [pg. 21]

file   A collection of data stored on disk that has a name, called a filename. [pg. 238]

file extension   The last part of a filename; consists of three characters that represent the type of file. For example, the extension for a Word file is .doc. [pg. 254]

filename   The name of a collection of data stored on disk. [pg. 238]

fill   The shading color used within a graphics object, drawing object, or text box. [pg. 218]

first line indent   Indents the first line of a paragraph. [pg. 124]

folders   Categories for organizing and storing files on a storage device, such as a data disk or hard drive. [pg. 31]

font   Style, weight, and typeface of a set of characters. The default font is Times New Roman. [pg. 61]

font size   The height of the characters, typically measured in points, where 72 points equal one vertical inch. [pg. 61]

footer   Document information, such as a filename or date, that appears at the bottom of every page. [pg. 167]

format (a disk)   A procedure that prepares a disk to store files. Formatting also identifies and automatically isolates any bad spots on the surface of the disk, and creates an area for a disk directory. [pg. 250]

Format Painter   A feature that helps you copy existing text formats to other text. [pg. 66]

formatting marks   Nonprinting symbols and characters that indicate spaces, tabs, and hard returns. You display these symbols by clicking the Show/Hide ¶ button on the Standard toolbar. These symbols are useful when selecting text. [pg. 73]

Formatting toolbar   The toolbar that contains a row of buttons that help you format text. For example, this toolbar helps you select a font, boldface text, and select text alignment. [pg. 4]

full menu   Refers to an entire pull-down menu from the menu bar. You display the full menu by pointing to the arrows at the bottom of the short menu. [pg. 6]

Full Screen view   This view displays the document for the entire screen. You do not see the title bar, toolbars, and other screen elements. [pg. 43]

graphical user interface (GUI)   A program interface, such as Microsoft Windows, that incorporates graphics to make the program easier to use. [pg. 238]

grayed-out   The status of an option or a button that appears in gray and is not currently available. [pg. 7]

gridlines   Horizontal and vertical lines that separate cells within a table. [pg. 184]

hanging indent   Paragraph format that keeps the first line of a paragraph at the left margin and indents the remaining lines from the left margin. [pg. 124]

hard return   Defines the end of a line where you press ⏎Enter. [pg. 73]

header   Document information, such as a filename or date, that appears at the top of every page. [pg. 167]

heading   Text between paragraphs or sections that helps identify the content of that section. [pg. 60]

Help   Onscreen assistance or reference manual. It provides information about features, step-by-step instructions, and other assistance. [pg. 19]

highlight   Places a color behind text, such as a highlighter pen, to draw attention to text. [pg. 70]

horizontal scrollbar   The scrollbar that adjusts the horizontal view of text going left to right. [pg. 5]

hypertext links   Underlined words or phrases that appear in a different color. In Help, clicking a hypertext link displays another topic. [pg. 20]

icons   **1.** Images on toolbars or within windows that represent various tasks. For example, the Print icon looks like a printer. [pg. 7]   **2.** Small pictures that represent objects or programs. Double-clicking a program icon starts the program. Right-clicking an icon displays a menu of options related to the icon. [pg. 238]

Insert Clip Art task pane   A window pane in which you search for and select clip art, photographs, movies, and sounds. [pg. 209]

Insert mode   When you type within existing text, Word inserts the new text and keeps the other text; it does not replace text to the right of the insertion point. [pg. 35]

insertion point   A blinking vertical line that shows the current location in the document or in a dialog box text box. [pg. 4]

kerning   Automatically adjusts spacing between characters to achieve a more evenly spaced appearance. [pg. 66]

keyword   Words associated with Microsoft's clip art, photographs, sounds, and movies. A user types a keyword to locate other clips that have some of the same characteristics. [pg. 210]

leader   A tab option that produces a series of dots, a dashed line, or a solid line between tabulated columns. [pg. 138]

left indent   An indent format that indents a paragraph from the left margin. [pg. 122]

line break   A marker that continues text on the next line, but treats the text as a continuation of the previous paragraph instead of as a separate paragraph. You insert a line break by pressing ⬆Shift+⏎Enter. [pg. 135]

line spacing   The amount of vertical space from the bottom of one text line to the top of the next text line. The default line spacing is single. [pg. 115]

manual page break   A break you insert to immediately start text at the top of the next page. [pg. 158]

margins   Amount of white space around the top, left, right, and bottom of text on a page. [pg. 153]

maximize   An action that resizes a window to occupy the entire screen. [pg. 243]

menu   A list of commands. [pg. 5]

menu bar   A row of menu names displayed below the title bar. Tasks are categorized by nine different menus in Word. [pg. 4]

message box   A box that displays information—for example, that a procedure has been completed or an error has occurred—but does not provide an opportunity for the user to respond, except to close the box. [pg. 242]

minimize   An action that keeps a window open but removes it from the screen display. [pg. 243]

mouse pointer   A small arrow on the display screen that moves as you move the mouse. [pg. 238]

nonbreaking hyphen   A special type of hyphen that prevents hyphenated words from separating by the word-wrap feature. For example, you can insert hard hyphens to keep 555–1234 from word-wrapping. [pg. 75]

nonbreaking space   A special type of space that prevents words from separating by the word-wrap feature. For example, pressing Ctrl+⬆Shift+Spacebar inserts a nonbreaking space to keep October 16 from word-wrapping. [pg. 74]

Normal view   This view shows text without displaying space for margins, page numbers, headers, or other supplemental text. [pg. 42]

object   A non-text item, such as a clip art image. [pg. 92]

Office Assistant   An animated image that provides onscreen assistance and help. You can click it and ask it a question to learn how to do something in Word. [pg. 21]

Office Clipboard   An area of memory designed to store items that you cut or copy from a document. The Office Clipboard holds up to 24 different pieces of data, which you can paste within the same application or other applications. [pg. 92]

opening   The process of retrieving a document from storage, such as from a data disk, and displaying it onscreen. [pg. 31]

operating system   A computer program that manages all the computer's resources, sets priorities for programs running at the same time, and has several built-in functions that manage files stored on a computer's disks. [pg. 238]

orphan   The first line of a paragraph that appears by itself at the bottom of a page. [pg. 165]

outline numbered list   A list that contains several levels of numbering in an outline format. [pg. 128]

Overtype mode   When you type in this mode, the text you type replaces existing text at the insertion point. [pg. 41]

paragraph spacing   Controls the amount of space before or after the paragraph. [pg. 118]

paste   To insert the contents of the Office Clipboard in the insertion point's location. [pg. 93]

Paste Options Smart Tag   An icon that appears when you paste text. When you click it, you can choose the formatting style for the text you paste. [pg. 94]

position   A font option that raises or lowers text from the baseline without creating superscript or subscript size. [pg. 66]

Print Layout view   This view shows you what the document will look like when it's printed. You see margins, page numbers, headers, and so on. [pg. 42]

Redo   Reverses an undo action. [pg. 100]

restore   An action that automatically resizes a window to its size before being maximized. [pg. 246]

Reveal Formatting task pane   A window pane that displays font characteristics, alignment, indentation, spacing, and tabs. [pg. 138]

reverse text effect   An appearance that uses a darker background with a lighter text color. For example, a yellow text font on a blue background creates a reverse text effect. [pg. 133]

right indent   Indents a paragraph a specified amount of space from the right margin. [pg. 122]

row   A group of table cells arranged horizontally. [pg. 182]

row height   The vertical space from the top to the bottom of a row. [pg. 189]

ruler   Shows the location of tabs, indents, and left and right margins. [pg. 5]

sans serif font   A font that does not have serifs. This type of font is useful for headings, so they stand out from body text. [pg. 61]

saving   The process of storing a document for future use. [pg. 13]

scale   Increases or decreases the text horizontally as a percentage of its size. [pg. 66]

ScreenTip   A little yellow box that displays the name of a button when you position the mouse on the button. ScreenTips also appear for AutoComplete and other tasks. [pg. 8]

scrollbox   An object within a horizontal or vertical scrollbar that you can drag to shift quickly the display within a window. [pg. 246]

scrolling   The process of moving the insertion point through your document. [pg. 33]

section break   A marker that divides a document into sections; section breaks allow you to have different formats, such as page numbering. [pg. 156]

selecting   The process of defining a section of text. After you select text, you can delete, format, or cut it. [pg. 38]

selection bar   The space in the left margin area where you see a right-pointing arrow, indicating that you can make a selection. For example, click once to select the current text line. [pg. 40]

serif font   A font that displays tiny little lines or extensions at the top and bottom of most characters in the font. The serifs guide the reader's eyes across the text. [pg. 61]

shading   A colored background, similar to highlight, except that the space within the area is also colored; it is also the background color within a table cell or group of cells. [pg. 131]

short menu   A pull-down menu from the menu bar (also known as an **adaptive menu**). When you first select from the menu bar, you see a short menu of the most commonly used tasks you use. The short menu adapts, based on your usage of the features. [pg. 5]

shortcut   A fast keyboard method for performing a task. For example, the keyboard shortcut for bolding text is Ctrl+B. [pg. 8]

shortcut menu   A menu that enables you to perform operations quickly without using a menu bar or toolbar. [pg. 241]

single-space   Text lines that are close together, one immediately above the other. [pg. 115]

sizing handles   Little black boxes that appear around a selected object, so you can change the size or move the object. [pg. 213]

Smart Tag   An icon that displays options when you click it. It might display a note to enter a name in the Microsoft Outlook Contacts folder or provide options for pasting text. [pg. 34]

soft return   Occurs when Word word-wraps text to the next line within a paragraph as you type it. [pg. 116]

spacing   A font option that controls the amount of space between two or more characters. [pg. 66]

Standard toolbar   The toolbar that contains a row of buttons that perform common tasks, such as save and print. [pg. 4]

Start button   Pressing this button provides a menu approach to opening and closing programs, managing files and folders, getting onscreen Help about Windows, and controlling system components; it is located at the left end of the Windows taskbar. [pg. 238]

status bar   Appearing above the taskbar, this bar displays the current page number and location of the insertion point. [pg. 5]

subfolder   A folder created within another folder. [pg. 250]

submenu   A menu that appears to the side of a main pull-down menu. It provides more specific options and features. For example, choosing View, Toolbars displays the Toolbars submenu that lists specific toolbars. [pg. 7]

suppress   Hides or removes something onscreen. For example, suppressing the page number prevents the number from displaying and printing on a page. [pg. 163]

synonym   A word that means the same as another word. Word contains a feature that helps you select appropriate synonyms for words. [pg. 102]

table   A series of rows and columns that organize data effectively. [pg. 182]

table alignment   The horizontal position of a table between the left and right margins. [pg. 196]

tabs   Markers that specify the position for aligning text when you press `Tab`. [pg. 134]

taskbar (Windows)   A bar that displays a button for each open file; generally located across the bottom of the Windows desktop. Use the taskbar to switch from one application to another. [pg. 238]

task pane   A window pane that displays frequently used features. It displays different tasks, based on what you are doing—such as options for creating a new document, recovering a document, inserting clip art, and applying styles and formatting. [pg. 5]

tight wrap   A wrapping style that lets text contour or wrap tightly around the outer edges of the image itself instead of the square border area that surrounds an image. [pg. 218]

title bar   Shows the name of the file you are currently working on, as well as the name of the application. Dialog boxes also have title bars that show the name of the dialog box. [pg. 4]

toolbar   A bar containing a set of buttons; each button on the toolbar performs a predefined task. [pg. 239]

Undo   Reverses an action that you perform in the document. Actions are undone in reverse sequential order; that is, the last action performed is the first reversed. [pg. 98]

vertical alignment   Positions text between the top and bottom edges on a page. [pg. 160]

vertical scrollbar   Moves up and down in a document. [pg. 5]

view buttons   Switches between different view modes, such as Normal, Web Layout, Print Layout, and Outline view. [pg. 5]

watermark   A washed-out graphic object or text that typically appears behind text. [pg. 225]

widow   The last line of a paragraph that appears by itself at the top of a page. [pg. 165]

window   An enclosed, rectangular area on the screen that enables you to see the output from a program. [pg. 238]

Windows   A group of operating systems developed for personal computers by Microsoft. [pg. 238]

Windows Explorer   A utility program that enables you to access programs and documents; as well as copy, move, delete, and rename files. [pg. 246]

windows, cascading   An arrangement in which open windows display in a stack—each window slightly to the right of, and slightly below, the previous window. [pg. 246]

windows, tiled   An arrangement in which open windows display horizontally—each window to the right of the previous one—or vertically—each window below the previous one. [pg. 246]

WordArt   A feature that creates interesting shapes and designs for text. Useful for creating banners and titles on fliers and advertisements. [pg. 227]

WordPad   A Windows utility program for creating small word-processing files in several formats. [pg. 252]

word-wrap feature   Continues text on the next line if it can't fit at the end of the current line. [pg. 11]

wrapping style   Specifies the way text wraps around an object, such as a clip art image. [pg. 216]

WYSIWYG   Stands for "What You See Is What You Get." This means that your printout will look like what you're seeing onscreen. [pg. 73]

zoom   Specifies the magnification percentage of the way your document appears onscreen. [pg. 43]

Index